CW01359980

LIBRARY OF HISTORICAL JESUS STUDIES

Editor
Robert L. Webb

Published under

LIBRARY OF NEW TESTAMENT STUDIES
334

formerly the Journal for the Study of the New Testament Supplement series

Editor
Mark Goodacre

Editorial Board
John M. G. Barclay, Craig Blomberg, Kathleen E. Corley,
R. Alan Culpepper, James D. G. Dunn, Craig A. Evans, Stephen Fowl,
Robert Fowler, Simon J. Gathercole, John S. Kloppenborg, Michael Labahn,
Robert Wall, Steve Walton, Robert L. Webb, Catrin H. Williams

JESUS AND LAND

SACRED AND SOCIAL SPACE
IN SECOND TEMPLE JUDAISM

KAREN J. WENELL

t&t clark

Copyright © Karen J. Wenell, 2007

Published by T&T Clark
A Continuum imprint
The Tower Building, 11 York Road, London SE1 7NX
80 Maiden Lane, Suite 704, New York, NY 10038

www.tandtclark.com

All rights reserved. No part of this publication may be reproduced or transmitted in any form or by any means, electronic or mechanical, including photocopying, recording or any information storage or retrieval system, without permission in writing from the publishers.

Karen J. Wenell has asserted her right under the Copyright, Designs and Patents Act, 1988, to be identified as the Author of this work.

British Library Cataloguing-in-Publication Data
A catalogue record for this book is available from the British Library

ISBN-10: HB: 0-567-03115-2
ISBN-13: HB: 978-0-567-03115-0

Typeset by CA Typesetting Ltd, www.publisherservices.co.uk
Printed on acid-free paper by Biddles Ltd, King's Lynn, Norfolk

Contents

Acknowledgements	vii
Abbreviations	viii

Chapter 1
LAND AS PROBLEM AND PROMISE — 1
  Interpreting Land as Sacred Space — 3
  Genesis 10 and Interpretations — 8
  Socially Constructed Mythical Places — 14
  A Plausible Jesus: Words and Actions in Place — 17

Chapter 2
THE TEMPLE AS CONTESTED SPACE — 21
  Text and Architecture — 23
  The Tabernacle in the Wilderness — 25
  Solomon's Temple — 27
  The Rebuilt Temple — 29
  The Second Temple at Home and Abroad — 31
  The Samaritan Temple at Gerizim — 35
  Qumran and the Jerusalem Temple — 37
  The Testament of Moses — 40
  The Temple Action: Destruction and Restoration or Destruction Only? — 44
  The Action in the Temple: Mark 11.15-18//Matthew 21.12-13//Luke 19.45-46 — 47
  Stones Torn Down: Mark 13.1-2//Matthew 24.1-2//Luke 21.5-6 — 50
  Destroy the Temple and Rebuild it: Mark 14.56-59//Matthew 26.60-61, 27.40; John 2.13-22; Acts 6.12-14 — 52
  Critique of Temple-Centred Space — 56

Chapter 3
EMBODIED SACRED SPACE: PURITY IN THE LAND — 61
  Purity Practices in the Second Temple Period — 68
  Leviticus and Bathing — 69
  The Rise and Fall of *Miqvaot* — 72
  Meaning, Hierarchy and the Cost of Purity — 76
  Interpretation of Purity Laws 1: The Sadducees and Pharisees — 79
  The Sadducees and Temple Purity — 80
  Pharisees: The 'Who' and 'Where' of Purity — 82

Interpretation of Purity Laws 2: Qumran, Samaritans and
John the Baptist 85
Qumran: Purity Confined to the Community 86
The Holy Land of Samaria? 91
John's Baptism of Repentance in the Jordan 92
Rejection of Purity, Rejection of Land? Jesus and Ritual Purity 97

Chapter 4
IMAGINED SPACE: JESUS' GROUP OF TWELVE 104
  Twelve Tribes and the Land in Judaism 106
  Twelve Tribes and Land: Keeping the Number
  of Territories Consistent 107
  Twelve Objects and Land: Unity and Disunity 110
  Twelve Leaders and Land: A Territorial Governing Role? 111
  Twelve Tribes, Land and Eschatological Expectations 113
  The Authenticity of a Group of Twelve 116
  The Twelve and Eschatology 121
  Twelve Thrones, Twelve Tribes: Matthew 19.28//Luke 22.30 122
  In the Palingenesia 124
  Matthew 8.11-12//Luke 13.28-29 128
  Gathering 129
  Comparative Aside: Twelve Leaders at Qumran 135
  Jesus' Group of Twelve 135

Chapter 5
JESUS AND LAND: MILLENARIAN DREAMS OF SPACE 139
  Experience of Land, Beliefs about Land 142
  Biblical Land and Beyond 146

Bibliography 148
Index of References 159
Index of Authors 166

Acknowledgments

The seed of an idea to investigate Jesus' relationship to the land was first presented to me by Scot McKnight along with the suggestion to read W. D. Davies' *The Gospel and the Land*. Over several subsequent years of study, the initial idea grew to become a doctoral thesis, and now is presented in book form with some further pruning and new growth.

I owe numerous debts along the way. I was fortunate to receive an Overseas Research Students award as well as a postgraduate research scholarship from the Faculty of Arts at the University of Glasgow. I am grateful to my examiners, Helen Bond and Louise Lawrence, for their suggestions for improvement of the work. I have also benefited from involvement with the Bible and Sacred Space group of the European Association of Biblical Studies, chaired by Jorunn Økland, with whom I am grateful to have shared conversations about spatial theory and its application to biblical studies. Postgraduate colleagues, especially Marije Altorf, Mark Brummitt, Angus Paddison and Susan Miller, provided numerous helpful discussions, as well as plentiful opportunities for laughter and distraction. I am grateful to John Barclay for his supervision and guidance during my second year of doctoral research.

I have the privilege at present of continuing to work alongside my PhD supervisor in the capacity of editing the *Expository Times*. Since beginning my doctoral studies, John Riches has allowed me to consider possibilities and avenues of thinking I had never previously imagined. His assiduous guidance takes 'centre space' in the work and development of this book.

Traditionally book authors' partners are owed words which extol their support, encouragement and long suffering. To Damian, all these and more are offered with deepest appreciation and love. This book is dedicated to my parents, Alan and Judy Wenell, for their belief that all things are possible.

ABBREVIATIONS

1 En.	*1 Enoch*
2 Bar.	*2 Baruch*
ABD	*Anchor Bible Dictionary* (ed. D. N. Freedman; 6 vols; New York: Doubleday, 1992)
Ant.	Josephus, *Jewish Antiquities*
BA	*Biblical Archaeologist*
BAR	*Biblical Archaeology Review*
BASOR	*Bulletin of the American Schools of Oriental Research*
BBR	*Bulletin for Biblical Research*
BibInt	*Biblical Interpretation*
C. Ap.	Josephus, *Against Apion*
CBQ	*Catholic Biblical Quarterly*
CRINT	**Compendia rerum iudaicarum ad Novum Testamentum**
DSD	*Dead Sea Discoveries*
Flaccus	Philo, *Against Flaccus*
Gos. Thom.	*Gospel of Thomas*
JAAR	*Journal of the American Academy of Religion*
JBL	*Journal of Biblical Literature*
JJS	*Journal of Jewish Studies*
JSJ	*Journal for the Study of Judaism in the Persian, Hellenistic and Roman Periods*
JSNT	*Journal for the Study of the New Testament*
JSP	*Journal for the Study of the Pseudepigrapha*
Jub.	*Jubilees*
Legat.	Philo. *On the Embassy to Gaius*
Life	Josephus, *The Life*
NTS	*New Testament Studies*
OTL	**Old Testament Library**
Pss. Sol.	*Psalms of Solomon*
Sib. Or.	*Sibylline Oracles*
SJT	*Scottish Journal of Theology*
T. Ab.	*Testament of Abraham*
T. Ash.	*Testament of Asher*
T. Benj.	*Testament of Benjamin*
T. Jud.	*Testament of Judah*
T. Levi	*Testament of Levi*
T. Naph.	*Testament of Naphtali*
T. Reu.	*Testament of Reuben*
T. Sim.	*Testament of Simeon*
TDNT	*Theological Dictionary of the New Testament* (ed. G. Kittel and G. Friedrich; trans G. W. Bromiley; 10 vols; Grand Rapids: Eerdmans, 1974–)

TynBul	*Tyndale Bulletin*
VT	*Vetus Testamentum*
War	**Josephus,** *Jewish War*

Chapter 1

LAND AS PROBLEM AND PROMISE

> Blessed are the meek, for they will inherit the land. (Mt. 5.5)

It is entirely possible that Jesus never uttered this beatitude, which appears only in Matthew's Gospel. Yet even if we consider it to be an addition which Matthew has borrowed from Ps. 37.11, the statement – which uses a particular phrase (κληρονομήσουσιν τὴν γῆν – inherit/ possess the land/earth) associated with fulfilment of the promise of land to Abraham[1] – begs thoughtful consideration of the relationship between Jesus and the land. Why, if Jesus is understood as a Jew of his time, would he ignore the promise to Abraham which was firmly part of Jewish tradition and beliefs and would have been a socially and politically relevant issue under Herodian and Roman rule? Or, why, as W. D. Davies concluded in his 1974 study, *The Gospel and the Land*, would it be appropriate to say that 'Jesus, as far as we can gather, paid little attention to the relationship between Yahweh, and Israel and the land'?[2] Would we not expect the gospel accounts of the life of Jesus to contain a greater amount of material which might illuminate his perspective on the Abrahamic land promise?

It is sometimes claimed that Christianity is a religion that moved beyond the particular territorial dimensions of Judaism to become a universal religion.[3] Some would consider this to be supersessionist in nature:[4] Judaism emphasizes the holiness of temple, city and land; Jesus

---

1. R. L. Wilken, *The Land Called Holy: Palestine in Christian History and Thought* (New Haven and London: Yale University Press, 1992) says of this phrase, that it 'became the standard formula to express the promise of the land to Abraham and his descendants' (p. 7). See also pp. 46–8 on the use of the phrase in Mt. 5.5.

2. W. D. Davies, *The Gospel and the Land: Early Christianity and Jewish Territorial Doctrine* (The Biblical Seminar, 25; repr., Sheffield: Sheffield Academic Press, 1994), p. 365. Originally published by University of California Press, 1974.

3. See, for example, David E. Holwerda's *Jesus and Israel: One Covenant or Two?* (Grand Rapids, MI: Eerdmans, 1995).

4. Peter Walker, in his discussion of Jerusalem, claims that the New Testament

fulfils and replaces these categories as a centre of holiness himself. The holiness of land and temple are transferred or subsumed in the person of Jesus. However, in the New Testament, there is no consistent or explicit statement of such views. Certainly the book of Hebrews in particular does speak of Jesus as the great high priest in very spatial terms and associates his post-resurrection existence with his priestly role over the true dwelling, or tabernacle, of God in heaven. The inheritance of salvation (κληρονομεῖν σωτηρίαν) in Heb.1.14 stands at a distance from Matthew's inheritance of the land. But this is precisely the point. There are different voices in the New Testament and these do not constitute a single attitude to land (or the temple). As Christianity emerged and developed, so did its understanding of the foundational spatial categories of Judaism such as land and temple. In the second century, Justin Martyr and Irenaeus each articulated what could be called chiliastic beliefs, which included the assigning of particular eschatological importance to the promise of inheritance of the land.[5] Various strands of Gnosticism at the same time (against whom Irenaeus argues in *Adversus Haereses*) would not have fostered such beliefs regarding the land. As ever, we are dealing with a situation of diversity and not a linear and consistent development of ideas. As John Riches has shown in his study of identity formation in Mark's Gospel and Matthew's re-reading of Mark, even within the Synoptic Gospels significant changes and shifts in the meaning of sacred space occurred.[6] The meaning of 'land' or 'temple' was never static, and different groups and authors take up and use such concepts in different ways – modifying, adapting, adding to and even deleting particular elements along the way. We should not predispose the discussion to the view that land had a set meaning, either within Jewish or later Christian beliefs. Therefore, I prefer to avoid the terminology of 'replacement' or 'supersession', and instead look for some of the diverse ways that spatial models were taken up, used and adapted around the time of Jesus.[7]

'endorses the supresessionist approach' ('Christians and Jerusalem, Past and Present', in B. Norman [ed.], *The Mountain of the Lord: Israel and the Churches* [London: Council of Christians and Jews, 1996], pp. 107–130 [128]). See also P. Walker, 'The Land in the New Testament', in P. Johnston and P. Walker (eds), *The Land of Promise: Biblical, Theological and Contemporary Perspectives* (Downers Grove, IL: InterVarsity Press, 2000), pp. 81–120; and T. D. Alexander and S. Gathercole (eds), *Heaven on Earth: The Temple in Biblical Theology* (Carlisle: Paternoster, 2004).

5. See Wilken, *Land Called Holy*, pp. 55–62 (including references).
6. J. K. Riches, *Conflicting Mythologies: Identity Formation in the Gospels of Mark and Matthew* (Edinburgh: T&T Clark, 2000).
7. See my discussion on this point in relationship to the temple in K. Wenell,

The primary purpose of this study is to offer an evaluation of the relationship between Jesus and land. However, broader analysis is also part of the aims, and the study will attempt to set views of the land within the context of the social world of Jesus and in relationship to the sacred spaces of that time. This relationship needs further definition, particularly in terms of the theoretical approach of the present investigation. Therefore, by way of introducing the issues, I propose first to explore the concept of sacred space and its place within a religious worldview, and to demonstrate how texts might be read for their use of models and concepts of sacred space. Secondly, I will look at some of the particular social issues to do with mythical appropriations of sacred space. And finally, I will outline the plan of the study and the methodology used for interpreting the historical Jesus.

Interpreting Land as Sacred Space (or Avoiding the IKEA Problem)

In order for land to be sacred, it must be interpreted and communicated as such.[8] This is as true for a land or landscape as it is for a mountain, a river or a purpose-built temple or church. Whether we are thinking of ancient or modern sacred spaces, the plain fact of diversity is a primary characteristic of what we might call 'sacred space'. There is no limit to the type or location of places which might be interpreted as sacred. Therefore, comprehensive definitions are not easy. An anthropological approach to sacred space has the advantage of being able to cope with this diversity by allowing for analysis and comparisons of many types of sacred spaces across history and geography (time and space). Yet, even within the field of anthropology, there has not always been a great degree of theoretical precision when it comes to sacred space.[9] We could

---

'Contested Temple Space and Visionary Kingdom Space in Mark 11–12', *BibInt* 15.3 (2007), pp. 291–305.

8. See Verónica Salles-Reese's illuminating study of the sacred character of Lake Titicaca from pre-Incan times to the present, *From Viracocha to the Virgin of Copacabana: Representation of the Sacred at Lake Titicaca* (Austin, TX: University of Texas Press, 1997). She states: 'A person [is not precluded] from having an individual experience of the numinous, that is, from experiencing a personal revelation. However, for that experience to be shared and understood by others, for it to be communal, it must first be conveyed through language. A mountain, for instance, may only be known as a deity if an individual characterizes it as such in some form of language – in written, oral, or other forms of symbolic representation' (p. 6).

9. See, for instance the 1972 article by Hilda Kuper, 'The Language of Sites in the Politics of Space', in S. M. Low and D. Lawrence-Zúñiga (eds), *The Anthropology of Space and Place: Locating Culture* (Oxford: Blackwell, 2003), pp. 247–63: repr. from

say that this is also true from an archaeological[10] and also a geographical[11] point of view when it comes to interpreting religious spaces.

This does not mean that sacred space is impossible to define, only that we must account for great differences in interpretation, even if we are speaking about characteristics which could be viewed as common to many sacred places such as connection with the gods, performance of ritual, relation to cosmogony, etc. From a history of religions point of view, Mircea Eliade views sacred space as constituting an irruption of the sacred into the world, breaking with the chaos of surrounding profane space. For Eliade, sacred space 'founds' the world for religions humans, yet also depends on 'historical moments and cultural styles'.[12] Critiquing Eliade's view of sacred space as space which is qualitatively, or essentially 'different', Jonathan Z. Smith emphasizes the human role in the creation of sacred places.[13] Human beings take an active role in defining the meaning of sacred space. As Smith states: 'Human beings are not placed, they bring place into being'.[14] Within human experience, 'the' meaning of particular sacred places is not static but is an essential part of the process by which humans create and understand themselves.[15] Changes can and do occur as the experience of the sacred is communicated and repeated through ritual and individuals and societies come to understand themselves in new ways. Therefore, not only are sacred spaces diverse in terms of types and locations, we must also account for the ways that the symbols and meanings given to places change and develop over time in a society.

American Anthropologist 74.3 (1972), pp. 411–25. Kuper states, 'It is clear that there is a good deal of imprecision and confusion in the anthropological use of the concept of "space"' (p. 252).

10. Note the comments of Garwood, Jennings, Skeates and Toms in P. Garwood, D. Jennings, R. Skeates and J. Toms (eds), *Sacred and Profane: Proceedings of a Conference on Archaeology, Ritual and Religion, Oxford, 1989* (Oxford: Oxford University Committee for Archaeology, 1991): 'the current conceptual and methodological situation with respect to the study of ritual and religion in archaeology ... seems to be characterized by a very wide range of interpretative and analytical approaches, and few threads of consistency in specific theoretical aims' (p. vi).

11. Chris C. Park, *Sacred Worlds: An Introduction to Geography and Religion* (London: Routledge, 1994), pp. 18–21.

12. Mircea Eliade, *The Sacred and the Profane: The Nature of Religion* (trans. W. R. Trask; San Diego, CA: Harcourt, 1959), pp. 62–3. See also pp. 20–26.

13. J. Z. Smith, *Map is Not Territory: Studies in the History of Religions* (Leiden: E. J. Brill, 1978), pp. 88–190. J. Z. Smith, *To Take Place: Toward Theory in Ritual* (Chicago: University of Chicago Press, 1987).

14. Smith, *To Take Place*, p. 28.

15. Smith, *Map is Not Territory*, pp. 138–44.

1. *Land as Problem and Promise*

And yet, many places in society have meaning, and many places – homes, marketplaces, government buildings – have symbolic associations which change over time. A British television programme about IKEA, aired during the Christmas season of 2004, explored the modern 'phenomenon' which is the home-furnishings giant IKEA and the impact it has made on global society. Alongside clips of a man dressed as a Viking playing an electric guitar at the entrance to an IKEA car park, there were numerous sound bites of organ music and visual cuts to the insides of gothic cathedrals. IKEA, so the show seemed to strongly suggest, presents a kind of modern sacred space. In my view, rejecting this example actually helps us to be precise. One's car or home or favourite globalized furniture store may be (and probably indeed is) a space of significance, but there is something more to sacred space. Whilst this type of popular appropriation of the concept of sacred space may be academically harmless, it draws our attention back to looking at the definition of sacred space – if IKEA does not properly represent sacred space, what does and what makes it so? For even some of the recent work on the interpretation of ancient spaces in the Bible and biblical world has focused on socially meaningful spaces rather than drawing out the meaning of sacred places in relationship to text and world.[16]

We may return then to sacred space and to the aspect of interpretation in order to attempt to define the scope of sacred space. Though many spaces may constitute focal points of human interpretation, the meaning of sacred space is specifically defined within a religious worldview. Anthropologist Clifford Geertz defines religion as a cultural system, 'a set of symbols which acts to establish powerful, pervasive and long-lasting moods and motivations... by formulating conceptions of a general order of existence'.[17] Religious individuals are thus placed; they will interpret their experience in light of beliefs and meaningful symbols, but such beliefs will also shape their experience, patterns of behaviour and actions. Again, from Geertz:

---

16. See the volume produced out of the research of the 'Constructions of Ancient Space' Group of the Society of Biblical Literature and the American Academy of Religion: D. M. Gunn and P. M. McNutt (eds), *'Imagining' Biblical Worlds: Studies in Spatial, Social and Historical Constructs in Honor of James W. Flanagan* (London: Sheffield Academic Press, 2002). See also the collected papers, bibliography and other relevant literature at the GAIR website: http://www.cwru.edu/affil/GAIR/Constructions/Constructions.html

17. C. Geertz, *The Interpretation of Cultures* (New York: Basic Books, 1973), p. 90.

> Meanings can only be 'stored' in symbols: a cross, a crescent, or a feathered serpent. Such religious symbols, dramatized in rituals or related in myths, are felt somehow to sum up, for those for whom they are resonant, what is known about the way the world is, the quality of the emotional life it supports, and the way one ought to behave while in it.[18]

Places – whether land, temple or heavenly realm – are significant symbolic resources within a religious system. If land, for instance, is believed to be holy, this will affect the behaviour of those who understand it in this way. The social experience of these same individuals will also have an impact on how they understand land to be holy. Thus, models *of* and *for* reality (in Geertz' terminology) are in operation. 'Placement' in the world is grounded in both sacred realities and social experience and in the interaction between these. Meanings (as mentioned above) will also change over time through interpretation and re-interpretation.[19] In the words of John Riches and Alan Millar, beliefs are 'grounded' in daily life, that is, '[theological] propositions must come down to earth and this they do via their links with experience and action'.[20]

How do we begin to discuss Jesus' relationship to sacred space and the interpretation of land as sacred space in terms of beliefs, experiences and actions? The first issue we must grapple with is one of reading texts. Whether we are speaking about the Hebrew Bible, Jewish texts of the Second Temple period or the Gospels, our primary reference point for understanding spatial conceptions of the sacred is through language, although archaeological data must also be taken into consideration wherever possible.[21] We must also be upfront in our recognition that the language of 'sacred space' is itself anachronistic. And yet, clearly the ancient world had concepts of separate spaces associated with divinity. In the Greek-speaking world, ἱερός was the most common term in sacral or cultic use.[22] Something (or somewhere) which was filled with divine power or belonged to the divine sphere of existence was ἱερός. Interest-

---

18. Geertz, *Interpretation of Cultures*, p. 127.
19. Geertz, *Interpretation of Cultures*, pp. 91–4.
20. J. Riches and A. Millar, 'Conceptual Change in the Synoptic Tradition', in A. E. Harvey (ed.), *Alternative Approaches to New Testament Study* (London: SPCK, 1985), pp. 37–60 (39). See also A. Millar and J.K. Riches, 'Interpretation: A Theoretical Perspective and Some Applications', *Numen* 28.1 (1981), pp. 29–53.
21. Seán Freyne's approach, for example, incorporates social description as a 'meeting place' for New Testament scholarship and archaeology. S. Freyne, 'Archaeology and the Historical Jesus', in J. R. Bartlett (ed.), *Archaeology and Biblical Interpretation* (London: Routledge, 1997), pp. 117–44 (117–20).
22. See the article on 'ἱερός' in *TDNT*, vol. III, pp. 221–47.

ingly, in the Septuagint, there is a conscious avoidance of ἱερός and the Hebrew *qadosh* is most commonly translated with the Greek ἅγιος, indicating separation or dedication to God. This shows us something about distinctions in terminology which will also have implications for distinctions in identity between Jews and non-Jews. Clearly there were also rules and practices associated with places characterized as sacred in the ancient world, and we must come to terms with such concepts and practices in order to comprehend how the sacred is understood for particular people of specific times and places. We may continue to use the English words 'sacred' and 'sacred space', but with an awareness that the concepts denoted by the words will vary from culture to culture. As Jane Hubert states:

> Although the translation of words and concepts in other cultures may be inexact, the concomitant concepts of separateness, respect and the rules of behaviour seem to be common to sacred sites in different cultures. But the nature of sacred sites themselves may be different, and thus difficult for those outside the culture to recognize, except by observation of the rules of behaviour that pertain to them.[23]

When considering *ancient* spaces, the rules of behaviour and concepts of sacred space must be observed in the ways we have already discussed – through interpretation of texts and material evidence. This study attempts to observe the rules and behaviour of sacred space by making use of such evidence.

For the land in particular, a survey of texts relating to 'land' may not be the best place to begin.[24] Though such surveys hold interest in their own right, they do not tell us what the land meant for individuals and groups at a later time (such as Jesus and his followers). And in any case, there is no unified meaning to discover. Norman Habel's book on land identifies *six* distinct ideologies of land in the Hebrew Bible, and this is not considered to exhaust the meaning of the concept of the land. We are reminded by Habel that we must look for the social interests of particular groups as they articulate ideologies of land. He clearly states:

23. J. Hubert, 'Sacred Beliefs and Beliefs of Sacredness', in D. L. Carmichael, J. Hubert, B. Reeves and A. Schanche (eds), *Sacred Sites, Sacred Places* (London: Routledge, 1994), pp. 9–19 (11). On the strangeness of culturally or geographically distant places (and even places within one's own culture), see also Amos Rapoport, 'Spatial Organization and the Built Environment', in T. Ingold (ed.), *Companion Encyclopedia of Anthropology* (London: Routledge, 1994), pp. 460–502.

24. Though note this approach in Davies, *Gospel and the Land*, pp. 3–74. This is also the approach of Jari Laaksonen, *Jesus und das Land: das Gelobte Land in der Verkündigung Jesu* (Åbo: Åbo Akademis Förlag, 2002), pp. 43–159.

> There is no monolithic concept of land in the Hebrew Scriptures. There is, rather, a spectrum of ideologies with diverse images and doctrines of land. These ideologies, moreover, are promoted by particular social groups with vested interests in promoting a given ideology to gain, regain, or maintain land.[25]

In forming such ideologies, social groups and individuals will take up particular *models* from Scripture, or sacred texts, such as models of land. Seth Kunin identifies several models of sacred space in the Hebrew Bible, including the dominant centralized model of tabernacle or temple, but also other models, including decentralized or local models within the texts.[26] These models in turn become foundational for other interpretations.[27] We might illustrate this briefly with an example of this process in the re-reading of Genesis 10 (Table of Nations) in *Jubilees* and Josephus' *Antiquities*. This will show us something of the variety of interpretations closer to the time of Jesus (more than a survey of texts in the Hebrew Bible would be able to provide).

Genesis 10 and Interpretations

Although the term 'holy land' itself occurs relatively late in Hebrew Scripture,[28] the land is part of the relationship between God and humanity almost from the very beginning of the Pentateuchal narrative, and therefore is firmly part of conceptions of the sacred and sacred space in these texts. After humanity's beginning in the earthly paradise of Eden, the great deluge entailed a new beginning for humans upon the earth. Genesis 10 describes how the peoples spread out over the earth. The table is presented as an ethnographic (according to their lands, languages, families and nations in vv. 5, 20 and 31) placement of peoples and nations: 'These are the families of the sons of Noah, according to their genealogies, in their nations, and from these the nations spread abroad on the earth after the flood' (Gen. 10.32). The table is a sort of map, showing spatial relationships and proximity between peoples, yet

---

25. N. Habel, *The Land is Mine: Six Biblical Land Ideologies* (Minneapolis: Fortress Press, 1995), p. 148.
26. S. Kunin, *God's Place in the World: Sacred Space and Sacred Place in Judaism* (London: Cassell, 1998), pp. 1–27, 68–71.
27. Kunin, *God's Place*, p. 11.
28. Wilken, *Land Called Holy*, pp. 17–19. Zechariah (2.12) was the first to describe the land in this way (τὴν γῆν τὴν ἁγίαν – LXX).

it is also able to relate proximity in terms of culture and language.[29] Shem's land is structurally at the narrative centre of the text, but this centrality is not emphasized. It is only later in the chapters which follow that the land comes into view. After the Tower of Babel incident in Genesis 11, the genealogy of Shem leads to the patriarch Abram. In verse 1 of chapter 12, God says to Abram: 'Go from your country and your kindred and your father's house to the land that I will show you'. The land is described as God's gift to Abram and his descendants (Gen. 12.7; 15.18) under the covenant of circumcision: 'And I will give to you, and to your offspring after you, the land where you are now an alien, all the land of Canaan, for a perpetual holding; and I will be their God' (Gen. 17.8). There is a much longer history of God, people and land in the Pentateuch and the other literature of the Hebrew Bible, but as we have noted, this will not provide us with an overall concept of land, and so a fruitful investigative route is to show how the text of Genesis 10 (which was closely connected with the God–people–land relationship established through the patriarch Abraham) could be formative for later spatial conceptions. Texts such as this were the sort of texts which could then become building-blocks, foundational to religious cosmology.

The author of *Jubilees* (2nd century BCE) offers a reinterpretation of Genesis 1 through to Exod. 24.18 (creation to Sinai), giving divine perspective on the events through the revelations of the 'angel of the presence' to Moses. *Jubilees* 8–10 retells the story of the Table of Nations from Genesis 10. Philip Alexander identifies how the author of *Jubilees* actually fits the Table of Nations from Genesis into an ancient Ionian world map.[30] The centre of the Ionian map is Delphi, but for *Jubilees*, it is Zion, 'in the midst of the navel of the earth' (*Jub.* 8.19). Ezekiel's model of sacred space has Zion at the centre or *omphalos* of the land with concentric circles of holiness extending outwards (Ezek. 38.12). Yet the *Jubilees* text does not appear to borrowing the Ezekiel's model with respect to the land. Other sacred places are incorporated into the map as well, and a triad of sacred spaces – the garden of Eden, Mount Sinai and Mount Zion – is established, where 'the three of these were created as holy places, one facing the other' (*Jub.* 8.19). Thus, with the garden of Eden containing the 'holy of holies and the dwelling of the

---

29. See P. S. Alexander, 'Geography and the Bible (Early Jewish)', *ABD* vol. 2, pp. 977–88. 'A genealogical tree as a geographical device cannot cope as well as a drawn map with spatial relationships, but it can show, in a way that a primitive map cannot, the political, linguistic, and cultural connections between peoples' (p. 980).

30. P. S. Alexander, 'Notes on the "Imago Mundi" of the Book of Jubilees', *JJS* 33 (1982), pp. 197–213, on this map, pp. 198–201.

Lord'[31] (*Jub.* 8.19), we have here 'a vision of a triangle of three holy places, facing each other and creating, as it were, a field of forces which renders the territory in between sacred'.[32] Unlike Genesis, where there was no specific claim to the land in the account of the Table of Nations, in *Jubilees* the sons of Noah divide up the earth in a manner which recalls Joshua's division of the land among the tribes.[33] However, one significant difference is that Noah's sons' division is done 'in an evil manner' (*Jub.* 8.8-9). The 'demons' had begun to mislead Noah's sons and grandsons (*Jub.* 7.26), as earlier the Watchers had brought evil and injustice to the earth (*Jub.* 5.1-2). However, Shem comes out the favourite in the story and is wronged by Canaan who seizes the land allotted to Shem (rather than the other way around!) 'from the bank of the Jordan and from the shore of the sea' (*Jub.* 10.29). Canaan is therefore cursed:

> You and your children will fall in the land and be cursed with sedition because by sedition you have dwelt and by sedition your children will fall and you will be uprooted forever. Do not dwell in the dwelling of Shem because it came to Shem and his sons by lot. (*Jub.* 10.30-31)

Shem is clearly the most loved by Noah (explicitly stated in *Jub.* 10.14), and even the land of Shem receives a favourable description in comparison with Ham and Japheth's lands: 'but it [Japheth's land] is cold, and the land of Ham is hot, but the land of Shem is not hot or cold because it is mixed with cold and heat' (*Jub.* 10.14). This Goldilocks-like description says that Shem's land is 'just right'.

So in *Jubilees*, we find considerable modifications and additions to the original Genesis narrative (as well as the spatial model of Ezekiel). Sacred space is re-conceptualized and claims to land are reinforced. Not only are the sacred Scriptures drawn upon as resources, but also the common geographical perspectives and knowledge of the day (the

---

31. See E. J. C. Tigchelaar on how *Jubilees* has reworked the text of Genesis 2–3 in relation to the holy of holies and Eden. Tigchelaar, 'Eden and Paradise: The Garden Motif in Some Early Jewish Texts (*1 Enoch* and Other Texts Found at Qumran)', in G. P. Luttikhuizen (ed.), *Paradise Interpreted: Representations of Biblical Paradise in Judaism and Christianity* (Leiden: E. J. Brill, 1999), pp. 37–57.

32. Riches, *Conflicting Mythologies*, p. 25. Though these sites 'mark out the central axes of the world' in Shem's territory, 'they do not coincide with the borders of the land' (p. 31). Compare James Scott's discussion of the *Jubilees* text and its relationship to Ezekiel 38.12. James M. Scott, *Geography in Early Judaism and Christianity: The Book of Jubilees* (Cambridge: Cambridge University Press, 2002), esp. p. 34.

33. See J. VanderKam, *From Revelation to Cannon: Studies in the Hebrew Bible and Second Temple Literature* (Leiden: E. J. Brill, 2000), p. 488. Also J. M. Scott, *Geography in Early Judaism*, pp. 33–43.

Ionian world map). We can imagine how a narrative such as this could have motivated a Maccabean ideology (and perhaps military actions coming out of this ideology) of conquest, expansion of the borders of the land, and purification of the temple. In terms of the future, *Jubilees* looks toward the final period of time:

> And jubilees will pass until Israel is purified from all the sin of fornication, and defilement, and uncleanness, and sin and error. And they will dwell in confidence in the land. And then it will not have any Satan or evil (one). And the land will be purified from that time and forever. (*Jub*. 50.5)

Other covenantal aspects are emphasized in *Jubilees*, such as obedience to the law, the practice of circumcision, observance of the Sabbath, feasts and the 'right' calendar. Yet, land is also visible, as the rightful territory of Israel and also as part of hopes for the future.[34]

Another author who took up an interpretation of Genesis 10 is Josephus in his *Antiquities of the Jews*, written sometime around 93 or 94 CE in Rome. Books 1–4 of the *Antiquities* cover the material of the Pentateuch, and in relationship to Genesis in particular, Josephus treats his subject fully, without making 'the kind of large-scale redispositions of the scriptural data' found elsewhere in his re-reading of the Pentateuch.[35] Josephus is concerned with updating the geographical information for his audience, and does so by explaining names which would remain recognizable and also names which were 'corrupted' or have no modern equivalent.[36] The story of Noah is pivotal for Josephus, for it marks the reason that Canaan did not remain in their land of settlement as did the other children of Noah. Rather than making Canaan the usurper of Shem's land as in Jubilees, Josephus explains the cursing of Canaan in this manner:

> Noah, on learning what had passed [cf. Gen. 9.24-25], invoked a blessing on his other sons, but cursed – not Ham himself, because of his nearness of kin – but his posterity. The other descendants of Ham escaped the curse, but divine vengeance pursued the children of Chananaeus. (*Ant*. 1.142)

Because of his father, Canaan's rights are forfeit (not explicitly spelled out in Gen. 9.24-25), though his name is still given to the land.[37] Otherwise, it seems to be a process of settlement which secures the

---

34. See Betsy Halpern-Amaru, *Rewritng the Bible: Land and Covenant in Post-Biblical Literature* (Valley Forge, PA: Trinity Press, 1994).

35. T. W. Franxman, *Genesis and the 'Jewish Antiquities' of Flavius Josephus* (Rome: Biblical Institute Press, 1979), p. 8.

36. On this, see Alexander, 'Geography and the Bible', p. 983.

37. Riches, *Conflicting Mythologies*, pp. 41-2.

places of the nations in their lands for Josephus (*Ant.* 1.122-143). Israel is an exception, having been given their land by God, in part as a result of the punishment for Ham's dishonesty. There is no suggestion of military conquest or demonic misbehaviour, rather Abram, at the age of seventy-five 'at the command of God went into Canaan, and therein he dwelt himself, and left it to his posterity' (*Ant.* 1.154; cf. *Jub.* 12.12-14). Josephus' view of spatial order is one that allows for different peoples to have their own places. In his view, the Hebrew Scriptures record the original founders of these ancient nations (*Ant.* 1.121). They are not the modern names that the Greeks have given, dating from 'yesterday or the day before' (*C. Ap.* 1.7), but the true and accurate reports of history. Abraham is more noteworthy for being the first to promote monotheism (*Ant.* 1.154-156) than for his role in the placement of Israel in the land. In fact, the depiction of the land of Israel is rather flat in *Antiquities*, as noted by Franxman:

> For all his obvious eagerness to take note of place-names, there is a contrasting lack of concern in making the territory with which he should have been the most familiar 'live' for his readers, and from his picture of the physical setting of his accounts of Abraham, Isaac, and Jacob thus emerges a rather vapid, two-dimensional sketch.[38]

Josephus consciously avoids an emphasis on the covenantal aspect of the land in general, and this reflects his social, political situation. In the very action of his writing, he must take care in what he says about the land so as not to suggest ideas about further revolt or messianism.[39] Yet it is interesting to note that even Josephus does not delete the land promise entirely:

> Even Josephus, whom we know would have cause for such a deletion [of the eschatological content of the land promise], includes the Land in the divine predictions he substitutes for the covenant structure and dangerously alludes to the Land functioning as a vibrant mother country in some future time.[40]

---

38. Franxman, *Genesis*, p. 13. See also B. Halpern-Amaru, 'Land Theology in Philo and Josephus', in L. A. Hoffman (ed.), *The Land of Israel: Jewish Perspectives* (Notre Dame, IN: University of Notre Dame Press, 1986), pp. 65–93.

39. See John Barclay, *Jews in the Mediterranean Diaspora: From Alexander to Trajan (323 BCE–117 CE)* (Berkeley: University of California Press, 1996): 'This [deletion of the covenanted status of land in Josephus] probably reflects political realism: in the aftermath of the War, it was impossible to represent the land as inviolable, and though he still owned property in Judea (*Life* 429), Josephus' Jewish identity now had to be defined in a Diaspora context' (p. 359).

40. Halpern-Amaru, *Rewriting the Bible*, pp. 126–7.

We may even wonder whether Josephus presents in his writings in some way a different view from what he might have held himself at an earlier point in his life, perhaps during his years of training for the priesthood, living within the land. Certainly, within the re-reading of Genesis 10 we have examined, we *do* find a conception of world order in relationship to Jewish traditions and beliefs, but there is no particular interest in setting out and identifying sacred space within that world order, and indeed the relationship to land is determined more through settlement than by divine right and decree.

Texts such as the *Jubilees* and *Antiquities* re-readings of Genesis 10 are extremely valuable for showing up precisely the sorts of ideology in relationship to sacred space which we have previously discussed.[41] Each text was written at a time when land was an important issue in society. For *Jubilees*, it reflects the Hasmonean period of victory and expansion in the land; for Josephus, the land had been lost to the Romans. Neither text reconstructs the historical circumstances of the time of Jesus, but we can see how biblical models are taken up and adapted in light of the (very different) experiences of the two authors. The original text of Genesis 10 provides a rich resource for interpretation a foundation for new appropriations and ideas. Each re-reading asserts that Israel is properly placed (by God) in the land, yet the ways this is expressed are quite different. Land was a key element in retellings of Jewish mythical history.

Looking at Strabo's *Geography* (1st century BCE) as instructive for ancient perspectives on space, it would seem that mythic histories, significant events of recent history, and particular beliefs were more formative for ethnic identity in terms of geography than were specific territorial boundaries. Strabo views the Jewish people as those who have a particular set of beliefs and who are located both in the land and the Diaspora. Strabo's understanding was that the area of the fertile crescent and the lands of Judea and Galilee were populated by different gods and had different myths and mythic figures from those of Graeco-Roman traditions.[42] From a Jewish point of view, it would be important for social identity to emphasize their religious distinctiveness from 'the nations', through such mythic elements and history. The conceptions of the sacredness of space within mythical histories of ancient people are significant, and require further theoretical understanding.

---

41. Scott strongly suggests that *any* 'description of Jewish geographical conceptions must deal with the Table of Nations in Genesis 10 and the influential tradition to which it gave rise' (*Geography in Early Judaism*, p. 23).

42. Katherine Clarke, *Between Geography and History: Hellenistic Constructions of the Roman World* (Oxford: Clarendon Press, 1999), pp. 322–5.

Socially Constructed Mythical Places
(or The Problem of the Sevateem Tribe)

Though tied to particular people and geographical locations, mythical histories and places are not confined to 'this world'. Within sacred writings, it could be argued that land is never merely equal to a physical territory, but is more significant for its part in the mythic relationship between God, people and land. This is confirmed by the fact that the descriptions which *do* include boundaries are not consistent or compatible. As Bruggeman puts it, 'land is never simply physical dirt'.[43] Already, we have seen how the original paradise of Eden was incorporated into the *Jubilees* narrative along with Zion and Sinai. This new triad of sacred spaces may seem to exist purely at the level of belief. However, even such mythical places are part of the social construction of the sacred. As part of a religious worldview, and with meaningful relevance to the present world and social experience, their importance is not diminished for their lack of strict 'mappability'. They are true religious places, the locus of meaning. John Gager describes religion in strikingly spatial terms:

> Religion, then, is that particular mode of world-building that seeks to ground its world in a sacred order, a realm that justifies and explains the arena of human existence in terms of the eternal nature of things. Whether this transcendent realm is the mythical world of remote ancestors, an ideal universe existing in some remote 'heaven', or an order of realities utterly unlike anything known in the present, it is what gives meaning and value – whether positive or negative – to human affairs in 'this world'.[44]

What can we know about such mythical spaces? How can we relate them to experience? Further insights may be found in the work of spatial-critical theorists.

Henri Lefebvre, a prominent figure in the field of critical spatiality and highly influential within the work of James Flanagan and the 'Constructions of Ancient Space' Group of the Society of Biblical Literature and American Academy of Religion,[45] outlines a 'history

---

43. W. Brueggeman, *The Land: Place as Gift, Promise and Challenge in Biblical Faith* (Philadelphia: Fortress Press, 1977), p. 2.

44. J. Gager, *Kingdom and Community: The Social World of Early Christianity* (Englewood Cliffs, NJ: Prentice-Hall, 1975), p. 10.

45. H. Lefebvre, *The Production of Space* (trans. D. Nicholson-Smith; Oxford: Blackwell, 1991), translation of *La Production de l'espace* (Paris: Éditions anthropos, 1974). See H. Molotch on the influence of Lefebvre in English-speaking scholarship, 'The Space of Lefebvre', *Theory and Society* 22 (1993), pp. 887–95.

of space' which begins with absolute space (including mythical and religious space) of nomadic and pastoral societies and continues up to the present (Western) capitalist society, which contains traces of absolute space and other modes of spatial production characteristic of past societies.[46] One of the most important dicta of Lefebvre's work is that all space is socially produced (*L'espace [social] est un produit [social]*).[47] Space is not passive, empty and waiting to be filled. Rather, it is active, productive, and has its own corresponding codes which are part of the relationship between individual members of a society and their space. Humans comprehend and negotiate in daily life the spaces of their social environment, and these spaces have been socially produced in terms of planning, construction and architecture, as well as in corresponding ideas or ideology. One of Lefebvre's examples describes how the image of the *rose des vents* was used in the development of Florence in the twelfth century at the time when a new town square, wharves and bridges were introduced by conscious planners in accordance with this particular *imago mundi*.[48] A symbolic meaning was written into practical space by those who planned and saw to completion the urban development of the city. Were we to make a comparison with Second Temple Judaism, Herod's temple in Jerusalem was clearly built at an ideological level in accordance with the image of the biblical description of the temple, with all its separations and areas of distinct holiness (of which more will be said in Chapter 2). Herod, his architects and planners, including perhaps those priests who took part in the construction of the holy of holies, worked out a 'representation of space' which could be implemented in the physical environment. Again, the temple is a more concrete example than some of the more 'representational' spaces we encounter within Second Temple Judaism, such as those described in our discussion of *Jubilees*.[49]

See also Jon Berquist's analysis of the use of spatial critical work (including that of Lefebvre) in relationship to Biblical Studies and ancient space: J. M. Berquist, 'Critical Spatiality and the Construction of the Ancient World', in D. M. Gunn and P. M. McNutt (eds), *'Imagining' Biblical Worlds: Studies in Spatial, Social and Historical Constructs in Honor of James W. Flanagan* (London: Sheffield Academic Press, 2002), pp. 14–29.

46. Lefebvre, *Production of Space*, pp. 116–22 (on 'absolute space'); pp. 236–41 (on the history of space).

47. Lefebvre, *La Production*, p. 35. (*Production of Space*, p. 26).

48. Lefebvre, *Production of Space*, pp. 118–20.

49. Lefebvre describes a threefold understanding of space which includes: spatial practice (*la pratique spatiale*), representations of space (*les représentations de l'espace*), and representational space (*les espaces de représentation*). These three

A danger which I would want to identify with regard to mythical spaces is in assigning them 'mere' symbolic value. An illustration of this may be found in one of the older incarnations of the British science-fiction television programme *Doctor Who*, where Tom Baker (as the Doctor) is visiting the Sevateem (Survey Team) tribe, and Leela, one of the 'savages' of the tribe, explains to him certain details about the central holy place of her planet and its location. The Doctor responds to her description by asking, 'Is that just some religious gobbledegook, or is that an actual place?' The inner sanctum turns out to be a megalomaniac computer located at the centre of a space ship; however, this scientific 'explanation' of the beliefs of the tribe need not diminish the significance of the place or make it any less formative to the fictional tribe in practical terms. This, I believe, is one of the difficulties in discussing places such as those which we encounter in apocalyptic literature, or for instance 'the kingdom' of the Gospels. How can we understand the importance of a place which does not exist, or does not exist in the 'real' world of scientific description? Here, Lefebvre may again provide helpful insight into the practical importance of mythical spaces. He states:

> Y a-t-il des mythes et symboles en dehors d'un espace mythique et symbolique, déterminé aussi *comme practique? sans doute pas.* [Are there myths and symbols outside of a mythic and symbolic space which is *also* determined as practical? Doubtless not.][50]

Mythic or symbolic spaces do not exist merely as part of highly symbolic language where they are not connected to 'real' (or social) space and also determined in practical ways. They too are firmly part of 'the ongoing social construction of the spatial' which Rob Shields describes as occurring 'both at the level of the social imaginary (collective mythologies, presuppositions) as well as interventions in the landscape (for example, the built environment)'.[51] We shall endeavour, therefore, to keep a balance, and to recognize that religious spaces, whether 'real' or mythical are truly social and socially produced. Though conceptual

---

terms correspond to space perceived (*espace perçu*), space conceived (*espace conçu*) and space lived (*espace vécu*). The three 'moments' of space come together in an individual (subject) for Lefebvre. I will deal here with the concepts only as they relate to the interpretation of mythical and social space. For a clear analysis of Lefebvre's understanding of space with relation to biblical texts, see R. Boer, *Marxist Criticism of the Bible* (London: T&T Clark, 2003), pp. 87–109.

50. H. Lefebvre, *La Production*, p. 140. (*Production of Space*, p. 118).

51. R. Shields, 'Spatial Stress and Resistance: Social Meanings of Spatialization', in G. Benko and U. Strohmayer (eds), *Space and Social Theory: Interpreting Modernity and Postmodernity* (Oxford: Blackwell, 1997), pp. 186–202 (189).

and theological, they are not *merely* so, and have a discernable impact on the 'real' world of human experience.

We might also note that Yi-Fu Tuan describes a category of '*oriented mythical spaces*', emphasizing that society may be organized and personalized in association with cosmological orientation, even including spaces which are described in unreal, vague or inaccurate terms. Such spaces, which 'lie at the conceptual end of the experiential continuum' are also 'pragmatic space in the sense that within the schema a large number of practical activities ... are ordered'.[52] In the sense that Second Temple Judaism was oriented toward Jerusalem, this also ordered the celebration of yearly festivals as well as tithing and other activities. The Jerusalem temple can be considered part of mythical space, with its attendant symbolic associations and the 'secret space' of the holy of holies, which must be imagined for all except the high priest. Yet, even more so, for Jesus and his followers, the *kingdom* functions as an orienting mythical space with practical implications for followers in their daily life and conduct. It is not a question of whether the kingdom is temporal or ethereal, now or not-yet, but rather *how* in practical terms it functions as *both* earthly *and* heavenly, present *and* future orienting space. How does the Abrahamic land promise fit into this notion of the kingdom? Does the temple play a central role in this vision? In order to attempt to answer such questions and to consider the full potential of the spatial concepts we have been exploring, we need to relate them to criteria which may be used to study the historical Jesus in order to determine what, if any, relationship he saw between God, people and land in his own spatial orientation and outlook.

A Plausible Jesus
Words and Actions in Place

The major texts I will be concerned with in the study which follows relate to three particular areas: the temple, purity and the Twelve. Jesus' action in the temple occurs in the earliest layer of tradition about Jesus, the Gospel of Mark (Mk 11.15-18; par. Mt. 21.12-13; Lk. 19.45-46), as does the statement of the stones of the temple torn down (Mk 13.1-2; par. Mt. 24.1-2; Lk. 21.5-6) and the claim of the false witnesses concerning the temple (Mk 14.56-59; par. Mt. 26.60-61; also Jn 2.13-22 and Acts 6.12-14). Regarding purity (a concept closely related to land

---

52. Yi-Fu Tuan, *Space and Place: The Perspective of Experience* (Minneapolis: University of Minnesota Press, 1977), p. 17, pp. 91–100; Philip Sheldrake, *Spaces for the Sacred: Place, Memory and Identity* (London: SCM Press, 2001), pp. 6–8.

in biblical law), Mk 7.15 is a key text which must be dealt with, also found in Matthew and Thomas (Mt. 15.11, *Gos. Thom.* 14). With regard to the Twelve, two Q sayings are key: the statement about the Twelve ruling the twelve tribes (Mt. 19.28; Lk. 22.30); and the gathering from east and west (Mt. 8.11-12; Lk. 13.28-29), which has implications for the tribal land as the central place of the gathering. The authenticity of the temple incident and the existence of the Twelve as a group are generally accepted, and Jesus' interaction with impure individuals and 'sinners' is also considered to be part of early tradition.

Of course, even using material which comes from our earliest sources about Jesus is never a guarantee that they go back to the 'real' historical figure. Gerd Theissen and Dagmar Winter therefore very sensibly emphasize that we always begin our study of the historical Jesus with an idea of what he was like, and this understanding is tested and revised through the evaluation of sayings and actions.[53] 'Authenticity' itself is too strong a term; it is not a matter of piecing together material which then provides a portrait of Jesus.[54] Rather, our discussions must consider the material in such a way that Jesus is recognizable within a first-century Jewish-Galilean context and also account for effects on the different streams of early Christian history.[55] Therefore, what we can know about Jesus and land in the end must be set firmly within the context of contemporary Judaism within 'the land'. It must also offer some explanation as to why the notion of the land was not central (and is even missing) from many strands of early Christian interpretation.

So, what we can know about Jesus and the land promise to Abraham requires more than an evaluation of certain texts. I propose, therefore, to take an integrated and comparative approach which incorporates various resources for Second Temple Judaism, both texts and archaeological evidence. Jewish groups such as the Pharisees, Sadducees, the community at Qumran and others were located and formed their ideologies within 'the land', and living among Jewish sectarianism within the land was clearly a different experience from living as part of Jewish communities of the Diaspora (themselves diverse according to locale).[56] Such groups offer valuable resources for comparison and allow us to appreciate the

---

53. G. Theissen and D. Winter, *The Quest for the Plausible Jesus: The Question of Criteria* (trans. M. E. Boring; Louisville, KY: Westminster/John Knox Press, 2002), p. 211.

54. Theissen and Winter, *Plausible Jesus*, pp. 191–201.

55. Theissen and Winter, *Plausible Jesus*, pp. 209–12.

56. Shaye Cohen, *From the Maccabees to the Mishnah* (Philadelphia: Westminster Press, 1987), p. 171.

different interpretations of Jewish Scripture and ideas. For instance, when the Qumran commentary interprets Ps. 37.11 in the following way, it says something quite different than the interpretation in Mt. 5.5:

> And the poor shall inherit the land and enjoy peace in plenty. Its interpretation concerns the congregation of the poor who will tolerate the period of distress and will be rescued from all the snares of Belial. Afterwards, all who shall inherit the land will enjoy and grow fat with everything... of the flesh. (4Q171ii.9-12)

As a community with strict rules for members who set up a physically separated way of life in the Judean desert, this commentary is applied to the group as the 'congregation of the poor'. Matthew 5.5 also identifies a group to whom the text applies, namely 'the meek'. However, this is set within the context of a very different type of group, one of a wandering charismatic preacher and his followers proclaiming a message of God's kingdom open to the 'tax collectors and sinners' of society in the towns and villages of Galilee. The words and actions of Jesus fit within a very different kind of space than other contemporary groups. And yet, such comparative resources are invaluable for highlighting these sorts of differences.

The plan of the next three chapters is to treat the themes already noted: temple, purity and the Twelve. In looking at the temple, I wish to highlight the great significance of the temple as the central sacred space in first-century Judaism, but also to show that it is a contested place. The boundaries of the temple emphasize separations and hierarchies of society and also allow for the true worship of Yahweh. Jesus' attitude toward the temple, in comparison with other groups such as the Pharisees, Sadducees and Qumran, shows that the temple was not a central focus of the kingdom he proclaimed. And yet, as we cannot simply say that Jesus' attitude toward the temple was the same as his attitude towards the land, there is scope to continue to look to other areas (e.g. purity and the Twelve) for further illumination.

The next chapter focuses on purity and the 'thinking of sacred space' in Second Temple Judaism.[57] Keeping purity regulations was always related to life in the land in the Hebrew Bible, and it was part of everyday life in Palestine at the time of Jesus. The archaeological evidence, particularly relating to *miqvaot* and stone vessels, points to a special interest in purity and the interpretation of purity laws within Jewish society. Jesus' attitude to purity practice is strikingly different from other Jewish groups, and

---

57. This phrase echoes Francis Schmidt's, *How the Temple Thinks: Identity and Social Cohesion in Ancient Judaism* (trans. J. E. Crowley; Sheffield: Sheffield Academic Press, 2001).

his major association of impurity is with 'unclean spirits'. There are important implications for keeping the land pure in the practice of ritual purity, which focuses on the purity of bodies. However, Jesus does not emphasize bodily purity, and again this points to a different understanding of purity, associated more directly with the impurity of spirits and less with the strict maintenance of group boundaries through ritual practices.

The group of the Twelve have an immediate symbolic connection to the land in their association with the twelve tribes of Israel. Jesus' deliberate choice of this group shows something of his understanding of order and governance in the kingdom. This chapter will develop the notion of the Twelve and show its importance for Jesus' expectations about the future in terms of a new, imagined space, namely God's kingdom. The group of twelve relates to the story of exodus and entry into the promised land and shares most in common with the so-called sign-prophets mentioned by Josephus. The Twelve suggest of a new gathering into the land. This vision is both subversive and indicative of a new understanding of sacred space which is characterized by itinerancy in the present, yet looks toward the coming of a 'future sacred space' under God's control and with social recourse for those who struggle for livelihood in the present.

By taking these three themes of temple, purity and the Twelve, I hope to show that there is good reason *not* to discount any consideration of the relationship between God, people and land for Jesus. Though the picture may be more symbolic, eschatological and imaginative than concrete, halakhic and mappable, it is nonetheless important to understand, and to understand spatially. Jesus himself was involved in the dynamic process of changing religious beliefs as he defined a community which would grow and develop in different directions after his death. As a millenarian prophet, Jesus symbolically utilizes notions of sacred space, particularly those closely related to the Abrahamic land promise, in strikingly different ways from his contemporaries; therefore he stands firmly within the diverse strands of social interpretation of the sacred spaces of his time.

Chapter 2

THE TEMPLE AS CONTESTED SPACE

The connections between temple and land are undoubtedly close. So close that in William Horbury's evaluation, entry into the land by Israel was to be immediately followed by worship at the sanctuary in the holy city in sources from the Hasmonean to the Herodian period.[1] Though it is entirely correct to identify close links between the land and the temple, and also the earlier, parallel camp and tabernacle, we need to pay particular attention to the symbolic associations and values placed on each of these as sacred space. The temptation is to link them so closely that they become equal: if we know something about how Jesus related to the temple, then we also know his views on the land. It is not uncommon that land and temple are discussed in close proximity to each other in studies of Jesus.[2] Peter Walker argues along these lines:

> For there is explicit New Testament teaching concerning the fulfilment of the temple in Christ. We can then work out from the clear to the unclear, from the temple through the city to the land, to see how the same phenomenon of fulfilment in Christ affects the issue of the land.[3]

---

1. W. Horbury, 'Land, Sanctuary and Worship', in J. M. G. Barclay and J. P. M. Sweet (eds), *Early Christian Thought in its Jewish Context* (Cambridge: Cambridge University Press, 1996), pp. 207–24.
2. See, for instance, S. Bryan, *Jesus and Israel's Traditions of Judgement and Restoration* (Cambridge: Cambridge University Press, 2002). J. Riches, 'The Social World of Jesus', *Interpretation* 50 (1996), pp. 383–93, S. Freyne, *Galilee, Jesus and the Gospels: Literary Approaches and Historical Investigations* (Dublin: Gill and Macmillan, 1988), 178–98.
3. P. Walker, 'Land in the New Testament', in P. Johnston and P. Walker (eds), *The Land of Promise: Biblical, Theological and Contemporary Perspectives* (Downers Grove, IL: InterVarsity Press, 2000), pp. 81–120 (116–17). Similarly, 'Within a first-century Jewish worldview the temple, the city and the land were understood as three interconnecting theological realia. They were like concentric circles. So a new approach to one aspect of this triad might well signify a new attitude towards the others as well' (p. 101).

In order to avoid this simple transference of meaning between temple, land and city, it will be helpful to turn to the biblical models of land and temple to see how they each behave as sacred space. For here, as we found with the Table of Nations, we will discover a wealth of symbolic resources which could be taken up again at later times, interpreted, modified, adapted, added to and even disregarded. The interpretation of sacred spaces around the time of Jesus was by no means determined. Meaning could be given in very different ways to different holy places (i.e. the tabernacle, Eden, land, temple).

In moving to look at the temple in particular, there is not one single text that establishes a central temple in Jerusalem. Indeed, if we follow Jonathan Smith, no rationale was necessary for the temple, for once it was accepted as sacred, it became 'a place of clarification – most particularly of the hierarchical rules and roles of sacred/profane, pure/impure'.[4] In later tradition, Adam, Noah and Abraham, all 'chronologically' before the temple in the biblical narrative, could become associated with the temple and Jerusalem.[5] The centrality of Jerusalem had been emphasized in Jewish writings particularly since the Persian restoration of Babylonian exiles in Jerusalem and the establishment of the second temple.[6] By the first century, the temple was, in Richard Horsley's words, '*the* sacred space' for ancient Jewish worship and contact with the divine.[7] From the year 6 CE, Rome ruled Judea directly, and yet the Roman garrison was located at Caesarea, while the city of Jerusalem was (for at least a large part of the year) left to the care of the Jerusalem hierarchy. Jerusalem was in many respects a unique city of the Roman Empire, with both religious and socio-political importance in the land as well as in the Jewish Diaspora.[8]

By focusing on the spatial significance of the temple, both as part of religious beliefs and social experience in the first century, we have the

---

4. J. Z. Smith, *To Take Place: Toward Theory in Ritual* (Chicago: University of Chicago Press, 1987), pp. 83–4.

5. See the discussion and examples in Smith, *To Take Place*, p. 84. The temple is asserted to be in the 'right place' through association with important events and figures of the biblical story.

6. R. A. Horsley, *Galilee: History, Politics, People* (Valley Forge, PA: Trinity Press, 1995), pp. 130–32.

7. Horsley, *Galilee*, p. 128.

8. M. Goodman, *The Ruling Class of Judaea: The Origins of the Jewish Revolt Against Rome A.D. 66–70* (Cambridge: Cambridge University Press, 1987). 'Jerusalem was peculiar as a *polis*, even if technically such at this period, because it was to a large extent administered from the Temple in its midst' (p. 46). See also M. Hengel, 'Judaism and Hellenism Revisited', in J. J. Collins and G. Sterling (eds), *Hellenism in the Land of Israel* (Notre Dame, IN: University of Notre Dame Press, 2001), pp. 6–37.

2. *The Temple as Contested Space*

opportunity to flesh out Lefebvre's notion that space is experienced differently by the 'producers' and the 'users' of space. Those with more direct control over the 'representations of space' relating to the temple (e.g., the Sadducees) have a very different relationship to the space than those majority of Jews who experienced the temple from a non-elite position. Though space may be 'a means of control, and hence of domination, of power', it is not completely mastered 'by those who attempt to use it in this way'.[9] Other interpretations, symbolic or 'representational' spaces, exist alongside and compete with the dominant understandings. There is evidence in the relevant literature that the temple was a contested space in the first century, meaning that it symbolized 'contrasted and opposed values' in society from different vantage points.[10] Therefore, by examination of some of the varied perspectives on the temple, we can see that, as a place of contested meaning, it is able to 'reveal broader struggles over deeply held collective myths'.[11] The Samaritans are perhaps a good example of this contested nature of the temple. Even when their own temple at Gerezim was destroyed by John Hyrcanus in an attempt to enforce Jerusalem as the central cult, they still held to the importance of a temple system, though not the *Jerusalem* temple cult. The Qumran community focused on and lived by a temple system, but not the present Jerusalem temple system. For Jesus, the action in the temple shows a contested meaning for the temple, even if that precise meaning tends to be elusive in light of the early interpretations of the action evidenced in the Gospels. Whether the temple action indicates the destruction and restoration of the temple or the destruction of the temple only, it still serves to indicate a critique of the temple system in the gospel traditions about Jesus. In each case, we need to look at the social situations and symbolic resources used by different groups. To begin, therefore, we will examine more closely some of the relevant models of sacred space in biblical tradition.

Text and Architecture

By the first century, the temple was experienced as the physical structure of Herod's rebuilding project (described in the writings of Josephus and

---

9. H. Lefebvre, *The Production of Space* (trans. D. Nicholson-Smith; Oxford: Blackwell, 1991), p. 26.

10. Hilda Kuper, 'The Language of Sites in the Politics of Space', in S. M. Low and D. Lawrence-Zúñiga (eds), *The Anthropology of Space and Place: Locating Culture* (Oxford: Basil Blackwell, 2003), pp. 247–63, here p. 253.

11. S. M. Low and D. Lawrence-Zúñiga, 'Contested Spaces', in Low and Lawrence-Zúñiga (eds), *Anthropology of Space*, p. 245.

the rabbis), but also as a subject of considerable treatment in Jewish apocalyptic literature, particularly writings of the so-called Pseudepigrapha.[12] There was the physical structure in Jerusalem, but also a heavenly entity, revealed to Moses. Jon D. Levenson comments:

> In short, what we see on earth in Jerusalem is simply the earthly manifestation of the heavenly Temple, which is beyond localisation. The Temple on Zion is the antitype to the cosmic in 'heaven', which cannot be distinguished sharply from its earthly manifestation. Thus, when Moses is to construct Israel's first sanctuary, the Tabernacle in the wilderness, he does so on the basis of a glimpse of the 'blueprint' or 'model' of the heavenly shrine which he was privileged to behold on Mount Sinai. (Exod. 25.9, 40)[13]

The tabernacle is then the closest of the earthly models to the heavenly ideal. As a model, the tabernacle is dynamic, and 'presents sacred space as it was thought to be, rather than as it existed'.[14] It may even be that the tabernacle of the Pentateuch, as an idealization placed in the formative period of mythical history, was actually 'based on the Temple itself'.[15] Even so, there are differences in the descriptions of the various structures (e.g. the tabernacle, Solomon's temple). Mark George argues that the tabernacle, first and second temples 'are not simply copies of one another, all reducible to one basic model'.[16] By this, he means to reiterate the diversity of social, political and cultural contexts out of which each of these spatial concepts emerged. An older, idealized model may be used to offer a critique in a new situation in a symbolic way. All of the structures (the tabernacle, first and second temples) show spatial distinctions; for each includes divisions according to different levels of holiness. They reinforce hierarchical structures of Jewish society from priests and kings to people of the land. Still, there are significant differences. Briefly, we will look at the structures of the tabernacle, first and second temples in order to highlight some of the differences in the structures and the hegemonic relationships that go along with them.

---

12. See Martin Goodman, 'The Temple in First Century CE Judaism', in J. Day (ed.), *Temple and Worship in Biblical Israel: Proceedings of the Oxford Old Testament Seminar* (London: T&T Clark, 2005), pp. 459–68.

13. J. D. Levenson, *Sinai and Zion: An Entry Into the Jewish Bible* (San Francisco: HarperSanFrancisco, 1985), p. 140. His remarks relate to Ps. 11.4, where we see that Yahweh has an earthly temple and a heavenly throne (cf. Mt. 5.34-35; 6.10).

14. S. Kunin, *God's Place in the World: Sacred Space and Sacred Place in Judaism* (London: Cassell, 1998), p. 22.

15. Kunin, *God's Place*, pp. 22–3.

16. M. George, 'Tabernacle and Temple Spaces', online: http://www.case.edu/affil/GAIR/Constructions/xtrapapers2000.html (accessed 6 November 2006).

The Tabernacle in the Wilderness

As far as the foundational narratives of the Pentateuch are concerned, the provision of a sanctuary was first realized with the institution of the tabernacle to be a place where God would dwell among the people (Exod. 25.8). This tabernacle was revealed to Moses by God (Exod. 25.8-9) and was to have particular specifications (Exodus 25–31). The different areas of the tabernacle include a most holy place (Exod. 36.35-37), the tabernacle itself (Exod. 36.8-13), an outer tent to the tabernacle (Exod. 36.14-18), an entrance (Exod. 36.37-38) and an outer court (Exod. 38.9-13). The specific dimensions of these spaces are given (Exod. 36.9-21; 38.9-18). Sacrifice was to take place at the tabernacle (29.38-43 and 30.7-10), and it was also a place for communication between God and Moses (25.22 – God says he will speak to Moses from above the mercy seat).[17] This tabernacle, a dwelling place of God, was established in the wilderness and was necessarily a *portable* shrine as the people moved in their wanderings. The tabernacle enters into the land with Joshua and the people and is set up at Shiloh (Josh. 18.1). Some of the tribes are allocated land from the threshold of the tabernacle (Josh. 18.1; 19.51). After this, as Koester affirms, 'in subsequent narratives the tabernacle all but vanishes' until 'David brings the ark of the covenant to his newly established capital of Jerusalem and places it in the tent that he had pitched for it (2 Sam. 6.17)'. This would serve to secure Jerusalem as a centre for worship and also political activity.[18] Still, there is resistance in the text to God dwelling in a permanent, fixed structure:

> Go and tell my servant David: Thus says the Lord, Are you the one to build for me a house to dwell in? I have not lived in a house since the day I brought up the people of Israel from Egypt to this day, but I have been moving about in a tent and a tabernacle. Whenever I have moved about among all the people of Israel, did I ever speak a word with any of the tribal leaders of Israel, whom I commanded to shepherd my people Israel, saying, 'Why have you not built me a house of cedar?' (2 Sam. 7.5-7)[19]

---

17. Craig Koester states that besides these two functions of the temple (sacrifice and divine revelation), God's presence in the tent would also be 'a sign of his covenant faithfulness, since it would fulfill his promise to dwell with Israel and to be their God (25.8; 29.45-46)'. (C. R. Koester, *The Dwelling of God: The Tabernacle in the Old Testament, Intertestamental Jewish Literature, and the New Testament* [Washington, DC: The Catholic Biblical Association of America, 1989], p. 7).

18. Koester, *Dwelling of God*, p. 12.

19. Koester, *Dwelling of God*, p. 13.

Under the tribal leaders (see also 2 Sam. 7.11 – 'judges over Israel'), the nation did not need a permanent house. The tent and tabernacle were sufficient. Bringing the tabernacle to the fixed structure in Jerusalem establishes continuity with the earlier, ideal model, but also indicates a different model of sacred space, to which some resistance is noted.

What sort of economy and leadership are associated with the tabernacle? A primary function of the tabernacle was to provide a place for the sacrifices of the tribal nation. In Leviticus and Numbers, the ordination of the priesthood and the organization of the camp are connected with the tabernacle.[20] Aaron and his sons are anointed at the tabernacle or tent of meeting (Lev. 8.1-10). While a census is taken among the tribes of those who are able to go to war (Num. 1.3), the Levites are excluded from the census and appointed over the tabernacle and all duties relating to it (Num. 1.47-50). The leaders of the tribes give offerings at the tent after Moses has set it up (Num. 7.2). In the wilderness tribal organization around the tabernacle, the nation was dependent on Yahweh even for its food and gathered manna from heaven for sustenance (Exod. 16.1-36) until they came to a habitable land, the border of the land of Canaan (Exod. 16.35).

The major figure associated with the tabernacle is certainly Moses (above the priests). It is he who receives the revelation concerning the tabernacle, and his authority is unquestioned as he is the one who exclusively receives revelation from Yahweh at the tent of meeting.[21] Dozeman points out that though Joshua is associated with the tent as it is brought into the land, 'he does not receive new revelation in the Tent of Meeting'.[22] The strong leadership of Moses in connection with the tabernacle and revelation indicate that the tabernacle was especially associated with Moses and the time in the wilderness, though it also comes to have significance for rest in the land under Joshua.[23] That is, the leadership of Moses and the movable presence of God in the wilderness mark a special time in the mythic history of the tribal nation.

Thus, in dealing with foundational narratives regarding a tribal Israel, the leadership of Moses, the economy of sacrifice and the movable

---

20. T. B. Dozeman, 'Masking Moses and Mosaic Authority in Torah', *JBL* 119.1 (2000), pp. 21–45 (39).

21. Dozeman, 'Masking Moses', p. 38.

22. Dozeman, 'Masking Moses', pp. 37, 38.

23. Koester points out the association of rest and the tabernacle as the promise that the nation would have rest from its enemies (Deut. 12.1-10) was fulfilled at least in part as 'the tent was set up at Shiloh only when most of "the land lay subdued" (Josh. 18.1)' (Koester, *Dwelling of God*, p. 14).

tabernacle are all mythically related to the origins of the nation. It is particularly worthwhile to emphasize that the tabernacle has its 'origins' outside of the land, in the wilderness. Though the land, with its sedentary as opposed to wandering existence, is the goal of the wilderness experience, the presence of Yahweh is with the nation and moves with them in the wilderness. Benjamin Sommer describes the tabernacle as *locomotive* as opposed to *locative*. The tabernacle is a centre for the sacred, divine presence, but it moves. In community, the shrine moves with the people. Thus, 'the divine presence...is not associated with any one locus, and it first became visible to Israel and first took up residence among them in the wilderness, not in the land of Israel'.[24]

Therefore, it was possible to think about the divine presence apart from one fixed location, even if the goal was a 'landed' existence. We will keep this in mind, particularly as the model of the tabernacle is said to be divinely revealed to Moses and is the model for the later temple. Looking even further ahead in the discussion, the idea of the movable presence of God with the people in the wilderness is significant for thinking about the itinerant existence of Jesus and his followers.

Solomon's Temple

In 2 Samuel, David is taken from shepherding to be prince of Israel (2 Sam. 7.8). The imagery is of a movement from pastoral existence to a fixed kingdom. It is said that David's descendant will build a house for God's name and God will 'establish the throne of his kingdom forever' (2 Sam. 7.13). Whereas previously the tabernacle was with the people in the wilderness and came to rest in Shiloh, it now comes to rest in Jerusalem (1 Kgs 6.19), and is a key feature of the establishment of a united monarchy and the first temple under Solomon. Thus, dynamic sacred space becomes static centralized sacred space, and the temple is now the centre of the promised land which is characterized by holiness. Seth Kunin highlights the differences in these models:

> Unlike the dynamic model which does not provide a firm foundation for the characterisation of geography, the static model with its centre fixed in Jerusalem provides a firm basis for the cognitive understanding of the land of Israel.[25]

In the 'landed' model, boundaries are fixed and centralized in a more permanent geography, but still with a tribal aspect in governance. Solomon

---

24. B. D. Sommer, 'Conflicting Constructions of Divine Presence in the Priestly Tabernacle', *BibInt* 9.1 (2001), pp. 41–63 (48).
25. Kunin, *God's Place*, p. 25.

has twelve officials over the tribes and their locations (1 Kgs 4.7-19). The assigning of districts within the land is followed by establishment of the borders of Solomon's kingdom (1 Kgs 4.20-28).[26] In the description of Solomon's temple, a rectangular shape is described (1 Kgs 6.2-20), with a vestibule and constructed area surrounding the temple. There is an inner sanctuary, a most holy place (1 Kgs 6.16, 21), and an entrance to the most holy place (1 Kgs 6.31-32) as well as to the nave of the temple (1 Kgs 6.33-35). As with the tabernacle structure, specific areas of sanctity are described.

As far as the economy and leadership of this temple are concerned, David and Solomon are essential to both. David brings the ark to Jerusalem (2 Samuel 6) and it is also David who desires to build a permanent house for the ark (2 Samuel 7). Throughout the description of the building of the temple in 1 Kings 6, Solomon is the integral to the entire process. 1 Kings 6.14 gives Solomon sole responsibility for the building project: 'So Solomon built the house and finished it'. Still, in the ceremony of dedication of the temple, it is the priests who carry the ark and place it in the holy place (1 Kgs 8.3-11).

In the context of the so-called Deuteronomistic History (Deuteronomy through to Kings), the temple of Solomon is of central importance and other holy places of worship must succumb to the centrality of worship in Jerusalem. Shiloh, for instance, is one of the 'outside' or competing centres for worship.[27] Roland Boer, in his treatment of the account of Samuel and the temple at Shiloh in 1 Samuel 1–2, points out how the sacred site at Shiloh must become subordinate to Jerusalem in the understanding of the 'historian' who compiled this work:

> But not only is the temple central in a chronological sense; it also functions as the only place for legitimate worship of Yahweh. The other places, especially the high places, but also the other shrines and minor places for worship are therefore illegal, not to be tolerated. And this applies even to those with some apparent pedigree, such as Bethel, Dan, and of course, Shiloh. So, a continual pattern becomes apparent in the 'Deuteronomistic History', in which worship must be carried out in Jerusalem, at the temple, and nowhere else, and yet alternative worship continues. The various shrines and high places become contested zones, the subject of polemic and theological condemnation.[28]

---

26. M. George, 'Tabernacle and Temple Spaces'.

27. See Kunin on 'non-centralized models of sacred space', *God's Place*, pp. 27–30.

28. R. Boer, *Marxist Criticism of the Bible* (London: T&T Clark, 2003), pp. 106–7.

Again, the Samaritan example compares with this, as Gerezim is a contested sacred space which, from a Judean perspective, must be eliminated in favour of Jerusalem.

Irrespective of its historical referent, the description of the building of Solomon's temple attempts 'to establish an ideological continuity between the beginning of the monarchy under David and Solomon and its end, and to suggest the possibility of restoration and a new beginning, perhaps under a restored Davidic ruler'.[29] The narrative, expressing such hopes, also opens up possibilities for new interpretations. For instance, the text of 2 Sam. 7.10 ('And I will appoint a place for my people Israel and will plant them, so that they may live in their own place, and be disturbed no more') was read by the community at Qumran in such a way as to express the ideology of the community regarding the last times and their own role as a 'community temple' (4 QFlorilegium).[30] The hope of a new Davidic era and kingdom would be continuous with the setting of the description of Solomon's temple within the Deuteronomistic History.

The Rebuilt Temple

The rebuilding of the temple is described in the book of Ezra. Interestingly, though, there is no description as to how the space of the temple was divided, as was the case for the tabernacle and Solomon's temple. It is, however, noted that this temple rests on the foundations of the first temple (Ezra 2.68; 5.15; 6.7). Therefore, it may be that the divisions of space were assumed to rely on the earlier narratives. It is not mentioned that the tabernacle is installed in this temple.[31] As for the location of the temple in *Jerusalem* (which was not emphasized in the description of Solomon's temple), it is crucial to Ezra's description of rebuilding. King Cyrus says after his decree that the temple should be rebuilt: 'Take these

---

29. J. Van Seters, 'Solomon's Temple: Fact and Ideology in Biblical and Near Eastern Historiography', *CBQ* 59 (1997), pp. 45–57 (57).

30. D. Vanderhooft, 'Dwelling Beneath the Sacred Place: A Proposal for Reading 2 Samuel 7:10', *JBL* 118.4 (1999), pp. 625–33. Vanderhooft states that 'the Qumran commentator suggests that the "house" he has in mind is not a physical structure but rather is constituted metaphorically by the elect community at the end of days; the midrash is thus reflective of a particular sectarian eschatology' (p. 627).

31. Victor A. Hurowitz, 'YHWH's Exalted House – Aspects of the Design and Symbolism of Solomon's Temple', in J. Day (ed.) *Temple and Worship in Biblical Israel* (London: T&T Clark, 2005), pp. 63–110. On the re-built temple in comparison to Solomon's, see p. 101. See also the larger discussion of the divine presence and symbolism of Solomon's temple.

vessels [taken from the Jerusalem temple to Babylon]; go and put them in the temple in Jerusalem, and let the house of God be rebuilt on this site' (Ezra 5.15). Cyrus plays an important role in the Jewish community's ability to return and rebuild the temple at Jerusalem. Jewish leaders and priests are specifically named (Ezra 3.2, 8–9, 12), indicating their social position and status.[32] The leadership of the new community consists of priests, Levites and other named individuals of particular families, and there is no Jewish king involved in the rebuilding of the temple.

In the descriptions of the tabernacle and Solomon's temple, there was a principle established of hierarchical divisions of sacred space which was 'built on' or modified by other descriptions, yet never rethought 'from scratch'.[33] For the first temple and the tabernacle, there are divisions of the holy and most holy spaces. The land, as the widest category of sacred space, is not merely equal in meaning to the temple. For the tabernacle, the land features as the goal of the wandering; for Solomon's temple, the land is part of the king's empire.[34] For the second temple, following the return to the land from exile, there is specific concern with location in Jerusalem and with the named individuals who are involved in the rebuilding of the temple. We are not arguing for the historical or archaeological accuracy of the descriptions (indeed there is scant evidence for Solomon's temple, let alone the tabernacle), but these biblical models are important to later understandings of sacred space. They are not the only biblical models (Ezekiel's descriptions of the temple, for instance), but they show the place of the temple for major events of the biblical narrative – wandering and entry into the land, the institution of kingship, and exile and return.

By looking at some of the aspects of leadership associated with the described spaces, we begin to observe that these types of texts display 'representations of space' and connections with status and hierarchy. This can also be observed in relationship to Herod the Great's temple. As with Cyrus' involvement with the rebuilding of the temple in Ezra, the first-century situation entailed Roman involvement with the temple system, as well as other groups such as Herodians and the high priest. Ordinary Jews of the land and Diaspora held the temple in high regard as the central place of worship and sacrifice. At different levels of interaction with the temple, the contested nature of the temple may

---

32. M. George ('Tabernacle and Temple Spaces') lists the people involved in the rebuilding and notes the importance for social practice of 'being named, and therefore recognized, as a participant'.

33. George, 'Tabernacle and Temple Spaces'.

34. Habel, *The Land is Mine: Six Biblical Land Ideologies* (Minneapolis: Fortress Press, 1995), pp. 22–5.

The Second Temple at Home and Abroad

By the beginning of the first century CE, Roman rule had been a reality in Palestine since 63 BCE. The memory of Hasmonean expansion of the borders of the land and the purification of the temple after the profanation by Antiochus Epiphanes was still fairly recent. Herod the Great (37–34 BCE) undertook to rebuild in Hellenistic style the temple in Jerusalem. This was the most impressive of his many building projects, and was hailed by Pliny as one of the great structures of the empire (*Natural History* 5.70). However, Josephus tells us that the temple was not completed until 64 CE, which was a mere six years prior to its destruction by the Roman armies. Jerusalem was an important cosmopolitan city, yet also different from other cities of the empire, with the temple in its midst. The distinctiveness of the city and temple would have had a considerable impact on the traffic of pilgrims to Jerusalem for festivals.[35] Pilgrimage, as well as the payment of the half-shekel temple tax (based on Exod. 30.11-16) show that among the diverse communities of the Diaspora, there were important links between the people, 'the Jews' and the land and temple.[36] Philo considers Jerusalem the 'mother city' of Jews in Europe and Asia, even though the settled regions of the Diaspora are considered to be their 'country' (*Flaccus*, 46). A writing such as the *Letter of Aristeas* (ca. 2nd century BCE – 1st century CE) from Alexandria in the Diaspora contained an imaginative geography (lacking historical references) of Jerusalem and the land of Israel.

If we look at the situation within 'the land', there were potential problems with Roman presence within the ideal boundaries of sacred space. According to Kunin's structural model of biblical sacred space, Rome, as part of the category of 'the nations' is in opposition to the category of Israel (land and people, which would include Jews in the Diaspora) and therefore should be separate and excluded from the realm of sacred space.[37] Yet, the reality of Roman rule meant that, although

---

35. M. Hengel, 'Judaism and Hellenism Revisited', in J. Collins and G. Sterling (eds), *Hellenism in the Land of Israel* (Notre Dame, IN: University of Notre Dame Press, 2001), pp. 6–37 (25). See also L. Levine, *Judaism and Hellenism in Antiquity: Conflict or Confluence?* (Peabody, MA: Hendrickson, 1999), p. 93.

36. John Barclay, *Jews in the Mediterranean Diaspora: From Alexander to Trajan (323 BCE–117 CE)* (Berkeley: University of California Press, 1996), pp. 417–23.

37. Kunin, *God's Place*, pp. 14–17.

the Jews were allowed considerable control over the temple and were permitted to exclude foreigners from entering the temple on pain of death, there were still areas where Rome asserted their position. Rome maintained a military presence in Jerusalem at Herod's Antonia fortress, located next to the temple (*Ant.* 18.92) on the northeast corner of the enclosure.[38] Josephus relates that troops were stationed the time of festivals in case of an uprising among the crowds (*War* 2.224; *Ant.* 20.106–107). While the military headquarters (and residence of the Roman governor) was at Caesarea,[39] the forces at the temple during the festivals would reinforce Roman interest in and control over the temple.

Another significant issue seems to have been the control of the high priest's garments. In *Antiquities* 18.90-95, Josephus describes various stages by which control of the high priest's vestments changed hands. First, he says they were in the hands of the high priests (in a tower near the temple) beginning with Hyrcanus (18.91). Then he says that Herod kept control of the vestments at Antonia when he became king, which practice was also continued by his son Archelaus (18.92-93). When the Romans 'entered on the government' (18.93), they took possession of the vestments and kept them, only allowing the priest to have them in his possession during the three yearly festivals (18.93-4). Vitellius, according to this account, finally returned the robes to the priests in the temple (18.90, 95). The issue of the vestments occurs again in Josephus' writings at the death of Agrippa when his kingdom (Judea, Samaria and part of Galilee) was placed under Roman procurators. Fadus, the first procurator,[40] wanted the leaders of Jerusalem to place the robes under Roman control (*Ant.* 20.6-14). An appeal to Claudius Caesar is made and the robes are allowed to remain in the control of the priesthood. Clearly, this was an issue of some importance to the chief priests and leading men of Jerusalem, and Fadus' assumption that he had the right to control the vestments was problematic because of the symbolic value of the issue.[41]

---

38. D. Mendels, *The Rise and Fall of Jewish Nationalism: Jewish and Christian Ethnicity in Ancient Palestine* (Grand Rapids: Eerdmans, 2nd edn, 1997), p. 290.

39. M. Stern, 'The Province of Judaea', in S. Safrai and M. Stern (eds), *The Jewish People in the First Century: Historical Geography, Political History, Social, Cultural and Religious Life and Institutions* (CRINT; Assen: Van Gorcum, 1974), vol. 1, p. 343.

40. J. S. McLaren, *Power and Politics in Palestine: The Jews and the Governing of their Land, 100 BC–AD 70* (Sheffield: JSOT Press, 1991), p. 127. See *Ant.* 20.2.

41. McLaren, *Power and Politics*, p. 128.

2. *The Temple as Contested Space*

Herodian influence on the temple was not without its problems as well. In the *Antiquities*, Josephus tells us that the respected men of Jerusalem built a wall to block Herod Agrippa's[42] view of the temple from his palace (*Ant.* 20.189-190). Agrippa and Festus the Roman procurator were displeased with the wall which not only blocked the view of the temple from the palace, but also the view of the Roman guards from the western cloisters (*Ant.* 20.192-193). Festus ordered that the wall be taken down and the Jews (ten principal men) petitioned Nero to keep the wall (20.193-194), and their request is granted in order to please Nero's wife, 'a religious woman' (20.195). Says McLaren:

> Despite Agrippa's official position as custodian of the Temple, it is implied in the account that he was not omnipotent in terms of what happened there. The construction work on the Temple was undertaken in direct defiance of him. Furthermore, when pressed, the Jews refused to remove the wall. It is apparent that Jews connected with the Temple did not perceive Agrippa as its overlord. His permission was not considered necessary to engage in structural alterations.[43]

We may also be reminded here of the earlier Herod's inablility to enter the temple sanctuary, even though he had been the instigator and support for the building project (*Ant.* 15.420). In the account of the building of the wall, Agrippa is not capable of stopping the action of the Jews in blocking his view of the temple. Though Nero presents an opportunity for Agrippa to appoint a new high priest (*Ant.* 20.195-196), the Roman authorities ultimately decide on the situation. Particularly significant is the influence and position of the leading men of Jerusalem with regard to the temple and the seeming lack of control by Herod Agrippa in this instance.

We should also mention the Sadducees as an important group in relationship to the temple. Though relatively little is known about the Sadducees – their history, leaders and beliefs – they are not an entirely indistinct group. They are mentioned as a group in Josephus, the rabbinical writings and the New Testament, yet none of these writings preserves any material produced by the Sadducees themselves. Since these sources come to us by way of opponents or outsiders, it is not surprising to find them 'necessarily selective and tendentious'.[44] We cannot be sure about the Sadducees connection with Sadok (*War* 2.451,

---

42. This is Agrippa II, ruling parts of Agrippa I's kingdom from 48–66 CE.
43. McLaren, *Power and Politics*, p. 148.
44. G. Stemberger, 'The Sadducees – Their History and Doctrines, in W. Horbury, W. D. Davies and J. Sturdy (eds), *The Cambridge History of Judaism* (Cambridge: Cambridge University Press, 1999), pp. 428–43.

2.628), nor with the precise moment of the Sadducees' nascence as a group. Josephus chronologically first mentions the Sadducees under John Hyrcanus (135–104 BCE, *Ant*. 13.288-98), but the other two passages where Josephus speaks of the Sadducees (*War* 11.119 and *Ant*. 18.11) could indicate that the Sadducees emerged as a group in the time of Herod.

As a group, the Sadducees probably made some impact on, as well as compromises with, Herod (e.g. *Ant*. 15.299-316; 20.199-200).[45] They maintained their position in society by cooperating with 'the salient tendencies of the institutions at that time'[46] (namely the Herodian family and the Roman administration). The New Testament mentions a Sadducee as 'captain of the Temple' (Acts 4.1) as well as indicating that the high priest 'party' was made up of Sadducees (Acts 5.17).[47] Whatever else we might say about the make-up of the Sadducees, they emerge as a small group with members of status, having high priests or potential high priest among their members, and centred in Jerusalem.[48]

Not only such 'powerful' groups in Jewish society, but also the general population had a stake in the temple and the protection of the central institution for the worship of God. Accounts of the Roman order to place a statue of Gaius in the temple at Jerusalem and subsequent Jewish protest are recorded in both Josephus (*War* 2.185-203; *Ant*. 18.261-304) and Philo (*Legat*. 207-276, 333). As a general outline of the story, Gaius orders Petronius (governor of Syria) to place a statue of himself (Gaius) in the temple. The Jewish leading men are involved and the population protests (differently in the accounts, but all regarding crops). Eventually, the order is withdrawn. Both Josephus and Philo refer to influential Jews who meet with Petronius over the conflict. The description of the protest of the populace varies. In *War*, they delay sowing their crops (*War* 2.200). In Philo, the fear is that they will burn their crops (*Legat*. 249). Perhaps the best known description is the one in the *Antiquities* where the crowd at Tiberias offer their throats to be

---

45. M. Stern, 'Social and Political Realignments in Herodian Judea', in L. I. Levine (ed), *The Jerusalem Cathedra: Studies in the History, Archaeology, Geography and Ethnography of the Land of Israel* (3 vols.; Jerusalem: Yad Izhak Ben-Zvi Institute, 1981), vol. 2, pp. 40–62 (51).

46. Stern, 'Social and Political Realignments', p. 51.

47. M. Stern, 'Aspects of Jewish Society: The Priesthood and Other Classes', in S. Safrai and M. Stern (eds), *The Jewish People in the First Century: Historical Geography, Political History, Social, Cultural and Religious Life and Institutions* (CRINT; Assen: Van Gorcum, 1976), vol. 2, pp. 561–630 (610).

48. Stemberger, 'The Sadducees', p. 434.

cut, for they would rather die than see the law transgressed (18.271). This protest is said to have lasted forty days in which time they did not till the ground, though it was the sowing season (18.272). It is not necessary to choose one of these accounts as more historical than the others, but it is significant that a large number of Jews 'protested as a united front'.[49] Their concern for the temple is apparent, important enough to defend with their lives.[50] There are other incidents which could be mentioned, such as the reaction to Pilate's placing of Roman standards into the Antonia fortress, where a group of protesters go to Caesarea to petition Pilate, again offering their necks rather than allow the transgression of the law (*Ant.* 18.55-59).

The point here is not to give a comprehensive picture of the complex relationships of the temple in the Roman period. However, it is possible to highlight different levels of involvement with the temple and the potential for conflict within the given political situation. As a central focus of contact with the sacred for Jews of the land as well as the Diaspora, the temple inspired devotion and loyalty; but control of the temple was also a contested issue, particularly during the first revolt and the period leading up to the revolt. Recognizing this, we now turn to look at examples of alternative temples, the Samaritan temple at Gerezim and the place of the temple for the Qumran community.

The Samaritan Temple at Gerizim

The Samaritan temple at Gerizim may be grouped with such sacred places as Bethel, Dan (1 Kgs 12.25-33) and Shiloh (1 Samuel 1–2). That is, these are alternative places of worship, not without some level of pedigree in the literature, but which become 'contested zones, the subject of polemic and theological condemnation'.[51] In Deuteronomy and Joshua, Mount Gerizim is the site of the declaration of blessings upon entry into the land (Deut. 11.29, 27.12; Josh. 8.33). Though there are no biblical references to a temple at Gerizim, Josephus relates that one was built by Sanballat and that he instituted a priesthood (*Ant.* 11.19-119, 304-347). Samaritan documents unfortunately come from the fourth century CE (and later), and therefore are not reliable sources of Samaritan practices or beliefs of the first century.[52] Therefore, the best evidence concerning the Samaritans

---

49. McLaren, *Power and Politics*, p. 126.
50. McLaren, *Power and Politics*, p. 126.
51. Boer, *Marxist Criticism of the Bible*, pp. 106–107.
52. Stanley Isser, 'The Samaritans and their Sects', in W. Horbury, W. D. Davies and J. Sturdy (eds), *The Cambridge History of Judaism,* vol. 3: *The Early Roman Period* (Cambridge: Cambridge University Press, 1999), pp. 569–95 (569–70).

during the Second Temple period comes from Josephus, who is actually quite hostile in his treatment of them and should be distrusted in many instances. There are three main passages where Josephus makes polemical statements against the Samaritans. One describes the Samaritan reaction to the proscription of Jewish practices by Antiochus Epiphanes (*Ant.* 12.257-264). In another, he describes their origins as Chouthaioi transported to Samaria from Persia by the Assyrian king of 2 Kgs 17.4, learning the Hebrew religion from Israelite priests (*Ant.* 9.277-279, 288-291). Finally, in book 11 of the *Antiquities*, Josephus talks about the Samaritans in relation to Alexander, calling them apostates from the Jewish nation (11.340). Josephus' statements suggest it would be unwise to trust his evaluation of the Samaritans.[53] He does, however, give the information that it was under John Hyrcanus that the temple at Gerizim was destroyed (*Ant.* 13.255-256) between 113 and 111 BCE.[54] This, according to Pummer, was 'motivated by expansionistic politics'[55] of the Hasmoneans, destroying rival sites to Jerusalem.[56]

There is some archaeological evidence for the Gerizim temple. The temple, according to such evidence, was similar in some respects to the Jerusalem temple. It has been suggested that there is evidence of Passover celebration at the site of the sacred precinct at Mount Gerizim and that the structure of the precinct was similar to the Jerusalem temple.[57] Coins dating from after the destruction of the Gerizim temple by John Hyrcanus show that the city continued for at least some years after the destruction of the temple.[58] Josephus suggests in *War* 3.307-315 that the Samaritans defended themselves against the Romans.

Another incident in Josephus suggests eschatological hopes among the Samaritans. In *Ant.* 18.85-89, the tale is told of an individual, a 'sign-prophet' who promises to reveal the hidden sacred vessels and

---

53. See R. J. Coggins, 'The Samaritans in Josephus', in L. H. Feldman and G. Hata (eds), *Josephus, Judaism and Christianity* (Detroit, MI: Wayne State University Press, 1987), pp. 257–73.

54. Y. Magen, 'Mount Gerizim and the Samaritans', in F. Manns and E. Alliata (eds), *Early Christianity in Context: Monuments and Documents* (Jerusalem: Franciscan Printing Press, 1993), pp. 91–148 (142–3).

55. Pummer states that 'John Hyrcanus' conquests were part of the Maccabeean policy which Alexander Janneus had intensified to attack and destroy the Hellenistic culture and eliminate the sacred sites which competed with the Temple in Jerusalem'. R. Pummer, *The Samaritans* (Leiden: E. J. Brill, 1987), p. 4.

56. Magen, 'Mount Gerizim', p. 143.

57. Magen, 'Mount Gerizim', p. 139.

58. O. R. Sellers, 'Coins of the 1960 Excavation at Shechem', *BA* 25 (1962), pp. 87–96 (96).

'signal the Era of Divine Favour'.[59] An important point, made by Isser, can be learned from this account, namely that 'many of the Samaritan religious community took seriously its eschatological traditions which involved the figure of Moses, the ancient tabernacle, and a restorer, all connected with Mount Gerizim'.[60] This millenarian figure takes up the spatial model of the tabernacle, and uses it in a way that asserts the sacredness of Gerizim. However, the group of followers and their leader are among the powerless in society, not the powerful, and Pilate kills and captures them, ordering those still alive to be slain (18.87). Though Pilate is ordered to answer to Rome for his actions (88–89), the damage has been done and the symbolic movement is quashed (as was also the case for other, non-Samaritan prophetic groups of this type).

Richard Bauckham describes the Samaritans and the Jews as each 'understanding their self-identity as Jewish while denying Jewish identity to the other'.[61] In spatial terms, this means that it is possible to suggest at the widest understanding of sacred space, in the distinction between Israel and the nations, each group includes the other in the realm of profane space among the nations. Josephus relates an incident in which Samaritans place human bones in the Jerusalem temple (*Ant.* 18.29), which would be a strong symbol of the profanity of the Jerusalem temple from a Samaritan perspective. It is fascinating how two groups, so closely related – geographically, in terms of sacred tradition and ethnicity – could draw such exclusive boundaries in terms of identity.

Qumran and the Jerusalem Temple

One of the distinctive features of the Qumran community is that they separated themselves from the Jerusalem temple and viewed themselves as a temple community awaiting the establishment of a new temple. Not unlike the Samaritan example, the boundaries of the sacred do not necessarily include all Jews in the present time of the community. As John Kampen states, 'Israel has not followed the correct law because it was rooted in the wrong temple'.[62] Proper prayers are only offered by the

---

59. Isser, 'Samaritans and their Sects', p. 176. Isser says these are the vessels of the tabernacle.
60. Isser, 'Samaritans and their Sects', p. 176.
61. R. Bauckham, 'The Parting of the Ways: What Happened and Why', *ST* 47.2 (1993), pp. 135–51 (141).
62. John Kampen, 'The Significance of the Temple in the Manuscripts of the Damascus Document', in R. A. Kugler and E. M. Schuller (eds), *The Dead Sea Scrolls at Fifty: Proceedings of the 1997 Society of Biblical Literature Qumran Section Meetings* (Atlanta: Scholars Press, 1999), pp. 185–97 (196).

community in the desert (1QS ix.4-5). They kept purity in an 'age of ungodliness' (that ungodliness affecting other Jews and not just non-Jews) and maintained an 'interim ethic' whereby they obeyed the Torah according to their interpretation.[63] Schiffman comments on CD vi.11-14, saying that '[it] provides that abstention from the Jerusalem cult was a condition for sectarian membership'.[64] In 1QS, the community themselves will be 'founded on truth' to be 'a holy house for Israel' chosen and accepted 'to atone for the land' (1QS vii.5-6, 10).[65] In the messianic age, the hopes of the community will be realized in the new Israel. They will usher in the promises for Israel centred on the temple, city and land. Interestingly enough, the inheritance of the land in Isaiah 60.21 (interpreted at Qumran) uses exactly the same terminology as Psalm 37.[66]

Again, we see that spatial models are utilized which order life according to the community rule. Though there is separation from the current temple and its leadership, there is still a concern with the temple and temple worship. Temple references are found in numerous documents of the Dead Sea Scrolls. Indeed, George Brook identifies no less than ten temples in various Qumran documents.[67] In the *Temple Scroll*, the future temple is modelled on Israel's encampment in tribes around the tent of meeting in the wilderness (Exodus 25–40) and Ezekiel's descriptions of the temple in Ezekiel 40–48.[68] As Jonathan Smith argues with regard to the Ezekiel text, so the Qumran text is also 'an endeavor in mapping the social configurations of an ideal cultic space'.[69] Francis Schmidt makes the suggestion that perhaps the choice of the camp as a

63. O. Betz, 'The Essenes', in W. Horbury, W. D. Davies and J. Sturdy (eds), *The Cambridge History of Judaism*, vol. 3: *The Early Roman Period* (Cambridge: Cambridge University Press, 1999), pp. 444–70 (453).

64. L. Schiffman, *The Halakhah at Qumran* (Leiden: E. J. Brill, 1975), p. 129.

65. See P. R. Davies, 'Space and Sects in the Qumran Scrolls', in D. M. Gunn and P. M. McNutt (eds), *'Imagining' Biblical Worlds: Studies in Spatial, Social and Historical Constructs in Honor of James W. Flanagan* (London: Sheffield Academic Press, 2002), pp. 81–98. Here, whether or not the holy of holies in the holy house (1QS 8.5-9) is meant to indicate the entire community or an inner group of it, 'in either case we have a radical redrafting of the geography of the land of Israel' (p. 94).

66. See the pesher on Psalm 37 (4Q171ii.4-5). R. L. Wilken, *The Land Called Holy: Palestine in Christian History and Thought* (New Haven: Yale University Press, 1992), p. 48.

67. G. J. Brooke, 'The Ten Temples in the Dead Sea Scrolls', in J. Day (ed.), *Temple and Worship in Biblical Israel: Proceedings of the Oxford Old Testament Seminar* (London: T&T Clark, 2005), pp. 417–34.

68. See Dwight D. Swanson, *The Temple Scroll and the Bible: The Methodology of 11QT* (Leiden: E. J. Brill, 1995), p. 3.

69. Smith, *To Take Place*, p. 48.

model was particularly appropriate to the community as they awaited the messianic times, recalling a period of origins when God directly intervened for his people.[70] Solomon's temple also serves as a model for the design of the temple and sanctuary in 11Q19 iii–xiii, xxx–xxxv. The temple here is ideal and 'part of the tradition that idealized the Solomonic structure', and yet 'the design is not entirely outside the range of possibility' in comparison with the descriptions of the holy area in Josephus and the rabbis.[71]

Again, we see the significance of the earlier models, and also the adaptation of such models. Maier says that the *Temple Scroll* has 'a centrifugal shifting of the functional design' wherein the middle court is a men's court and the court of Israel is part of the outer court. The boundary for foreigners and impure people moves to outside the entire complex.[72] There is also 'the consequent application of the scheme of concentric squares combined with the function of a sanctuary for the twelve tribes'.[73] Therefore, the status of men is elevated and the belief is reinforced that not only foreigners, but also those who are considered by the community to be the impure of Israel, are excluded from the sacred.

This tells us something about how the Qumran community envisions the order of the new era. They prepare for it by their arrangements within the community in the present. So, Schmidt:

> The calendar of the Community already organized temporality according to the rhythm of the celestial liturgies: community times, sacred and profane, at odds with the Jerusalem calendar, are in unison with the angelic festivities. But, as long as the conditions will not be realized for the building of the new Temple, the Community will not have a Sanctuary where such an organization of the sacred is distributed in its architectural space.

Therefore, Jerusalem may continue to stand at the centre of the world, but matters of law and living are centred in the community itself.[74] If Qumran had anything like a functioning high-priestly role, that

---

70. F. Schmidt, *How the Temple Thinks: Identity and Social Cohesion in Ancient Judaism* (trans. J. E. Crowley; Sheffield: Sheffield Academic Press, 2001), p. 145.

71. J. Maier, 'The *Temple Scroll* and Tendencies in the Cultic Architecture of the Second Commonwealth', in L. Schiffman (ed.), *Archaeology and History in the Dead Sea Scrolls: The New York University Conference in Memory of Yigael Yadin* (Sheffield: JSOT Press, 1990), pp. 67–82 (77).

72. Maier, 'The Temple Scroll', p. 77.

73. Maier, 'The Temple Scroll', p. 77.

74. This is argued by P. R. Davies, 'Space and Sects', p. 89. He compares the attitude of Qumran (the *Damascus Document/Temple Scroll*) with the respect Paul held for the Jerusalem church.

role was quite unlike the role of the high priest in Jerusalem and was specifically related to the existence and practices of the community, such as meals and meetings together.[75] Clearly, spatial were contested, defined and redefined within the organization and beliefs of the community at Qumran.

The Testament of Moses

References to the temple occur with some frequency in the *Testament (Assumption) of Moses*, and certainly the meaning and role of the temple is at issue for the author in a way which conflicts with the present temple. This Jewish work of the early first century CE has as its overall framework Moses' appointment of Joshua to take the people into the land. When they enter the land, Joshua is to give each tribe their individual portions (*T. Mos.* 2.2), but soon a distinction is made between 'two holy tribes' and the ten tribes (*T. Mos.* 2.4-5). It would seem that the author identifies with the two tribes and that the ten tribes are viewed negatively. One set of verses in particular draws attention to the distinction:

> And in those times he will inspire a king to have pity on them and send them home to their own land. Then some parts of the tribes will arise and come to their appointed place, and they will strongly build its walls. Now, the two tribes will remain steadfast in their former faith, sorrowful and sighing because they will not be able to offer sacrifices to the Lord of their fathers. But the ten tribes will grow and spread out among the nations during the time of their captivity. (*T. Mos.* 3.6-9)

Here, we cannot be sure who is meant by 'some parts of the tribes' nor can we say with certainty why the two tribes were not able to offer sacrifices. Daniel Schwartz thinks that these verses refer to the return of some Israelites to the land and Jerusalem under Cyrus. Therefore, only the 'some' return, while the two and the ten remain in the Diaspora. From among the Jews that remained in the Diaspora, 'those of the two tribes remained faithful while the ten tribes sank into oblivion among their Gentile neighbours and so are not referred to again'.[76] Thus, for

---

75. Davies cites evidence in making this judgement: '1QS refers to the "sons of Zadok" as having authority over the *yahad*, while 1Qsa describes the presence of the high priest at the meal of the congregation. But the role of a sectarian high priest (and obviously not the high priest of the Jerusalem Temple), while it does imply the relocation of sacerdotal functions from the Jerusalem Temple to the community, remains consistent with the essential vertical dimension of the sectarian liturgy. Other than the regular meetings and meals, and texts of prayers and blessings, we have no clear description of any liturgical ceremonies'. Davies, 'Space and Sects', p. 96.

76. D. Schwartz, 'The Tribes of As. Mos. 4:7-9', *JBL* 99.2 (1980), pp. 217–23 (22).

2. The Temple as Contested Space

Schwartz, both the two and the ten tribes would refer to Diaspora Jews. The two tribes mourn their inability to sacrifice because they are not near enough to the temple to do so.[77] Kyu Han takes a different view, saying that the verses may be understood metaphorically so that the two tribes stand for 'the righteous who are set apart, and who have spiritual leadership until the appointed time (the eschatological restoration): at the *eschaton* the people of God will be reduced to a smaller group, consisting of only a part of the "two tribes"'.[78] Furthermore, the reason for the sadness over sacrifice is 'the *unacceptability* of the offering due to the hindrance of the "ten tribes" (4.9)'.[79] It would be difficult to decide between these two views as there is no mention that the ten tribes have interfered in the sacrifice of the others. Likewise, there is no statement that locates the two tribes with certainty.[80]

However, the wider claim that the temple is condemned in the *Testament of Moses* should be considered. In 'prophesying Israel's history' the author pays particular attention at two points to the destruction of the temple. The fall of Jerusalem and captivity are described:

> in those days a king against them from the east and (his) cavalry will overrun their land. And with fire he will burn their city with the holy Temple of the Lord and he will carry off all the holy vessels. And he will exile all the people and will lead them to his own land, yea the two tribes he will take with him. (*T. Mos.* 3.1-3)

Both 2 Chronicles (36.7) and Jeremiah (27.18-22) mention the holy vessels of the temple, but neither describes the burning of the city or temple. Again, the burning of the temple is described in ch. 6 of the *Testament of Moses*:

> There will come into their land a powerful king of the West who will subdue them; and he will take away captives, and a part of their temple he will burn with fire. He will crucify some of them around their city. (*T. Mos.* 6.8-9)

John Collins believes that this is a reference to the Romans setting fire to the cloisters of the temple under Varus in 4 BCE (*Ant.* 17.261-262;

---

77. D. Schwartz, 'The Tribes of As. Mos.', p. 222.
78. K. Han, *Jerusalem and the Early Jesus Movement: The Q Community's Attitude Toward the Temple* (London: Sheffield Academic Press, 2002), p. 109.
79. Han, *Jerusalem*, p. 109.
80. See also J. J. Collins, *The Apocalyptic Imagination: An Introduction to Jewish Apocalyptic Literature* (Grand Rapids, MI: Eerdmans, 2nd edn,1998). Regarding the issue: 'In view of the elliptic nature of the text, it is not possible to be certain [whether the statement rejects the worship of the Second Temple or refers to the distance of those in exile]' (p. 133).

War 2.49).[81] However, Tromp makes the observation that in the *Testament of Moses* the next verse (7.1) speaks of the times ending after these events. The end would come soon after the partial destruction of the temple (6.8) no matter if the burning of the temple was thought to be in the past or future for the author.[82] Kyu Han notes the negative attitude toward the temple in this document as well as the fact that there is no mention of renewal of the temple.[83] Unlike *1 Enoch* which describes a new temple, the *Testament of Moses* does not mention a new structure and does not give attention to the importance of the cult and sacrifices, but rather to the misdeeds of the priests and the pollution of the temple (5.3-6; 6.1; 7.6-8).

At the end of the writing, a future kingdom is inaugurated by Taxo, which appears throughout the whole creation (*T. Mos.* 10.1). As for the location of this kingdom, the nation is raised:

> And God will raise you to the heights. Yea, he will fix you firmly in the heaven of the stars, in the place of their habitations. And you will behold from on high. Yea, you will see your enemies from the earth. (*T. Mos.* 10.9-10)

No temple is mentioned here, and there is no central focus. Indeed, the land is not mentioned either, as Israel is removed from the earth and elevated to the realm of the stars. Impurity is removed as the people are placed in the heights. The tabernacle also plays a rather prominent role from the start of the text:

> Moses called to himself Joshua, the son of Nun, a man approved by the Lord, that Joshua might become a minister for the people in the tent of testimony which contained all the holy objects, and that he might become the minister for the people in the tent of testimony which contained all the holy objects, and that he might lead the people into the land which had been promised to their fathers, (the land) which he, in the tent, had declared by covenant and oath that he would give them through the leadership of Joshua. (*T. Mos.* 1.6-9)

The move of the tabernacle to the place of the first temple is also described:

---

81. Collins, *Apocalyptic Imagination*, p. 129. Though note Tromp, who finds the argument of a correspondence between 6.8 and Varus unconvincing and consequently 'it is not clear whether the Roman intervention alluded to in 6.8 was something the author was expecting or something he had recently experienced' (J. Tromp, *The Assumption of Moses: A Critical Edition with Commentary* [Leiden: E. J. Brill, 1993], p. 117).

82. Tromp, *Assumption of Moses*, p. 117.

83. Han, *Jerusalem*, pp. 108–14.

> The twelve tribes will move the tent of testimony to the place where the
> God of heaven will build a place for his sanctuary. (*T. Mos.* 2.4)

The temple is defiled by idols set up in the temple by the ten tribes, and the holy vessels are carried off when the city and temple are burned (*T. Mos.* 3.2). The vessels are not returned when the temple is rebuilt (*T. Mos.* 4.7-8; cf. Ezra 5.15). Though the author is negative about the first and second temples, the tabernacle is treated as a valid structure.[84] Koester says this about the author's view of the (second) temple and the tabernacle:

> He depicts the temple as a place of apostasy, but associated the tabernacle
> with God's covenant promises (1.7-9). These promises were fulfilled under
> Joshua and provide assurance of divine help in the end times (2.1; 12.13),
> as do the eschatological secrets that were revealed in the tent of meeting
> and preserved in the *Testament of Moses* itself.[85]

Therefore, though the *Testament of Moses* is negative toward the present temple and its leadership, and sees its destruction as a sign of the last times, there is not a denial that God's presence could legitimately reside in a sacred shrine. The tabernacle (and initially the first temple) is a valid shrine according the *Testament* and is part of the fulfilment of God's past promises to the nation in an ideal time. The author recalls positively an earlier time when the twelve tribes were under the leadership of Moses (and Joshua) and had the tent of meeting as their sacred shrine. In the eschatological kingdom, when Israel is raised to the heights, they are apparently in the presence of God, the Heavenly One, who will arise from his throne and from his holy habitation (10.3). This may tell us that for the author of the *Testament*, the presence of God is in heaven and no longer in any earthly structure. In particular, God's presence is no longer residing in the second temple. If Israel is raised to heaven as well in the end time, they would have no need for a shrine in which to worship. There would be definite political as well as spatial implications to such a view. The space described in the *Testament of Moses* is highly symbolic; we could say it seeks to criticize the spatial structures of society. In any case, the denial of the validity of the present temple meant a harsh criticism of the structures of power centred at the temple.

This is a fitting place to begin to examine in more detail Jesus' relationship to the temple. We have seen the importance of earlier spatial

---

84. Koester, *Dwelling of God*, p. 46.
85. Koester, *Dwelling of God*, p. 46.

models, such as the tabernacle, in later interpretations of the Second Temple period. We have noted the conflicts relating to control of the temple under Roman rule. In very interesting ways, the biblical spatial models could be used to criticize, and to reveal as contested space, the present Jerusalem temple in the experience of the Samaritans, the community at Qumran, or the author of the *Testament of Moses*. For Jesus, too, the temple is a space of conflict and contested values. And yet, even if Jesus 'fits' with those who offer a critique of the temple, this begs a further question: what is the content of that criticism? To this investigation we now turn.

The Temple Action:
Destruction and Restoration or Destruction Only?

There is much less debate over the authenticity of Jesus' action in the temple than over the meaning of that action.[86] The question of whether the action indicates destruction or purification corresponds to whether one thinks that Jesus breaks with the temple or wishes to see its reform.[87] A further question, raised by the evaluation of E. P. Sanders, revolves around whether destruction (a break with the temple) would also entail eventual restoration of the institution of the temple in the eschaton. Logically, it is unproblematic to think that the temple action could indicate both a critique of the temple system and a break with it. However, the only example we have seen thus far of this is the possibility that the *Testament of Moses* takes such a stance. As we saw in the examples of the Samaritans and Qumran, it is possible to criticize the current Jerusalem temple and leadership *without* breaking with the notion that there ought to be a temple and priesthood. Yet Jesus son of Ananias ('a country person' – *War* 6.300) seemingly pronounces a damning sentence on the temple without any indication of the temple's subsequent restoration.

Included in E. P. Sanders' list of 'almost indisputable facts' is that 'Jesus engaged in controversy about the temple'.[88] Indeed, Jesus' action

---

86. Though note H. de Jonge, 'The Cleansing of the Temple in Mark 11:15 and Zechariah 14:21', in Christopher Tuckett (ed.), *The Book of Zechariah and its Influence* (Aldershot: Ashgate, 2003), pp. 87–100. De Jonge believes the story belongs to post-Easter, pre-Markan tradition.

87. Schmidt, *Temple Thinks*, pp. 254–6.

88. E. P. Sanders, *Jesus and Judaism* (Philadelphia: Fortress Press, 1985), p. 11. Such actions of Jesus are, for Sanders, to be valued over particular sayings, though he also treats sayings in his study (see pp. 10–14 for his approach to sayings).

at the Passover celebration is most certainly linked to the reason for his being put to death, else, as Crossan puts it, 'why then, why there, why thus?'[89] We find reference to the controversy in Mk 11.15-19 and parallels, Mk 13.2 and parallels, Mt. 26.61//Mk 14.58, Mt. 27.39 and Mk 15.29. It does seem that a temple conflict is 'deeply implanted in the tradition'.[90] Sanders argues strongly that the temple system was not corrupt in the way envisioned by scholars such as A. E. Harvey. Thus:

> There was not an 'original' time when worship in the temple had been 'pure' from the business which the requirement of unblemished sacrifices creates. Further, no one remembered a time when pilgrims, carrying various coinages, had not come. In the view of Jesus and his contemporaries, the requirement to sacrifice must always have involved the supply of sacrificial animals, their inspection, and the changing of money.[91]

Further, as the action would not have had a concrete result (i.e. stopping the temple trade), it would be seen as a symbolic action. And yet this symbolic action needs further explanation. As Dale Allison puts it, 'the turning over of tables in the temple is...less an illuminating episode than an episode that needs to be illuminated'.[92] Sanders assumes that it would not be possible to attack what was ordained by God without thinking in terms also of restoration for the temple in the eschaton.[93] But Marcus Borg's criticism of Sanders is valid: 'evidence that eschaton and new temple are frequently linked within Judaism says nothing directly about Jesus; he may or may not have made the connection, or may have made it in a different way'.[94] This is, in fact, one of Borg's reasons for not accepting that Jesus worked with the framework of 'restoration eschatology', as he believes we cannot be sure that Jesus expected a

---

89. J. D. Crossan, *The Historical Jesus: The Life of a Mediterranean Jewish Peasant* (San Francisco: HarperSanFrancisco, 1991), p. 372.

90. Sanders, *Jesus*, p. 61.

91. Sanders, *Jesus*, p. 63. See also pp. 63-8 as well as E. P. Sanders, *Judaism: Practice and Belief 63BCE–66CE* (London: SCM Press, 1992) where Sanders argues against modern scholarship's tendency to emphasize the corruption of the temple system (pp. 91-2).

92. D. C. Allison, *Jesus of Nazareth: Millenarian Prophet* (Minneapolis: Fortress Press, 1998), p. 98.

93. Sanders, *Jesus*, pp. 70-71. He says, 'On what conceivable grounds could Jesus have undertaken to attack – and symbolize the destruction of – what was ordained by God? The obvious answer is that destruction, in turn, looks towards restoration' (p. 71).

94. M. Borg, *Jesus in Contemporary Scholarship* (Harrisburg, PN: Trinity Press, 1994), p. 76.

new temple to replace the current one.[95] As an alternative understanding, Borg suggests that the action should be associated with what it is said to be associated with in Mark – namely money. It was the money-changers against whom the action was directed and these were in the service of the elite Jerusalem oligarchy.[96] Therefore, he concludes as follows:

> The temple action was not the invocation of eschatological restoration. Neither was it a cleansing, a purification of the temple, but virtually the opposite. It was anti-purity rather than pro-purity: a protest against the temple as the centre of a purity system that was also a system of economic and political oppression.[97]

Though aspects of Borg's explanation of the temple incident as 'a protest against oppression' would fit with some of the levels of conflict over control of the temple we have explored above, it is unconvincing in eliminating the eschatological significance of the temple action. It is entirely plausible that a protest against the temple and indication that it would come to an end may be just as eschatological in orientation as a belief in the destruction and restoration of the temple (i.e. in Sanders' view). Again, the *Testament of Moses* suggests an eschatological scenario of a kingdom in which a restored temple may not be a significant feature.

Crossan raises further questions about peasant attitudes toward the temple in the first century:

> Were they for it, or against it? Was it the place of prayer and sacrifices, or the place of tithes and taxes? Was it divine dwelling or central bank? Was it the link between God and themselves, between heaven and earth, or the link between religion and politics, between Jewish collaboration and Roman occupation?[98]

Put another way, the temple, as sacred space ('divine dwelling'; religious) and social space ('central bank'; political) could easily have engendered ambiguous responses from peasants.[99] For Crossan, the temple action concretized or enacted Jesus' vision and programme in Galilee. Before making any judgements as to the best understanding of the temple action, we will first look at the main passages in some detail.

---

95. Borg, *Jesus in Contemporary Scholarship*, p. 76: If we were confident that Jesus expected a new temple that would physically replace the old one, then we could say that Jesus was operating within the framework of restoration eschatology; but, of course, this is what Sanders is seeking to demonstrate, not something already established.

96. Borg, *Jesus in Contemporary Scholarship*, pp. 113–14.

97. Borg, *Jesus in Contemporary Scholarship*, p. 116.

98. J. D. Crossan, *Who Killed Jesus? Exposing the Roots of Anti-Semitism in the Gospel Story of the Death of Jesus* (San Francisco: HarperSanFrancisco, 1996), p. 50.

99. Crossan, *Who Killed Jesus?*, p. 50.

The Action in the Temple:
Mark 11.15-18//Matthew 21.12-13//Luke 19.45-46

All of the synoptic versions of Jesus' temple action begin with Jesus driving out merchants in the temple, and end with quotations from Isaiah and Jeremiah. Markus Bockmuehl argues that these texts, including the quotations, should be regarded as authentic.[100] His interpretation follows what he believes to be the point of the Isaiah passage. He says that it 'speaks of the universal access to Temple worship for all the nations'.[101] Though some biblical passages do seem to give a role to the Gentiles in the future gathering to Jerusalem and the temple, others certainly exclude them. Even in Isaiah, it is apparently not *all* Gentiles who are spoken of, but those foreigners and eunuchs who had joined themselves to the Lord by following the custom of the Sabbath and keeping the covenant of the Lord (Isa. 56.3-7). However, we do not doubt that the phrase 'house of prayer for all nations (οἶκος προσευχῆς πᾶσιν τοῖς ἔθνεσιν – LXX)' could be interpreted as universal or used for the purpose of making a universal statement with regard to the temple.

More importantly, there is the possibility that an eschatological temple is indicated in these few verses. The discernment of such a temple depends on reading the Isaiah quotation as speaking of an eschatological temple that 'will be'. In light of the varied eschatological interpretations of the temple we have already looked at, it seems tenuous to assert (even with some doubt) for this synoptic saying that 'Jesus' point here may be the reference to the eschatological Temple to which all the Gentiles will come to pray'.[102] If Jesus *did* have a belief in such a temple, this would not be particularly strong evidence of it, even if the Scripture quotation of Isa. 56.7 is authentic (a point we do not believe to be provable). Furthermore, what is '*the* eschatological Temple to which all Gentiles will come to pray'? Bryan is correct to point out that expectations regarding 'the relationship between the eschatological Temple and the Second Temple' are not uniform.[103] Further, the emphasis in the passage seems to be more on the present state of temple affairs than on offering an alternative to the temple. Bauckham asserts that even an eschatological temple should not be disassociated from criticism of the present situation:

---

100. M. Bockmuehl, *This Jesus: Martyr, Lord, Messiah* (Edinburgh: T&T Clark, 1994), p. 73.
101. Bockmuehl, *This Jesus*, p. 73.
102. Bockmuehl, *This Jesus*, p. 73.
103. Bryan, *Israel's Traditions*, p. 189.

> [Jesus] cannot have thought of the description 'a house of prayer for all nations' as one which could apply only to the eschatological temple in the messianic age. The temple authorities could not be accused of contradicting a divine intention which was meant to be fulfilled only in the eschatological temple. The thought must be rather that what is going to be fully realized in the messianic age – in the pilgrimage of the nations to Zion – has been God's intention for the temple all along. In that case *pasin tois ethnesin* must have had some referent in the present'.[104]

Saying 'my house will be called a house of prayer' (as in Matthew and Luke) or saying 'my house will be called a house of prayer for all nations' (as in Mark) certainly makes use of a phrase that provides a statement of God's intention for the temple. Therefore, using it in a context that follows an action against money-changers and sellers in the temple indicates that God's intentions are not fulfilled by what *they* are doing. If, by calling the Twelve (an action we will explore in Chapter 4), Jesus thought that God would gather the nation together into the land, then it may be that the temple structure was not needed in the eschaton, particularly if it was exploiting groups of people in the present. It may be that what is indicated here is that what was written *at the time of Isaiah* ('my house will be called a house of prayer for all the nations') had not been fulfilled *in the present* according to Jesus' action in the temple against those buying and selling. This is further emphasized by the Jeremiah quotation, which equates the character of what the money-changers and sellers are currently doing in the temple with robbery. In the *future*, this state of affairs will be radically changed through God's action, as indeed was a major concern in Jewish apocalypses.[105]

Regarding the Jeremiah quotation, Bockmuehl regards it as significant because it has parallels with Qumran texts where robbery is mentioned in connection with the temple (1QpHab x.1 and 4QpNah i.11)[106] and that Jeremiah 7 goes on to say that God will destroy the Jerusalem temple (Jer. 7.14). Thus, for Bockmuehl, the action and the Scripture quotation go together in that they both indicate the destruction

---

[104]. R. Bauckham, 'Jesus' Demonstration in the Temple', in B. Lindars (ed.), *Law and Religion: Essays on the Place of the Law in Israel and Early Christianity* (Cambridge: James Clark & Co, 1988), p. 85. See also Steven Bryan, who says, 'the failure of the standing Temple to be the eschatological Temple stands at the heart of his indictment of the Temple'. Bryan, *Israel's Traditions*, p. 189.

[105]. J. J. Collins, 'Temporality and Politics in Jewish Apocalyptic Literature', in C. Rowland and J. Barton (eds), *Apocalyptic in History and Tradition* (London: Sheffield Academic Press, 2002), pp. 26–43.

[106]. Bockmuehl, *This Jesus*, p. 73, and n. 42 on p. 201.

2. The Temple as Contested Space

of the Jerusalem temple.[107] Even in Jeremiah, however, the emphasis is on the current attitudes toward the temple as a safeguard rather than on the destruction of the temple (Jer. 7.3-14). Richard Bauckham is correct to point out that Mk 11.17 'is an antithetical saying which contrasts God's intention for the temple (*gegraptai*) with what the temple authorities (*humeis*) have made of the temple'.[108] It is also interesting to note that Bauckham also draws our attention to the contrast between two descriptions of the temple in the Isaiah and Jeremiah quotations – between 'house of prayer' and 'cave of robbers'.[109] Thus, we can join the two points together and align God/what is written (*gegraptai*) with 'house of prayer' and notice the contrast with you (*humeis*) and 'house of robbers'. It is because of what the 'you' have made of the temple that it will serve as no protection when God destroys it (cf. Jer. 7.4, 10, 14). Thus, the quotation of Isaiah and Jeremiah is meant to illustrate that Jesus' action of driving out money-changers and sellers is a criticism of what people have made of the temple and their attitudes toward it in contrast to what God intends for the temple. Certainly, the description of the temple action does not give clear evidence for a renewed temple. It does seem to clearly indicate a critique or protest against the present temple situation. As I have argued elsewhere, the naming of the temple in this way is significant to the meaning of the incident:

> There is a clear contrast between a house of prayer, οἶκος προσευχῆς, and a cave of robbers, σπήλαιον λῃστῶν. This naming (or renaming) of the temple conveys a strong symbolic indication that the institution is being criticized in its present existence.[110]

The values of Jesus' kingdom are contrasted with the values of the temple as a σπήλαιον λῃστῶν. Different sets of values are in conflict, showing the temple as a contested space.

If Jesus' action is a *symbolic* action indicating destruction *and* restoration, then it must be said that it does not have any symbolic element

---

107. Bockmuehl, *This Jesus*, p. 74.
108. Bauckham, 'Jesus' Demonstration', p. 83.
109. Bauckham, 'Jesus' Demonstration', p. 83. He pays particular attention to what the distinction is *not* between – 'house of prayer' and place of sacrifice – so as to contrast these two functions of the temple. Therefore, for Bauckham, the sacrificial cult is not what is being criticized or downplayed in favour of prayer in the temple (pp. 83–4). However, it seems more interesting to notice what the distinction *is* between – namely, a place for prayer and a place of robbers. The former is affirmed and the later denounced.
110. K. Wenell, 'Contested Temple Space and Visionary Kingdom Space in Mark 11–12', *BibInt* 15.3 (2007), pp. 291–305 (299).

which naturally points to restoration.[111] For Sanders, the restoration must occur, for the 'temple service was commanded by God' and 'Jesus knew what he was doing' so he must have understood the restoration to follow destruction.[112] The only way that Sanders can hold together the notion that the temple was ordained by God with Jesus' 'attack and symbolic destruction' of the temple is that he also looked toward the restoration of the temple. However, this need not be the case. As John Riches puts it:

> All might agree that the Temple Mount was or had been a sacred place, but this would not preclude radical disagreement at any particular time on the question whether or not the divine presence dwelt there.[113]

Attack and symbolic destruction of the temple might quite easily go together without a restored temple if Jesus' action in the temple implicates the values and position of the present temple and its leadership. There is good reason to question whether God's presence still resided in the temple for Jesus if God's οἶκος προσευχῆς has now become a σπήλαιον λῃστῶν. Though the quotations may be added by Mark, the essential contrast is clear. It is not impossible that Jesus meant that the temple was to end without an alternative to replace it. As for the description of it which we have just examined, it seems most naturally to be an action of protest against the temple system and its leadership – a central part of the current spatial order.

Stones Torn Down: Mark 13.1-2//Matthew 24.1-2//Luke 21.5-6

Normally, this saying does not receive a great deal of attention in evaluations of Jesus' action in the temple and the meaning of that action. In Mark, Jesus says this after the temple action. The reason for drawing particular attention to it here is that it highlights the destruction of the temple without any reference to the restoration of the temple. A distinction can be made between this statement, which predicts that the temple will not remain standing, and the action in the temple, which indicates a protest or threat against the temple system but does not include a prediction.[114] Sanders raises the question of whether prediction (as in this

---

111. J. Riches, 'Apocalyptic – Strangely Relevant', in W. Horbury (ed.), *Templum Amicitiae: Essays on the Second Temple Presented to Ernst Bammel* (Sheffield: JSOT Press, 1991), pp. 237–63 (246).

112. Sanders, *Jesus*, p. 71.

113. Riches, *Conflicting Mythologies: Identity Formation in the Gospels of Mark and Matthew* (Edinburgh: T&T Clark, 2000), p. 38.

114. K. H. Tan, *The Zion Traditions and the Aims of Jesus* (Cambridge: Cambridge University Press, 1997), pp. 185–6.

saying) or threat of the destruction of the temple was intended by Jesus. In the end, he uses both together:

> Thus we conclude that Jesus publicly predicted or threatened the destruction of the temple, that the statement was shaped by his expectation of the arrival of the eschaton, that he probably also expected a new temple to be given by God from heaven, and that he made a demonstration which prophetically symbolized the coming event.[115]

Here again, we have the argument that Jesus must have thought in terms of a new temple as this was the natural conclusion to destruction. Once more, there is no way to be sure that a new temple was part of what was indicated in Jesus' temple action and the sayings that go with it.[116]

Therefore, Mk 3.1-2 points us toward examining on its own merits what the meaning of destruction would be. By emphasizing the restoration of the temple, Sanders misses the element of judgement which should be connected to destruction.[117] The old temple would have to be destroyed merely in order for the new one to come into being.[118] Hooker is right to insist that a reason for the temple's destruction must be given.[119] The mention of stones and buildings indicates that the current physical structure was not going to remain standing. It would come crashing down, stone by stone.

When Jesus speaks of the temple's future destruction, this should be seen as related to the tearing down of authority structures that go with the present temple. It is this aspect that we want to highlight above considerations of which aspect of the current temple was viewed critically by Jesus. The temple *itself* was viewed critically by Jesus. The present state of the temple was highly problematic. Its time would come to an end and with it the end of the reign of the governing authorities. Thus, the structure was under judgement and would be destroyed in the coming eschaton.

When we combine the belief that the present temple would be destroyed with the calling of the twelve disciples to be the new leaders of the nation (Chapter 4), the likelihood that Jesus intended a renewed temple in the eschaton grows more doubtful. The new rulers were not to be priests for a (new) temple, but leaders (or judges) modelled on

---

115. Sanders, *Jesus*, p. 75.
116. Riches, 'Apocalyptic', p. 246.
117. M. Hooker, *The Signs of a Prophet: The Prophetic Actions of Jesus* (London: SCM Press, 1997), p. 45. She takes the point from Sanders that Jesus was not condemning the sacrificial procedures of the temple, but she asserts that 'he is wrong in ignoring the notion of judgment implicit in the events in the temple' (p. 45).
118. Sanders, *Jesus*, p. 71.
119. Hooker, *The Signs of a Prophet*, p. 45.

the tribal leaders. There are to be new authority figures, but they are not to be temple authorities. Thus, when Jesus (cf. Qumran and the author of the *Testament of Moses*) offers his own alternative, it contains both affirmation of the Twelve as future leaders and denial of the continuance of the present temple. He does not deny that the Twelve would rule or judge the nation, but he does deny that the physical structure of the Jerusalem temple would remain standing.

Destroy the Temple and Rebuild it: Mark 14.56-59//
Matthew 26.60-61, 27.40; John 2.13-22; Acts 6.12-14

Besides the interpretations of Mark and John (2.13-22), the evidence in Mk 14.56-59 and parallels is for a temple built in three days. Does this tell us that Jesus expected a renewed, eschatological temple? The *Psalms of Solomon, Sibylline Oracles, Testament (or Assumption) of Moses, 1 Enoch, Testament of Levi* and some Qumran Literature all offer critical views of the temple. However, with the possible exception of the *Testament of Moses*, they all portray a positive view of, or allegiance to, the temple in some form. These texts do not determine the meaning of the gospel text, but they do have the potential to shed light on the possibilities for interpretation.

In *1 Enoch*, part of the section known as the Dream Visions contains an imaginative telling of the history of Israel from creation and Adam to the Maccabean campaigns, followed by a judgement and institution of a new temple. Here, towers are representative of the temple, including the first and second temples. Kyu Han has most interestingly pointed out the differences in these descriptions and noted that while the portrayal of the first temple is positive (*1 En.* 89.50), the picture of the second temple is characterized by impurity (*1 En.* 89.73).[120] The view of the first temple is most interesting, suggesting that perhaps it served as a positive model. Also of note is the description of the new Jerusalem at the judgement and subsequent beginning of the new age. Interestingly, the 'tower' which refers to the temple is not mentioned. From *1 Enoch*, we have:

---

120. Han, *Jerusalem*, pp. 99–100. See also D. Bryan, *Cosmos, Chaos and the Kosher Mentality* (Sheffield: Sheffield Academic Press, 1995). Bryan compares *1 Enoch* to the Deuteronomistic history, saying: 'Like the Deuteronomistic history, the construction of the First Temple [in *1 Enoch*] is taken to be the high point in Israel's history, and thereafter events go downhill. In the *Animal Apocalypse*, of course, the descent continues after the exile until the Antiochan crisis, which is the prelude to the *eschaton*' (Bryan, *Cosmos*, p. 178).

2. *The Temple as Contested Space* 53

> Then I stood still, looking at the ancient house being transformed: All the pillars and all the columns were pulled out; and the ornaments of that house were packed and taken out together with them and abandoned [*lit.* they took them out and abandoned them] in a certain place in the South of the land. I went on seeing until the Lord of the sheep brought about a new house, greater and loftier than the first one, and set it up in the first location which had been covered up – all its pillars were new, the columns new; and the ornaments new as well as greater than those of the first, (that is) the old (house) which was gone [*lit.* which he had taken out]. All the sheep were within it. (*1 En.* 90.28-29)

This text is often mentioned as evidence for a belief in the destruction of the second temple and restoration of the temple in the eschaton.[121] Can we be sure that the second temple is mentioned at all in this description? There is also no mention of the impurity of the second temple (as in 89.73) as reason for the removal of the house. It may be that there is no temple in the new age,[122] or that the tower is not explicitly mentioned, but is implied, and thus 'no doubt included'.[123] Scholarly opinion is divided,[124] and yet we might ask whether we should expect a clear answer from the text. J. J. Collins, speaking about the ways that the transformation of the world were imagined in apocalyptic literature, states that the texts are certainly concerned with the earthly political order, yet 'their concern does not fine its primary expression in the construction of a new world order'.[125] What is important is the disjunction between the present world and the 'purity and incorruption' of the heavenly world or future age.[126] Although *1 Enoch* is concerned with

---

121. See especially Craig Evans, 'Predictions of the Destruction of the Herodian Temple in the Pseudepigrapha, Qumran Scrolls, and Related Texts', *JSP* 10 (1992), pp. 89–147 (on *1 Enoch*, pp. 94–5). Evans states that 'the destruction of the second Temple and its replacement with a new, eschatological Temple seem to be envisioned' in *1 Enoch* (Evans, 'Predictions', p. 94). Besides the verses we have discussed (*1 En.* 90.28-29), Evans also includes 91.11-13 as evidence for the same (p. 95). See also Sanders, *Jesus and Judaism*, pp. 81–2, 88; Han, *Jerusalem*, pp. 99–100; D. Bryan, *Cosmos*, p. 182; and cf. L. Gaston, *No Stone On Another: Studies in the Significance of the Fall of Jerusalem in the Synoptic Gospels* (Leiden: E. J. Brill, 1970), p. 114.

122. VanderKam, *Enoch: A Man for All Generations* (Columbia, SC: University of South Carolina Press, 1995), p. 84.

123. M. Black, *The Book of Enoch* (Leiden: E. J. Brill, 1985), p. 278.

124. See M. Knibb, 'Temple and Cult in Apocryphal and Pseudepigraphal Writings from Before the Common Era', in J. Day (ed.), *Temple and Worship in Biblical Israel: Proceedings of the Oxford Old Testament Seminar* (London: T&T Clark, 2005), pp. 401–16 (407).

125. Collins, 'Temporality and Politics', p. 40.

126. Collins, 'Temporality and Politics', p. 40.

the present state of the temple and Jerusalem, this does not necessitate that the new world and a new temple must be defined in precise detail. The point is its newness (*1 En.* 90.29) and the fact that God would act to bring this about. In a description which is proceeded by the judgement of stars with sexual organs like horses (90.21) and has broken with the description of the past history of the nation to describe the eschaton, it hardly seems impossible that this vision does not focus on the 'historical' second temple and describes a new vision of a temple-less Jerusalem of the future. The author seems to give a positive value to the first temple,[127] and also to the tabernacle model (*1 En.* 89.36). There is also the possibility that, as Tiller suggests, the 'house' of *1 En.* 89.36 refers to the camp rather than the tabernacle; in both this instance and in *1 En.* 90.29, all the sheep dwell within the house.[128] Perhaps in light of a connection with the model of the camp in the wilderness, it is not unreasonable to suggest an expansion of Jerusalem in the future age to include all Israel (land and people?) in a geographically expanded realm characterized by the presence of God.

In any case, there are serious difficulties with placing a high value on *1 En.* 90.28-29 as evidence for a belief in the destruction (of the second temple) and restoration of the temple (in the eschaton). In fact, picking up pillars, packing up ornaments, removing them and then replacing them with grander ones hardly sounds like a particularly destructive act at all. It sounds more like the renovation or improvement of an old structure. This is not to say that a text like *1 Enoch* does not criticize the second temple and its leadership (89.73 certainly indicates that it does). Rather, we mean to emphasize that some of the apocalyptic texts which *do criticize* the second temple draw from alternative models such as the tabernacle and camp, or the first temple in thinking about the future and God's presence with his people in the new age.

In another example, a new temple with a long history is referred to in *2 Bar.* 4.1-7. The building which will be revealed (4.3) was shown to Moses on Mount Sinai (4.5), to Abraham (4.4) and to Adam 'before he sinned' (4.3). The structure was prepared by the Lord 'from the moment that I decided to create Paradise'. (4.3). The building is decidedly *not* the building 'in your midst now' (4.3). Bryan notes that 'the eschatological Temple will be the heavenly tabernacle shown to Moses on Sinai as a model for the wilderness tabernacle'.[129] The text

---

127. Han, *Jerusalem*, p. 102.
128. P. A. Tiller, *A Commentary on the Animal Apocalypse of 1 Enoch* (Atlanta, GA: Scholars Press, 1993), pp. 40–51.
129. Bryan, *Israel's Traditions*, p. 192.

emphasizes that the origin of that temple goes all the way back to the moment of the *decision* of creation. That same structure existed continuously (including its revelation to Moses) and will be revealed at a future time. Both Paradise and the structure, though once taken from Adam (4.3), are preserved with the Lord (4.6). In *Jubilees* also, the Lord is the one to build his temple (*Jub.* 1.17, 27). In the *Testament of Benjamin*, we find the following:

> But in your allotted place will be the temple of God, and the latter temple will exceed the former in glory. The twelve tribes shall be gathered there and all the nations, until such a time as the Most High shall send forth his salvation through the ministration of the unique prophet. (*T. Benj.* 9.2)

In the *Sibylline Oracles*, God is called the founder of the greatest temple (5.431). The emphasis for the temple in the new age is on divine intervention. A new structure may be thought of as present with or built by God, even without a clear description of what that temple would actually be like.[130]

For Sanders, Mk 14.58 is central. He says, 'the saying indicates an expectation that God himself would shortly construct a physical, eschatological temple in Jerusalem'.[131] There are, however, serious questions as to what sort of temple might be indicated in the words placed on the lips of accusers: 'I will destroy this temple that is made with hands, and in three days I will build another, not made with hands'. It seems to go too far, in light of the diverse descriptions in Jewish apocalyptic literature regarding the new age, to suggest anything too concrete for this text in terms of a new temple.[132] This new temple, built in three days, need not conform in any real or physical sense to the present temple in Jerusalem. The human impossibility of building a temple in three days, highlighted in Jn 2.20, emphasizes the divine origin of the temple. Looking to later interpretation, Acts reports that the disciples were gathered in Jerusalem to await the 'promise of the Father', and that the disciples asked the risen Jesus, 'Is this the time you will restore the Kingdom to Israel?' (Acts 1.6), and yet the temple (or new temple) is not mentioned here, and indeed conflict occurs at the location of the temple throughout the book of Acts (4.1-22; 5.16-33; 21.26-36).

The temple 'not made with hands' found in Exod. 15.17 is connected to the model of the camp in the wilderness. We hear of this temple in Moses' song at the escape from the Egyptian army. This is the begin-

---

130. See here Sanders, *Jesus*, p. 87. Thus, in *Jub.* 1.17, God is to build the temple.
131. Sanders, *Jesus*, pp. 71-6.
132. Bryan, *Israel's Traditions*, p. 232.

ning of life as the camp in the wilderness: 'You brought them in and planted them on the mountain of your own possession, the place, O Lord, that you made your abode, the sanctuary, O Lord, that your hands have established'.[133] Speaking of a sanctuary or temple not made with hands could also recall promises regarding the land as the goal of the period of wandering in the wilderness. The sign-prophets, described by Josephus, echo themes of the exodus and entry into the land of Israel. It is at least possible that Jesus and his group saw themselves as enacting a time before the entry into the land, in which case it might be entirely appropriate to speak of a temple not made by human hands as related to the goal of the exodus, and part of the new age. The calling of twelve disciples as tribal leaders would fit with this model.

If Jesus did say something like the phrase attributed to him by his accusers in the gospels regarding a new temple not made with hands, perhaps all we can know about such a temple is that it compares with *Jubilees*' simple statement: 'I will build my sanctuary in their midst' (1.17). The quotations from Isaiah and Jeremiah in the accounts of the temple incident do not flesh out the picture of what Jesus may have envisioned regarding a renewed temple. The emphasis is on a disjunction between the ideal and the present existence of the temple. There is a conflict of values which point to the temple as a contested place for Jesus.[134] And yet, these values need to be drawn out. What was this conflict between the kingdom and the present order?

Critique of Temple-Centred Space

There are good reasons to doubt that there was a central focus on the temple in the traditions about Jesus we have looked at. If Jesus, as a millenarian figure, offers an alternative vision of the new age, then that vision need not be fully worked out. Are there reasons why Jesus might reject the temple-centred cult in his vision of the future kingdom? Sean Freyne suggests that Herodian political powers colluded with the Jerusalem priesthood and aristocracy who maintained 'the fiction of the theocratic ideal of the temple-state'.[135] Both Galilean Herodians and Jerusalem aristocracy endorsed the notion of a market economy where

---

133. See Bryan, *Israel's Traditions*, pp. 191, 192–3, 199.
134. Wenell, 'Contested Temple Space', pp. 303–305.
135. S. Freyne, 'Jesus and the Urban Culture of Galilee', in D. Hellholm and T. Fornberg (eds), *Texts and Contexts: Biblical Texts in their Textual and Situational Contexts: Essays in Honour of Lars Hartman* (Oslo: Scandinavian University Press, 1996), pp. 597–622 (611).

resources stream to the centre, which was not a shared or reciprocal system of exchange.[136] Freyne contrasts this with the impulses of Jesus' vision:

> By contrast, Jesus' vision of shared goods and rejection of the normal securities, including money (Mt. 6.19-21, 24; Lk. 12.33-34; 16.13; *Gos. Thom.* 47.1-2; 76.3), which apart from land was the most important commodity in the market economy, though utopian in its intention *did provide an alternative vision.* This vision viewed the world of human relations, based on status maintenance, in a very critical light and instead allowed for oppressors and oppressed to relate as equals.[137]

This ideal vision was one which God would bring about. The present situation needed an alternative. Transformed leadership, and indeed transformed space, were called for. For Lefebvre, *in order for* society to change, space must be changed. Thus, Lefebvre's statement bordering on injunction: To change life we must first change space.[138] This is not unlike the Qumran covenantors, who create their own space in the desert to 'prepare the way of the Lord'. The sign-prophets and the author of the *Testament of Moses* also propose changes to space in action and alternative vision. The vision Jesus offers is an alternative theocracy, the kingdom of God. Yet, as Theissen reminds us: 'God, was not, after all, to rule quite alone'.[139] Jesus endorsed 'wandering charismatics' as the new leaders of the nation. We will have more opportunity to discuss this new leadership in the chapter discussing Jesus' group of twelve, but for now note that Jesus does not propose a new temple leadership, a replacement priesthood.[140] In comparison, Jesus' kingdom is able to evoke an ideal situation of 'all Israel sharing in the fruits of the land' which, as Freyne argues, had appeal in Galilee

---

136. Freyne, 'Jesus and the Urban Culture', p. 609.
137. Freyne, 'Jesus and the Urban Culture', p. 618, emphasis added.
138. Lefebvre, *Production*, p. 190.
139. G. Theissen, *The First Followers of Jesus: A Sociological Analysis of the Earliest Christianity* (trans. John Bowden; London: SCM Press, 1978), p. 61.
140. This does not exclude the possibility that Jesus critiques the temple leadership, the priests. As noted by Ithamar Gruenwald, traditions such as the parable of the Good Samaritan, the action in the temple and prediction of its destruction, and the involvement of priests, or the high priest, in the trial of Jesus may indeed point to the conclusion that 'one of the chief targets in Jesus' criticism of the Judaism of his time was the priesthood' (I. Gruenwald, 'From Priesthood to Messianism: The Anti-Priestly Polemic and the Messianic Factor', in I. Gruenwald [ed.], *Messiah and Christos: Studies in the Jewish Origins of Christianity Presented to David Flusser* [Tübingen: Mohr, 1992], pp. 75–93 [82]).

among Jewish peasants at this time.[141] The temple, for Jesus and his followers, represented a system whose values were in contrast to the real-life situation of those who worked the land in the country (cf. Mt. 20.1-16; Mk 12.1-9; Mt. 18.23-35).[142] They were fixed on a new world, but one that also overlapped with the present world. Therefore, a vision which does not focus on the temple and which instead provides a broader view of all the land with unknown Galileans at the head of the tribes is seen as a more appropriate kind of 'world' for them to live in when justified in the eschaton. In the language of millenarianism, of apocalyptic, a new order for society can be offered, a new imagination of space that critiques the present arrangements.

Space and hegemonic powers are always connected,[143] and therefore the connection between the current leadership and current spatial arrangements for the temple is significant. Likewise, the new alternative of the ideal kingdom is a spatial arrangement connected to a different leadership. The imagined space of a millenarian prophet need not conform to the present societal arrangements, whether spatial or constitutional. In fact, alternative spatializations may serve to critique hegemonic powers within contested space, and the definition of a new community in a utopian movement confronts prevailing conditions and entails entering into 'a space of rules which one acknowledges, respects, and obeys'.[144] Jesus' rule of love of God, neighbour and enemy does not draw tight boundaries around the community akin to Qumran's exclusion of those who do not obey the community rule as 'outside'. The idea that Jesus and his group break from a temple-centred system and do not imagine a restored cult is not as implausible as Sanders suggests. It seems that the very structures (hierarchical and spatial) of society are challenged by the calling of the Twelve and the temple action. Abandoning the temple need *not* mean abandoning the presence of and rule of God. God had certainly been powerfully with his people in the wilderness when they had no

141. Freyne, 'Jesus and the Urban Culture', p. 616.
142. Goodman, *Ruling Class*, pp. 46, 51–6.
143. E. Soja, *Postmodern Geographies: The Reassertion of Space in Critical Social Theory* (London: Verso, 1989). Commenting on Foucault's treatment of space, Soja quotes from an interview where Foucault was asked 'whether space was central to the analysis of power, he answered: Yes. Space is fundamental in any form of communal life; space is fundamental in any exercise of power' (Soja, *Postmodern Geographies*, p. 19). The interview can be found in P. Rabinow (ed.), *The Foucault Reader* (Harmondsworth: Penguin, 1986), pp. 239–56. See also M. Foucault, 'Of Other Spaces', *Diacritics* 16.1 (1986), pp. 22–7.
144. D. Harvey, *Spaces of Hope* (Edinburgh: Edinburgh University Press, 2000), p. 239.

2. *The Temple as Contested Space*

temple structure. The *Testament of Moses* shows us the possibility of Israel being raised to the heights in the presence of God after the end of the temple system. We cannot be sure exactly what Jesus expected to happen in the new arrangement.

The space produced in the first century was organized around a central temple, powerful in its own right, yet in many ways subordinate to the Roman Empire. However, the temple also held great significance as a sacred place of worship, both for the Diaspora and the land. As John Riches states:

> The language of 'centre', applied to temples and palaces, has an ideological function: it serves to justify existing relations of power within a given society. But, one has to ask, could it have fulfilled those functions (and perhaps not only those), if it had not had a conventional cosmological sense which was well understood by those whom it was intended to hold in subservience?[145]

Within this common cosmological understanding, disagreements about the current temple and God's presence within it were by no means excluded.[146] We could perhaps compare the re-readings of sacred space at the time of Jesus to Deleuze and Guitarri's discussion of the use of maps as opposed to 'tracing':

> The map is open and connectable in all of its dimensions; it is detachable, reversible, susceptible to constant modification. It can be torn, reversed, adapted to any kind of mounting, reworked by an individual, group, or social formation. It can be drawn on a wall, conceived of as a work of art, constructed as a political action or as a meditation... A map has multiple entryways, as opposed to the tracing, which always comes back 'to the same'.[147]

In first-century Judaism other 'temples' – symbolic, imagined, or remembered – survive alongside the central temple, critiquing it and perhaps inspiring increasing interest in heavenly worlds.[148] New articulations about the temple are not simply tracings of earlier models, though they do draw on them. All are social constructions of the spatial. 'Imaginary'

---

145. Riches, *Conflicting Mythologies*, p. 21. The context of this statement is a critique of Jonathan Smith's preference for emphasizing the 'anthropological functions' of myth over concern with cosmological aspects of myth (in *his* – Smith's – critique of Eliade). See Riches, *Conflicting Mythologies*, pp. 118–21.

146. Riches, *Conflicting Mythologies*, p. 38.

147. In discussion of the 'rhizome' and the principles of tracing. Gilles Deleuze and Félix Guittari, *A Thousand Plateaus: Capitalism and Schizophrenia* (trans. Brian Massumi; London: The Athlone Press, 1988), p. 12.

148. J. J. Collins, *Apocalypticism in the Dead Sea Scrolls* (London: Routledge, 1997), p. 134.

spaces are no less significant than physical political structures of society. They are not mere gobbledegook.

Jesus did not simply trace the common view of temple and land. Though Peter Walker claims that Jesus took the temple as his model,[149] this remains uncertain from the comparisons and evidence we have seen thus far. However, another aspect of meaning with regard to Jewish conceptions of sacred space needs to be considered, and that is the ritual practice associated with these different models of space. How does Jesus' alternative vision fit with the 'thinking of the temple' and the purity system of the first century? Purity, it may be argued, was not only the 'thinking of the temple' but also the 'thinking of the land'. We cannot 'work out from the clear to the unclear, from the temple through the city to the land'[150] to discover the importance of land in the alternative space of the kingdom offered by Jesus. As we have seen, the temple was not the central model or focus of this new space, but it remains to be seen how the kingdom relates to the widest category of Jewish sacred space, Israel, including both people and land.

---

149. P. Walker, 'Christians and Jerusalem, Past and Present', in B. Norman (ed.), *The Mountain of the Lord: Israel and the Churches* (London: Council of Christians and Jews, 1996), pp. 107–130 (126).

150. P. Walker, 'Land in the New Testament', pp. 116–17.

Chapter 3

EMBODIED SACRED SPACE: PURITY IN THE LAND

The sacredness of the land is not the same as the sacredness of the temple, though they are related within the same symbolic system. In Seth Kunin's structural model which serves as a corrective to the more common model of concentric models of holiness, the holiness of Israel (people and land) is opposed to the profane space of the nations. Oppositions also occur at the level of Israel (people and land) and the Levites and tabernacle court; between the Levites and the tabernacle court and the priests and the holy place; between the priests and the holy and the high priest and the holy of holies. All the levels of opposition within Israel are within the largest realm of the sacred (people and land), with the nations excluded. At the final level, 'the final terms, priests and High Priest, suggest both difference and relationship'.[1] Thus, each level produces two circles which are distinct from each other and exclude the other. This model shows clearly the different levels of operation of the sacred, and demonstrates the need to compare at the correct level: Israel is opposed to the nations; the high priest is not opposed to the nations, but is distinguished from the priests, with both priests and high priest part of the wider category of Israel.

At the broadest level of distinction, between Israel and the nations, purity is a key part of the relationship between God, people and land. Thus, the distinctions between sacred and profane, pure and impure, define the relationship. These are the building blocks for the 'thinking of the temple' in the analysis of Francis Schmidt, and they also apply at the broadest level of distinction as the 'thinking of the land'. Purity may be viewed as a *spatial practice* which recalls and reinforces beliefs. To illustrate this principle, in a Catholic or Anglican church, the reserved sacrament is the real presence of Christ and therefore individuals may genuflect when entering and leaving (and at other times) to acknowledge

---

1. S. Kunin, *God's Place in the World: Sacred Space and Sacred Place in Judaism* (London: Cassell, 1998), p. 15.

Christ's presence. A physical practice (genuflection) acknowledges the sacredness of place (tabernacle or ambry).[2] By performing purity rituals, it is possible to recognize through bodily expression the sanctity of place (e.g. temple, land).[3]

As a spatial practice, purity must also be set in social context. That is, purity is certainly part of the interpretation of sacred space, but it must also be related to specific social situations. If Leviticus indeed envisages a 'religion of the body' where 'purity and impurity appear as possible states of man's bodily existence oriented toward God and creation, towards holiness and everyday life',[4] then the ways Levitical purity laws are interpreted in different contexts are instructive. Purity laws and their interpretations have the potential to 'show up' cosmology and ethos in that they offer a model for organizing everyday life according to accepted beliefs, namely to do with God's holiness. The reality of social life shapes beliefs and *vice versa*: how (and if) purity is interpreted in different contexts. For example, under Antiochus Epiphanes, with the temple profaned and Jewish practices banned, the possibilities were limited. Prior to the revolts, Roman rule allowed for a relatively large degree of freedom of practice. Purity is *as* connected to the particular beliefs (e.g. regarding God's holiness) of an individual or group as it is to societal relations of power and gender, to morality and indeed to spatial perception.[5]

---

2. The Orthodox practice of reverencing and kissing icons is another example which could illustrate a relationship between practice (physical gestures) and sacred space.

3. See J. Økland, *Women in Their Place: Paul and the Corinthian Discourse of Gender and Sanctuary Space* (London: T&T Clark, 2004), pp. 31–5.

4. M. Poorthuis and J. Schwartz, 'Purity and Holiness: An Introductory Survey', in M. J. H. M. Poorthuis and J. Schwartz (eds), *Purity and Holiness: The Heritage of Leviticus* (Leiden: E. J. Brill, 2000), pp. 3–26 (5, 7–8). See also Lefebvre, who discusses the relationship between an individual and space in terms of the relationship between an individual and their own body: 'The relationship to space of a "subject" who is a member of a group or society implies his relationship to his body and vice versa' (H. Lefebvre, *The Production of Space* [trans. D. Nicholson-Smith; Oxford: Blackwell, 1991], p. 40). He illustrates this using his three 'moments' of space, saying that there are practices of the body (physical gestures), representations of the body (scientific understanding of how the body works and relates to nature), and symbols of the body (i.e. a 'moral' body, thought of as not having sexual organs). 'The "heart" as lived', states Lefebvre, 'is strangely different from the heart as thought and perceived' (*ibid.*).

5. Poorthuis and Schwartz view purity and impurity as possible states which may reflect societal norms for behaviour. They state: 'This awareness may stimulate reflections upon the relation between perceptions of the body and society at

3. *Embodied Sacred Space: Purity in the Land*

Both the sacred and the social aspects of purity practices are important to our study. Different emphases regarding purity may help us to decipher different attitudes toward 'the land' in the Second Temple period. This suggestion will need to be developed further. First, however, we will examine the priestly ideology in Leviticus, and in so doing, highlight the connections between 'the land' and purity practices within that ideology.[6] This will help us to identify some of the conventional associations between purity and land in texts which were also resources available to later (i.e. first-century) interpreters.

In Leviticus, bodily purity is connected to a conception of separation and holiness (Hebrew – *qadosh*), which involves making distinctions between clean and unclean people, animals and things. As Mary Douglas has demonstrated for biblical purity laws, it is not necessary to determine whether (and how) these individual prohibitions do or do not 'make sense' (i.e., why one animal is unclean and not another).[7] Rather, we may view purity as part of a larger system of thought requiring relationships of ritual separation. Even if we think of 'secular contagion', the 'rules' will not need to follow either logic or the principles of scientific knowledge.[8] It is just as difficult to understand why someone would wash a television screen after it had been watched by a person with HIV as it is to understand why land animals must chew their cud, have divided hoofs *and* be cleft-footed in order to be clean and fit for eating (Lev. 11.2-8) without a broader framework for thinking about prohibitions within a particular society.[9]

---

large, upon gender relations and power structures, upon man's attitude toward the environment and upon the intertwined relations between sickness, moral behavior and subsequent healing rituals' (Poorthuis and Schwartz, 'Introductory Survey', p. 7).

6. Following Habel's approach, we will not look for the particular social and historical context of the text of Leviticus. Rather, we will attempt to highlight the ideologies promoted within the text. To quote: 'It is the ideology of that text [here, he uses Joshua as an example], rather than the actual history behind it, that has had, and continues to have, an influence on generations of readers of that text' (N. Habel, *The Land is Mine: Six Biblical Land Ideologies* [Minneapolis: Fortress Press, 1995], p. 6).

7. M. Douglas, *Purity and Danger: An Analysis of the Concepts of Pollution and Taboo* (London: Routledge, 1966), pp. 50–51: 'There must be contrariness between holiness and abominations which will make over-all sense of all the particular restrictions'.

8. See M. Douglas, 'Sacred Contagion', in J. F. A. Sawyer (ed.), *Reading Leviticus: A Conversation with Mary Douglas* (Sheffield: Sheffield Academic Press, 1996), pp. 86–106.

9. Douglas, 'Sacred Contagion', pp. 94–5.

Keeping with the notion that a god-granted land is considered a sacred space,[10] the broader framework for purity should also be related to spatial definitions. Separation (i.e., between God's people and the nations) and distinction (i.e., between clean and unclean animals) is part of a system of thought which also establishes boundaries for purity. In Leviticus, the land – 'their' land, the land that flows with milk and honey, the land which could vomit settlers out – is the location for purity. Entering and possessing the land requires holiness and obedience:

> You shall keep all my ordinances, and observe them, so that the land to which I bring you to settle in may not vomit you out. You shall not follow the practices of the nations that I am driving out before you. Because they did all these things, I abhorred them. But I have said to you: you shall inherit their land, and I will give it to you to possess, a land flowing with milk and honey. I am the Lord your God; I have separated (*badal*) you from the peoples. You shall therefore make a distinction between the clean (*tahor*) animal and the unclean (*tame*), and between the unclean (*tame*) bird and the clean (*tahor*); you shall not bring abomination on yourselves by animal or by bird or by anything with which the ground teems, which I have set apart (*badal*) for you to hold unclean (*tame*). You shall be holy (*qadosh*) to me; for I the Lord am holy (*qadosh*), and I have separated (*badal*) you from the other peoples to be mine. (Lev. 20.22-26)

In ch. 18, the land is shown to react to the defilement of its former inhabitants:

> Do not defile (*tame*) yourselves in any of these ways, for by all these practices the nations I am casting out before you have defiled (*tame*) themselves. Thus the land became defiled (*tame*); and I punished it for its iniquity, and the land vomited out its inhabitants. But you shall keep my statutes and my ordinances and commit none of these abominations, either the citizen or the alien who resides among you (for the inhabitants of the land, who were before you, committed all of these abominations, and the land became defiled [*tame*]); otherwise the land will vomit you out for defiling it (*tame*) as it vomited out the nation that was before you. For whoever commits any of these abominations shall be cut off from their people. So keep my charge not to commit any of these abominations that were done before you, and not to defile (*tame*) yourselves by them: I am the Lord your God. (Lev. 18.24-30)

It is interesting that here the land itself is not called a holy land.[11] The 'nations' made the land impure, but the land itself is not said to possess

---

10. J. Bereton, 'Sacred Space', in M. Eliade (ed.), *The Encyclopedia of Religion* (New York: Macmillan, 1987), pp. 526–35 (527).

11. See R. L. Wilken, *The Land Called Holy: Palestine in Christian History and Thought* (New Haven: Yale University Press, 1992). He discusses how it was

the quality of holiness or even purity explicitly. This holiness is in relationship to the people and their purity or defilement before God. Land is gift (Lev. 20.23), but as such it is highly dependent on the holiness and practices of the people (Lev. 18.24-30), rather than on its own inherent holiness. Still, 'the land' remains a prominent component of the passage. It is not only God in relationship with the people around which issues of holiness and defilement circle. Rather, it is God in relationship with the people in keeping or losing the gift of the land; they remain in it or are spewed out from it.

For the Abrahamic land promise, kinship with Abraham is emphasized alongside circumcision (Genesis 17); in Leviticus, keeping separate from the nations by certain moral and ritual practices is emphasized. Though there are differences in these ideologies and their requirements, they each focus on the land as given by God.[12] In these and other ideologies in the Hebrew Bible, land is connected with practice. If any ideology must in some way refer to space,[13] land is highly important as a spatial referent within the ideologies of the Hebrew Bible.

What, we might ask, is the significance that the Levitical ideology is a *priestly* ideology? Does it merely function to make the people of the land (the 'masses') consent to their position, to their exclusion from the most holy realms of the sanctuary? Is it only a justification for priestly privilege?[14] Certainly, there is a hierarchy to the Levitical 'system'. The priest's roles are assigned by virtue of their descent from

---

Zechariah who first used the descriptive 'holy land' though Ezekiel had such a notion in his description of a holy district (Wilken, *Land Called Holy*, pp. 17–19). Second Maccabees contains the second use of the term holy land and the first use of the term in Greek (Wilken, *Land Called Holy*, pp. 24–5). It is indeed striking that with the Levitical emphasis on holiness and also on the relationship between God, people and land, that the land itself is never called holy whereas both God and people are described as such.

12. See Habel's charts of comparison of different ideologies of land. Habel, *The Land is Mine*, pp. 149–57.

13. Lefebvre seems to answer in the negative in one of his many rhetorical questions: 'What is an ideology without a space to which it refers, a space which it describes, whose vocabulary and links it makes use of, and whose code it embodies?' He presses this even further and says, 'Ideology *per se* might well be said to consist primarily in a discourse upon social space' (Lefebvre, *Production*, p. 44).

14. See W. Herzog, 'The New Testament and the Question of Racial Injustice', *American Baptist Quarterly* 5.1 (1986), pp. 12–32. 'In ancient agrarian societies, the masses lived in misery while their ruling elites controlled vast amounts of wealth. One major dilemma for such ruling classes was to develop justifications for their privileged position persuasive enough to convince the peasants to acquiesce to their poverty' (p. 14).

Aaron. Whilst Levites have duties relating to the sanctuary, priests are strictly descendants of Aaron and only they may become high priest. It would seem that rather than mere justification of priestly roles, the 'system' of Leviticus would allow for a certain sense of awe at the holiness associated with the priests and the most sacred spaces.[15] A diagram adapted from Philip Jenson's *Graded Holiness* illustrates the connections between the ideology of holiness, sacred space, people and sacrifice.[16]

Holiness Gradient	Most Holy	Holy	Clean	Unclean	Especially Unclean
Spatial Realm	Holy of Holies	Holy Place	Court	Camp	Outside Camp
People	High Priest	Priest	Levites, Israelites	Minor Impurities	Major Impurities
Sacrifice	Sacrifice to God	Sacrifice (priests)	Sacrifice (non-priests)	Purification 1 day	Purification 7 days

(Increasing Holiness) →

Priests are supported by this 'system' (i.e., they partake of sacrifices) and they are connected to the most holy places, but ordinary Israelites may also gain access to redemptive media by obeying the laws of purity. The command in Lev. 10.10 to 'distinguish between holy and common, between unclean and clean' establishes three states of being and certain 'steps' between them as shown by Milgrom:[17]

```
Holy (qadosh)
      Desecrate/Desanctify (hillel/hiqdish)
Holy (qadosh)                    Pure/Common (tahor/hol)
      Sanctify (qiddesh)                    Pollute (timme)
      (anointment, commandment)   Pure/Common (tahor/hol)         Impure (tame)
                                        Purify (tiher)
                                        (ablution, sacrifice)
```

The holy and the impure are to have no contact according to the 'system' of Leviticus. In order to obey the command, 'be holy as I am holy',

---

15. See, for instance, Sanders' imaginative but helpful description of ordinary people bringing sacrifices to the Temple (E. P. sanders, *Judaism: Practice and Belief 63BCE–66CE* [London: SCM Press, 1992], pp. 112–16).
16. P. Jenson, *Graded Holiness: A Key to the Priestly Conception of the World* (Sheffield: Sheffield Academic Press, 1992), p. 37.
17. J. Milgrom, 'The Dynamics of Purity in the Priestly System', in M. J. H. M. Poorthuis and J. Schwartz (eds), *Purity and Holiness: The Heritage of Leviticus* (Leiden: E. J. Brill, 2000), pp. 29–32 (30).

3. Embodied Sacred Space: Purity in the Land

persons could 'move along' the scale towards holiness by performing the various rituals of bathing and sacrifice to purify themselves and obey the commandments in order to sanctify themselves.[18] Priests and Levites are necessary to the process and connected to the most holy spaces. Ordinary Israelites also participate, relying on the roles of the priests and Levites, and entering into the courts of the sanctuary when they are pure. The spatial distinctions corresponding to unclean, clean and holy are also connected to a hierarchy of persons and to specific practices. For the 'people of the land', their holiness is most related to the largest category distinction between Israel and the nations.

In Leviticus, God is present with the Israelites in a portable sanctuary – the tent of meeting. They are outside the land in the wilderness, yet, as in Leviticus 18 and 20, there is an emphasis on entering and possessing the land. Bodily purity with its codes and practices is part of an ideology of holiness which is not merely concerned with people and their bodies, but with people and their bodies in specific spaces, looking towards settlement in the land which God will give them and how to behave once they enter it. The vocabulary and codes for purity and holiness are linked to the vocabulary and codes for space in passages such as Lev. 18.24-30 and 20.22-26. Therefore, a religion of the body emerges from the text as well as the notion of a territorial religion – the body in relationship to its environment. If the land cannot withstand defilement and the people are to be holy as God is holy, then separation at different levels is required and this emphasis on separation is formative for the identity of the people *as a people*. This particular ideology comes from the top of the holiness gradient (from the priests) and is thereby closely connected to hierarchies in society.

Furthermore, when we are talking about land as sacred (as Hubert does in relationship to indigenous peoples), we need to recognize that holding an entire land as sacred within a religious system is different from holding a particular site as sacred:

> Although the whole landscape may be considered sacred, there are differences between this and the sacredness of sites that have particular significance. Not every stone or plot of earth can be treated with the same degree of respect... when the land comes under threat then the sacred sites, sacred places and sites of special significance become identifiable, even to outsiders.[19]

---

18. Milgrom, 'Dynamics of Purity', p. 30.
19. J. Hubert, 'Sacred Beliefs and Beliefs of Sacredness', in D. L. Carmichael, J. Hubert, B. Reeves and A. Schanche (eds), *Sacred Sites, Sacred Places* (London: Routledge, 1994), pp. 9–19 (18).

The boundaries of purity in relationship to the temple are on a level which allows them to be kept within a distinct sphere. The purity of the entire land cannot be kept with the same level of regulation. Nevertheless, when we look at the purity descriptions in the Hebrew Bible, the keeping of the laws of purity are related to the entire land, though there are, of course, specific behaviours which apply to the holiest places. Yet even so, purity is never *only* applied to the temple, it is also the 'thinking of the land'.

Purity Practices in the Second Temple Period

Certainly, there was a keen interest in the interpretation of purity laws during the Second Temple period. The Mishnah shows a great concern with purity and though codified in the 2nd century CE, it preserves traditions and interests prior to the destruction of the temple and the Bar Kochba revolt. The New Testament also contains early references to purity debates, for example Gal. 2.11-18. Jewish works from the Diaspora, notably Tobit (2.9 – after burying a corpse) and Judith (12.6-10 – after contact with Gentiles, before prayer) mention washing for purification. The practices mentioned in the rabbinic writings and the Diaspora relate to the specific practice of non-priestly purity, to which particular attention must be paid in relationship to Jesus.

Archaeological data gathered from the period also reveals some evidence for the practice of non-priestly ritual purity, particularly within 'the land'. Stone baths called *miqvaot* are suitable for immersion and are thought to have been used for ritual washing. These are described in the tractate on *miqvaot* in the Mishnah (also the tractate in the Tosefta) and appear in the archaeological record at various locations in Galilee and Judea.[20] Also of significance are stone vessels which are an innovation at this time (i.e., not prescribed in biblical law) and are found throughout the land. Both baths and stone vessels show a heightened concern with

---

20. Though numerous *miqvaot* have been identified, there is still debate over exactly what classifies as a *miqveh*. For example, see the following debate over finds at Sepphoris: H. Eshel, 'A Note on "Miqva'ot" at Sepphoris', in D. R. Edwards and C. T. McCollough (eds), *Archaeology and the Galilee: Texts and Contexts in the Graeco-Roman and Byzantine Periods* (Atlanta: Scholars Press, 1997), pp. 131–3; H. Eshel and E. M. Meyers, 'The Pools of Sepphoris: Ritual Baths or Bathtubs?', *BAR* 26.4 (July/August, 2000), pp. 42–9; E. M. Meyers, 'Yes They Are', *BAR* 26.4 (July/August, 2000), pp. 46–8; H. Eshel, 'We Need More Evidence', *BAR* 26.4 (July/August 2000), p. 49. Continuing the discussion, Ronny Reich writes in favour of Eric Meyer's identification of *miqvaot* at Sepphoris in 'They *Are* Ritual Baths: Immerse Yourself in the Ongoing Sepphoris Mikveh Debate', *BAR* 28.2 (March/April 2002), pp. 50–55.

purity practices. This evidence shows a widespread phenomenon which is not restricted to Jerusalem and the temple.[21] Many of the structures and artefacts may be dated to the period before the destruction of Jerusalem. For instance, at the site of the town of Jotapata in Galilee, which was destroyed in the Jewish war and remained unoccupied afterwards, there have been found fragments of stone vessels and (possibly) *miqvaot*.[22] We have already suggested that purity practices are spatial practices and connected to holiness within the land. The discussion of purity in the Second Temple period will help us to set this in context and show some of the different ways that purity was interpreted at this time.

Leviticus and Bathing

Washing and waiting until evening are important features of regaining purity in the Levitical laws. Sometimes the unclean person does both. Sometimes it is only a waiting period without bathing. People, clothes, homes and indeed 'any article that is used for any purpose' (Lev. 11.32) may be washed to restore their purity (e.g., Lev. 11.1-43).[23] Along with washing, waiting for evening is also a normal requirement. Many times, the text dictates that people and items are 'unclean until evening' and sometimes several days must pass; the longest waiting period is for a woman who must wait 66 days to be made clean again after the birth of a daughter (Lev. 12.5). Many people are instructed to wash: leprous persons (Lev. 14.1-34); a man with a discharge (Lev. 15.13); anyone who touches the man with the discharge or anything that was under him (Lev. 15.4-15); a man and a woman who have had sex, including an emission of semen (Lev. 15.16-18);[24] a man who touches something that

---

21. Eyal Regev makes a strong case for the practice of non-priestly purity in E. Regev, 'Non-Priestly Purity and its Religious Aspects According to Historical Sources and Archaeological Findings', in M. J. H. M. Poorthuis and J. Schwartz (eds), *Purity and Holiness: The Heritage of Leviticus* (Leiden: E. J. Brill, 2000), pp. 223–44a.

22. See Regev, 'Non-Priestly Purity', p. 232; D. R. Edwards, 'Jotapata' in E. M. Meyers (ed.), *Oxford Encyclopedia of Archaeology in the Near East* (5 vols.; Oxford: Oxford University Press, 1997), vol. 3, pp. 251–2.

23. According to Maimondes in the *Hilkhot Miqvaot* tractate, references in the Torah to washing clothes and bathing in water are to be interpreted as to be carried out by immersion in a ritual bath. See Y. Magen, 'Ritual Baths (*Miqva'ot*) at Qedumim and the Observance of Ritual Purity Among the Samaritans', in F. Manns and E. Alliata (eds), *Early Christianity in Context: Monuments and Documents* (Jerusalem: Franciscan Printing Press, 1993), pp. 181–92 (190).

24. It is interesting that the rabbis assume that a menstruant should immerse after the end of her period (e.g. *m. Miqvaot* 8.5). See T. Kazen, *Jesus and Purity Halakhah:*

a woman with a regular or irregular discharge touched (Lev. 15.19-30; *she* does not wash); anyone who eats an animal that dies of itself or is torn by wild animals (Lev. 17.15).

These regulations apply to men and women of the general community and are not specific to any group in particular (i.e., priests or Levites). Spatially, there are connections to the sanctuary, but often this is not explicitly mentioned or emphasized.[25] The idea that these laws were to be practiced in everyday life even when contact with the sanctuary was not imminent is certainly reasonable from the descriptions.[26] Washing to do with sexual contact would presumably be a fairly normal and regular reason for washing. Other reasons for washing may have been less common and ordinary, but we do not know the extent of this, that is, for lepers and those with irregular discharges, which according to Leviticus were certainly a concern.[27]

Priests are instructed to wash under special circumstances. They bathe to put on their vestments (Lev. 16.2, 23), or after burning a sin offering for the Day of Atonement (16.27). Priests are not to eat sacred food on the Day of Atonement unless they have washed their whole bodies in water. They wash and then wait for the sun to set before they eat (Lev. 22.4-7). They also bathe after the burning of the animal in the ceremony of the red heifer (Numbers 19). In Leviticus 22, priests are to make sure they are clean before they eat of the 'sacred donations'. If they are in a state of uncleanness (i.e., according to the regulations for all Israelites,

---

Was Jesus Indifferent to Impurity? (Stockholm: Almqvist & Wiskell International, 2002), p. 151. The only women who are specifically instructed (i.e., as women) to immerse in Leviticus are those who have sex as in Lev. 15.16-18. Waiting and offerings are required for childbirth and discharges (Lev. 12; 15) and it is men who are required to wash after coming in contact with menstruating women, not the women themselves (Lev. 15.20-24). Therefore, the practice by the time of the rabbis is remarkable.

25. According to Jacob Milgrom, a 'holiness source' (Leviticus 17–26 – including food laws) was more concerned with the camp and land rather than the tabernacle/temple. J. Milgrom, *Leviticus 1–16: A New Translation with Introduction and Commentary* (New York: Doubleday, 1991). In Num. 19.13-22, those who fail to purify themselves (including bathing) after contact with a corpse defile the sanctuary and are cut off from Israel. Women who are impure from child birth or menstrual impurity (Leviticus 12 and 15) are not allowed to touch holy things or enter the sanctuary (though bathing is not involved). Those with leprous diseases (Leviticus 13) are not prohibited from the sanctuary but from the camp. Men with discharges do not bring offerings to the sanctuary, but wash and are unclean until evening (Leviticus 15). The tabernacle 'in their midst' (Lev. 15.31) is in view and would be defiled by breaking the regulations.

26. Regev, 'Non-Priestly Purity', pp. 242–3.

27. See Kazen, *Jesus and Purity*, pp. 107–54 on lepers and those with discharges in the Second Temple period.

3. *Embodied Sacred Space: Purity in the Land*

see above), then they cannot partake in the sacred food. They must wait until evening and wash (their whole body) in water if they have a discharge, a leprous disease, come in contact with a corpse or a man who has had an emission of semen, touch an unclean 'swarming' thing or 'any human being by whom he may be made unclean' (22.4-5).

Exodus describes a water basin between the tent of meeting and the altar for the priests to wash their hands and feet (Exod. 30.18-21; 40.30-32; see also 29.4). Though there were extra requirements for priests, there are plentiful reasons why any Israelite (including priests) could be considered unclean. Bathing in particular was required for many of the impurities and applied to all Israelites (though more often for men than women), while the priests also washed on other occasions in connection to cultic ceremony. The concept of a *tebul yom*, described by the rabbis, was an 'in between' state where one had bathed and was waiting for sunset. This state reduced impurity by one degree.

Leviticus does not describe any certain built structure for bathing; it only gives the simple instruction to 'bathe in water' (i.e., Lev. 15.20-24; 17.16; Num. 19.19). Leviticus 15.13 says to wash in living (*hay*) water and Lev. 11.36 says that 'a spring or cistern holding water will be clean'. The development of *miqvaot* in the Second Temple period shows a particular interest in the laws regarding immersion. The rabbinic requirements for *miqvaot* (from the Mishnah and Tosefta tractates *Miqva'ot*) are summarized by Magen in these three points:

1. It must be organically connected with the soil, otherwise it is useless. (Accordingly, many known baths are cut into floor or basement bedrock.)
2. The water – either rain or spring water – must flow into the ritual bath of its own; therefore, water drawn up and conveyed in vessels may not be used.
3. The minimal amount of water in the ritual bath must be forty *seah*.[28]

Presumably, prior to the development of *miqvaot*, natural bodies of water could have been used for fulfilment of ritual purity laws.[29] In fact, there is no reason to believe that they were not, even after the development

---

28. Magen, 'Ritual Baths', p. 182. Estimates for the equivalent of 40 *seahs* of water range from 60 gallons to 250 gallons! See E. M. Meyers, 'Yes They Are', pp. 46–8.

29. See Reich, 'Ritual Baths', p. 430: 'In the early stages of the practice [of immersion], a state of purity was achieved through immersion in a natural body of water – a spring, river or lake. Eventually, however, the demand for pools of natural water to service the community was met via the introduction of the *miqveh*'.

of *miqvaot*. However, the interpretation 'beyond Leviticus' suggests a special concern with this practice. So, the biblical laws for bathing, and even the rabbinic laws, 'are sufficiently vague to allow considerable ingenuity in the matter of transferring "pure water"'.[30] In the next section, we will explore *miqvaot* in context of when they begin to appear in the archaeological record for 'the land'.

The Rise and Fall of Miqvaot

Notions about 'the land' were closely related to notions of purity in Second Temple Judaism. This era (with the possible exception of a brief time under the Hasmonean rulers) was marked by the domination of foreign rulers. Though it may be tempting to simply assume that it was the Hasmoneans who raised issues of purity and created the need for new 'purity innovations' such as *miqvaot*, we should also set alongside this the fact that *miqvaot* were introduced at a time when building various structures for holding large amounts of water was part of architectural development.[31] Among these, we could include baths, cisterns, pools, and *miqvaot*.

The public bath was a feature of the classical Greek world and originated in the 4th century BCE. From this time, public baths and hot baths were part of the built environment (i.e., 'spatial practice') and these were also used within the Roman Empire.[32] Public baths had particular characteristic elements:

> The major features of Roman baths include an exercise courtyard (peristylum) or larger gymnasium (palaestra), a dressing room (apodyterium), a cold room (frigidarium), often with a plunge bath, and a warm room (trepedarium) that led to a hot room (caldarium).[33]

Though these are the main common features, there was a large amount of diversity in the design of baths and they could be large (*thermae*) or

---

30. E. M. Meyers, 'Aspects of Everyday Life in Roman Palestine with Special Reference to Private Domiciles and Ritual Baths', in J. R. Bartlett (ed.), *Jews in the Hellenistic and Roman Cities* (London: Routledge, 2002), pp. 193–220 (213).

31. For Lefebvre, there is a 'creative capacity' associated with the production of space (*Production*, p. 115), re: 'a social reality capable...of producing that space'. In terms of architectural form, Lefebvre believes that the Romans utilized the spatial principles of ancient Greece in their architecture by taking what was essential to Greek buildings (i.e., the 'orders' – Doric, Ionic and Corinthian used in the building of Greek temples) and using them for decorative purposes.

32. A. Killebrew, 'Baths', in E. M. Meyers (ed.), *Oxford Encyclopedia of Archaeology in the Near East* (5 vols.; Oxford: Oxford University Press, 1997), vol. 1, pp. 283–5.

33. Killebrew, 'Baths', p. 285.

3. Embodied Sacred Space: Purity in the Land

smaller (*balnae*), public or private, attached to a military camp, sanctuary, or to a residence – either private or imperial.[34] It is no surprise that ritual baths were introduced in Palestine in the 2nd century BCE since this was the time when Hellenistic culture was increasingly permeating 'the land' to the distress of the Hasmoneans. The earliest examples from this period are Beth-Zur and Gezer (the 'Syrian Bath-house'), according to Ronny Reich.[35] Also among the earliest structures are private baths in Jericho and Masada. Herod built bath houses at his palaces (Jericho, Herodium, Masada, Kyros and Macheros). These baths copied the Roman feature of the *hypocaust* which is 'a floor supported on small columns and heated from below'.[36] Because of halakhic difficulties with using a Roman bath-house, Jewish examples (Hasmonean and Herodian) may have replaced the Roman cold bath (*frigidarium*) with ritual baths or *miqvaot*.[37] Thus, Reich believes that a *miqveh* necessarily accompanied baths because of a concern with purity:

> The only conceivable way to use the hot bath-house while maintaining a high degree of purity was, therefore, by installing a *miqweh* in every bath-house or very close to it. The affluent, who could afford to install in their houses a room with a *hypocaust* to serve as a hot bath-room, had no difficulties in this respect. Excavations in the Upper City of Jerusalem have revealed that every private house in the Second Temple Period was provided with at least one *miqweh* (usually more than one). In every case, a *miqweh* was situated close to each of the hot bath-rooms of the private house.[38]

Because of the concern of transmitting impurity through water,[39] bathing constituted a significant 'danger'. As we saw in Leviticus, it was possible to become impure by coming into contact with impure people (e.g., menstruating women, men who had had an emission, lepers, etc.). Water containing potentially impure bodies was of particular concern.[40]

Another concern relating to the architecture of ritual baths was retaining and storing annual rainfall. Cisterns had become so numerous in the Hellenistic, Roman and Byzantine periods that they could be found in households, supplying families with water for the whole year.[41] Elaborate

---

34. Killebrew, 'Baths', p. 285.
35. R. Reich, 'The Hot Bath-House (*balneum*), the *Miqweh*, and the Jewish Community in the Second Temple Period', *JJS* 39.1 (1988), pp. 102–7 (102).
36. Reich, 'Hot Bath-House', p. 102.
37. Reich, 'Hot Bath-House', p. 106.
38. Reich, 'Hot Bath-House', p. 106.
39. See Regev, 'Non-Priestly Purity', p. 229.
40. Reich, 'Hot Bath-House', p. 103.
41. T. Tsuk, 'Cisterns' (trans. Ilana Goldberg), in E. M. Meyers (ed.), *Oxford*

water systems such as the one at Sepphoris brought water supplies from outside cities.[42] Similarly, nearby Petra was known for its water system, so that Strabo commented on the skills of Petra's engineers in this regard (*Geography* 16.4.21). Petra (a Nabataean site) even had a pool near the so-called Great Temple. This pool may have been modelled on the larger pool complex built by Herod at Herodium.[43] In areas where water was limited, an extravagance like a pool would send a message of prosperity to inhabitants and those passing through a city such as Petra.[44]

Whether we think of the extravagance of a pool or the practicality of cisterns (used for keeping rainwater for 'drinking, washing, livestock, irrigation, and agricultural installations'[45]), water installations and new ways of moving and storing rainwater were developing in the early Roman period. It is therefore appropriate that a special water installation for keeping Levitical purity laws would be introduced at the same time as these various 'water structures' were part of the architectural (built) environment. They could serve not only to distinguish Jewish practice from Graeco-Roman practice, but they might also have an element of being able to impress others by their installation and construction.[46]

Examples of *miqvaot* have been found at Jerusalem, Jotapata, Sepphoris, Qumran, Masada, Jericho, Herodium and Gezar.[47] They have also been discovered in Samaria.[48] Many of the excavated *miqvaot* have been found in cities (e.g., Jerusalem, Jotapata), palaces and fortresses

Encyclopedia of Archaeology in the Near East (5 vols.; Oxford: Oxford University Press, 1997), vol. 2, pp. 12–13 (13).

42. See T. Tsuk, 'Bringing Water to Sepphoris', in *BAR* 26.4 (July/August 2000), pp. 35–41.

43. Leigh-Ann Bedal ('A Pool Complex in Petra's City Center', *BASOR* 324 [November 2001], pp. 23–41) states: 'The plans of the Herodian and Petra garden/pool complexes are virtually identical, although the Herodium complex is constructed on a significantly grander scale' (p. 37). See also chapter 3 (Description of the Excavations at Lower Herodium During the Years 1972, 1973 and 1987) in E. Netzer, *Qedem 13: Greater Herodium* (Monographs of the Institute of Archaeology, The Hebrew University of Jerusalem; Jerusalem: Publications of the Hebrew University of Jerusalem, 1981).

44. Bedal, 'Pool Complex', p. 39.

45. Tsuk, 'Cisterns', pp. 12–13.

46. That is, *miqvoat* were not practical in the sense that they did not store water for drinking, washing, etc. (see above). These were 'ritual' rather than 'practical' structures.

47. E. Netzer, 'Ancient Ritual Baths (*Miqvaot*) in Jericho', in L. I. Levine (ed.), *The Jerusalem Cathedra: Studies in the History, Archaeology, Geography and Ethnography of the Land of Israel* (3 vols., Jerusalem: Yad Izhak Ben-Zvi Institute, 1981), vol. 1, pp. 106–119.

48. See Magen, 'Ritual Baths', pp. 181–92.

3. Embodied Sacred Space: Purity in the Land

(Masada and Jericho) and private homes (the upper city of Jerusalem). However, ritual baths have apparently also been found on a Hasmonean farm in the region of Qalandiya (West Bank),[49] as well as in villages.[50] *Miqvaot* are not an urban phenomenon, nor are they a Judaean phenomenon. They seem to have been in use fairly widely throughout the land and were particular to it.[51] The work done in particular by Eric Meyers, Carol Meyers and Kenneth Hoglund in Sepphoris shows that the *miqvaot* located there are different in construction from *miqvaot* in Jerusalem or Jericho for instance. This may be compared to differences in pottery by region.[52]

Still, there are problems with establishing a list of excavated *miqvaot*.[53] We can identify two related reasons for this. First of all, there is the problem that not all of the finds have been published.[54] Secondly, due to the similarities between *miqvaot* and other contemporary 'water installations', there can be considerable disagreement as to what constitutes a *miqveh* and what constitutes simply a bath or cistern.[55] There were considerable variations on the designs for building *miqvaot*. We can certainly agree with Sanders that all of them could have been derived from Leviticus as there is room for interpretation in the text.[56] They could be single or double pools with single or double (divided) steps. They might have water supplied by a water supply system, or they

---

49. Magen, 'Ritual Baths', pp. 190–92.

50. Reich, 'Ritual Baths', p. 431.

51. This may be said cautiously based on the existing evidence, though more data and greater agreement about identification are needed before claims as to the spread and the ubiquity of *miqvaot* may be said to be certain. Reich notes the particularity of *miqvaot* to the land (Galilee and Judea): 'Frequently used in the Second Temple period in Judea (Judah) and the Galilee, *miqva'ot* were absent from the Late Hellenistic and Early Roman world. Like Jewish inscriptions and symbols, the *miqveh* is a clue (an architectural one) for identifying a Jewish presence at sites', Reich, 'Ritual Baths', p. 431. See also E. Netzer, 'Ancient Ritual Baths', where he comments, 'These baths seem to have first been built at this time; no comparable institution is known from the biblical period. The plan of such *miqvaot* was far from fixed, and a wide range of models appear to have fulfilled this ritual requirement' (p. 106).

52. R. Reich, 'They *Are* Ritual Baths', p. 53.

53. Reich estimates 300 *miqvaot* for the period before the Mishnah and the Talmud. R. Reich, 'The Synagogue and the *Miqweh* in Eretz-Israel in the Second-Temple, Misnaic, and Talmudic Periods', in D. Urman and P. V. M. Flesher (eds), *Ancient Synagogues: Historical Analysis and Archaeological Discovery* (Leiden: E. J. Brill, 1995), pp. 289–97 (296).

54. Hanan Eshel notes the problem of unpublished data for Sepphoris. See Eshel, 'We Need More Data', p. 49.

55. See Eshel, 'Pools of Sepphoris: Ritual Baths or Bathtubs?', pp. 46–8.

56. Sanders, *Judaism: Practice and Belief*, p. 222.

might have the feature of an *otsar* (a storage pool for water which could be used to 'purify' the ritual bath next to it by allowing contact between the two pools via a connecting pipe). The pools with an *otsar* may be considered to be Pharisaic because they are discussed in the Mishnah. These have been found at Masada, Herodium, Jericho and Jerusalem.[57]

It is perhaps wise to be cautious in evaluating the decline of *miqvaot*,[58] though Reich suggests that it may have been connected to the destruction of the Jerusalem temple in 70 CE.[59] However, even if the temple was important to the widespread use of *miqvaot* before 70, this does not tell us that purity was *only* practiced in preparation for entering the temple.[60] The existence of *miqvaot* at a considerable distance from Jerusalem (e.g., in the Galilee) as well as in Samaria (where presumably no one was preparing to offer sacrifices at the Jerusalem temple) and Qumran (connected to the community meal), indicates fairly strongly that the practice of bathing in *miqvaot* had broader uses than only in relationship to temple worship. As already noted, in Leviticus itself, bathing was not always explicitly connected to the sanctuary. There are implications for the meaning of *miqvaot* and how these structures relate to the notion of the land as sacred and social space.

Meaning, Hierarchy and the Cost of Purity

Does the widespread use of these structures in Second Temple Judaism tell us anything about land as sacred and social space? Eyal Regev suggests that the meaning of non-priestly purity is related to the individual and personal sanctity.[61] But even pure individual bodies are also part of the larger category of the sacredness of people and land in distinction from the nations. If ritual marks space as sacred, bathing in *miqvaot* could be connected to a wider concern with purity and to the holiness of the land, devotion to Yahweh and belief in his holiness.[62] Connected

57. Reich, 'Ritual Baths', p. 430.
58. Cf. Regev, 'Non-Priestly Purity', who rightly notes that the decline in *miqvaot* and stone vessels seems to conflict with the rabbis concern with (non-priestly) purity laws (pp. 233–5).
59. Reich, 'Ritual Baths', p. 431. See also R. Reich, 'Synagogue and *Miqweh*', pp. 296–7. Magen, 'Ritual Baths', pp. 162–3.
60. This is argued by Sanders, *Practice and Belief*, pp. 222–9.
61. E. Regev, 'Pure Individualism: The Idea of Non-Priestly Purity in Ancient Judaism', *JSJ* 31.2 (2000), pp. 176–202 (190–92).
62. M. Borg, *Conflict, Holiness and Politics in the Teachings of Jesus* (Harrisburg, PA: Trinity Press, 1994), pp. 71–7.

3. *Embodied Sacred Space: Purity in the Land* 77

to these beliefs, as John Riches has shown, is the notion that 'doing' purity meant not doing as the Gentiles do. And, here in particular we find implications for the social aspect of purity. That is, bathing in *miqvaot* meant distinguishing Jews from Gentiles and maintaining separate practices. The Romans might bathe for the 'general good' of purity,[63] but Jewish bathing in *miqvaot* was something distinguishable from this, based on the interpretation of biblical purity laws.

Gentiles were kept from entering the sacred sanctuary in Jerusalem, but what was the significance of the presence of Romans throughout the land? It was not possible to place signs at the borders of the land identifying the space as holy and restricting entrance. What might be possible, though, was distinctive practices, marking space and signifying holiness as part of the relationship between God, people and land. The practice of purity does emphasize distinctions, and *miqvaot* are not portable, but 'located' structures. Thinking of life in the camp described by Leviticus, *miqvaot* would certainly not fit within that model. Cut into rock, they could hardly be moved. Therefore, it is reasonable to suppose that they indicate a claim – if not to land itself – to the right to practice purity in the land and thereby maintain its holiness as its inhabitants.

Finally, if space has connections to social hierarchies, how do *miqvaot* fit with this principle? In Leviticus' priestly purity system, priests had a high level of responsibility and were closely connected to the holiest spaces. By the first century, priests certainly used *miqvaot* and probably interpreted them differently from the Pharisees in terms of their construction,[64] but were they responsible for them? Did they see to their construction and expect their use throughout the land? Certainly, it seems unlikely that *miqvaot* were introduced as part of a peasant ideology or a lower class 'revolutionary' idea as to the proper interpretation of Leviticus. The earliest Hasmonean *miqvaot* known so far were part of palaces. This does not mean that there was not a shared ideology, or concern with purity, only that the 'inspiration' to build a structure hewn in bedrock, holding 40 *seah* of undrawn water would not have originated among the 'common people' of the land, though it became part of common

---

63. Sanders notes that a lot of people (ancient people – Jews and 'pagans') were interested in purity (*Practice and Belief*, pp. 229–30). However, it was Jews and not 'pagans' who were interested in the interpretation of *Leviticus*. Certainly, Sanders would agree with this point, but the importance of purity as biblical interpretation (and part of *distinctive* Jewish religious identity, not merely for the good of purity in general) should be stressed.

64. The baths in the upper city of Jerusalem are of the single pool variety, in contrast to the 'Pharisaic' interpretation.

practice. There may be a connection between these purity structures and the elite who could afford to build them for their convenience. Still, we must make sense of the expansion of purity practices to reach beyond the temple, palaces, fortresses and private homes of the powerful. There seems to have been an enthusiasm for keeping purity even apart from the temple and more widely than just with the priests.[65] Indeed it is possible that the Pharisees had a role here. This necessitates further exploration, but the practice of non-priestly purity seems to have been fairly broadly influential and should be thought about in terms of the framework we have discussed for understanding purity as part of a concern with the holiness of the land.

Elite members of society could, in a sense, 'afford' to be pure. There is a certain cost involved with building *miqvaot*, cut into stone and perhaps connected to a water system supplying rainwater.[66] Another purity 'innovation' with labour intensive production associated with it is stone vessels. Such vessels, made either by hand or by lathe, were thought by the rabbis to be unable to contract impurity and workshops for the production of these items have been found in both Galilee and Judea, particularly in the environs of Jerusalem.[67] Similar to *miqvaot*, stone vessels are not discussed in relationship to keeping purity in Leviticus. Ceramic vessels, however, had to be broken if they became defiled according to Leviticus (e.g., 6.28; 11.33; 15.12).[68] They could not be used again as could stone vessels according to rabbinic interpretation.[69] Again noting the potential

---

65. See the discussion of Regev, 'Non-Priestly Purity', pp. 223–44.

66. In discussion of the irrigation system of the Hasmonean kings at Jericho, Netzer says, 'While these were intended primarily for the irrigation of royal plantations and gardens, they also made possible the construction and maintenance of luxurious winter palaces, with their full complement of swimming pools, bath houses and miqvaot' ('Ancient Ritual Baths', p. 108).

67. Y. Magen, 'Jerusalem as a Center of the Stone Vessel Industry During the Second Temple Period', in H. Geva (ed.), *Ancient Jerusalem Revealed* (Jerusalem: Israel Exploration Society, 1994), pp. 244–56 (245–7). A particular soft limestone was used in the Second Temple period for artefacts include ossuaries, tables and small vessels such as measuring cups (which were common (see p. 245). The Mishnah – *Kelim* 10.1; 4.4 – says that stone was clean because it were not fired. Thereby, vessels made of sun-dried dung and earth were also regarded as clean.

68. D. Adan-Bayewitz, *Common Pottery in Roman Galilee: A Study of Local Trade* (Ramat-Gan, Israel: Bar-Ilan University Press, 1993), p. 231. See also M. Ben-Dov, *In the Shadow of the Temple: The Discovery of Ancient Jerusalem* (trans. I. Friedman; New York: Harper & Row, 1985), pp. 155–7.

69. See Magen, 'Jerusalem as a Centre'. He makes a connection with the emergence of a stone vessel industry. 'Due to the strictures governing ritual cleanness it was more worthwhile to purchase a vessel which could not become unclean, for once a vessel

cost associated with purity, it could be quite expensive to replace pottery which had become defiled. Adan-Bayewitz suggests that potters would be able to provide a large number of vessels to 'observant consumers'.[70] Some would have been able to afford to replace pottery, purchase stone vessels (and stone tables[71]) and build their own *miqvaot* whilst others likely would not have been able to. The cost of being particularly careful about purity would certainly have been one factor contributing to a range of observance.

Interpretation of Purity Laws 1: The Sadducees and Pharisees

Having seen that purity laws were interpreted in new ways in the Second Temple period, we now turn to focus on some of the variations of interpretation among particular groups. William Herzog sees the Pharisees and Sadducees as the two groups controlling the redemptive media of Second Temple society, the Sadducees in their control of the temple and the Pharisees by their control of the Torah 'through their oral interpretation of its regulations'.[72] As in the diagram showing the purity system (see p. 66 above), washing, sacrifice and obedience to the commandments were the ways to maintain contact and relationship with Yahweh. These correspond to these two areas of 'control' for the Sadducees and Pharisees – temple and Torah. These are also interrelated, for 'the Temple was the centre of holiness, and the holiness of Temple, land and people depended on the careful observance of Torah'.[73]

---

became ritually unclean it had to be taken out use – especially a pottery vessel, which had to be broken. As a consequence of this halakhic precept of strict observance of the purity laws both inside and outside the Temple, a stone vessel industry began to develop in the Second Temple period' (p. 253).

70. Adan-Bayewitz, *Common Pottery*, p. 231. Perhaps stone vessels could be used to store wine (Jn 2.25). There seems to have been concern that wine and oil were produced in a state of purity as evidenced by the discovery of *miqvaot* at the sites of oil and wine production. See also Magen, 'Ritual Baths', pp. 181–92; D. Adan-Bayewitz and I. Perlman, 'The Local Trade of Sepphoris in the Roman Period', *Israel Exploration Journal* 40.2-3 (1990), pp. 153–72.

71. Tables have been found in the Upper City of Jerusalem. See Magen, 'Jerusalem as a Center', pp. 249, 252. See also Hillel Geva 'Twenty-Five Years of Excavations in Jerusalem, 1967–1992: Achievements and Evaluation', in H. Geva (ed.), *Ancient Jerusalem Revealed* (Jerusalem: Israel Exploration Society, 1994), pp. 1–28 (12–13).

72. Herzog, 'Racial Injustice', p. 14.

73. Borg, *Conflict, Holiness and Politics*, p. 76. He goes on to say: 'Moreover, the two major renewal movements (Pharisees and Essenes) were both committed to an intensification of holiness' (pp. 76–7). Sanders seems to have missed the point that observance of the Torah was related to the holiness of the land as well as the

The Sadducees and Temple Purity

Related to the location of the Sadducees in Jerusalem and their concern with the affairs of the temple, we may draw out a connection between the Sadducees and the purity of the temple. Josephus identifies the difference between the traditions of the Sadducees and the Pharisees as related to the authority of their traditions (*Ant.* 13.297). Josephus further says that the Sadducees do not believe in fate but hold that human actions determine whether one receives good or evil (*Ant.* 13.173; cf. *War* 2.164-5). They believe that soul and body die together (*Ant.* 18.16; *War* 2.165) and do not believe in punishment and rewards in Hades (*War* 2.165). In Goodman's view, the belief-system of the Sadducees was primarily accepting of the status quo.[74] It would follow that they were also influential in the maintenance or definition of the status quo.

The temple was the focus of the Sadducees, and although this was a highly respected institution in the land and the Diaspora, in many ways they themselves may have been isolated from most of the Jewish population. Bowker says of the Sadducees, 'they were in fact creating another isolation – in addition to the geographical isolation of the Temple as an enclave of holiness, they were in effect isolating Torah from the lives of most people'.[75] This would have made them a visible and yet perhaps distant group for most people participating in the temple cult. The popular election of a high priest by the Zealots at the end of the war (*War* 4.147-157) suggests that not everyone was pleased with the 'pool' from which the high priest was chosen. In Josephus' account of Simon's elevation to the high priesthood (*Ant.* 15.299-316) the backdrop where the scene is played out is the upper city of Jerusalem (15.318). It is not difficult to imagine Simon, high priest with the record for longest term in office under Herod,[76] living in a home like the ones uncovered

---

temple. He believes purity was performed for access to the temple in view of Josephus (*C. Ap.* 2.198; *War* 5.227). He says that purity laws regulated 'what must be done after contracting impurity in order to enter the temple' (E. P. Sanders, *Jesus and Judaism* [Philadelphia, PA: Fortress Press, 1985], p. 182). Further, 'purity is related to the temple and sacrifices, and impurity does not limit ordinary associations, except for very short periods of time' (Sanders, *Jesus*, p. 182). See also *Judaism, Practice and Belief*, pp. 71, 228.

74. M. Goodman, *The Ruling Class of Judaea: The Origins of the Jewish Revolt Against Rome A.D. 66–70* (Cambridge: Cambridge University Press, 1987), p. 79.

75. J. Bowker, *Jesus and the Pharisees* (Cambridge: Cambridge University Press, 1973), p. 18.

76. See Goodman, *Ruling Class*, pp. 42, 139.

by archaeological excavations in the upper city of Jerusalem, furnished with single-pool *miqvaot*, stone tables and vessels.[77]

In the end, we have a limited picture of the Sadducees, but one that indicates a group with considerable power in the Second Temple period. As such, they exert a certain control over society's space, particularly the sacred space of the temple. They are connected to the high priesthood, an office which had limits to its power at the time. Though it may have been possible to retain power over many aspects of the cult, Rome did not allow complete freedom for the office as evidenced by the retention of the high priest's robes (*Ant.* 20.6; 18.403-408; 18.90-95). High priests would have had to concede on some issues in order to maintain relations with Rome and their own positions. Still, the Sadducees, at least in part, were likely to have a significant role in the conventions and use of sacred space that others like the Pharisees might choose to debate and modify.[78] For them, obeying the law meant not accepting the new halakhic interpretations of the Pharisees. Nor did they accept beliefs about resurrection and fate as mentioned in Josephus (*War* 2.162-165 and *Ant.* 13.172-173). The temple was part of their sphere of influence. In this realm, they attempted to assert their authority and claim what control they could over 'the means of redemption', attempting 'to maintain their position of control by diplomacy and compromise'.[79] When that institution was destroyed in 70 CE so was the foundation of power for this group, whatever their membership may have been. They did not have a popular base of support to rely on after the revolt. In Goodman's words, they did not need to rely on the 'theological succour' many Jews accepted (i.e., beliefs about resurrection, fate).[80] Such views would have contributed to a divide between a group like the Sadducees and the people at the same time that theological beliefs among the people formed the ideological glue for their support of the temple. Turning to the Pharisees, they may have had more success among the people in some of the areas where the Sadducees had failed. Though they did not have the same amount of control of the central sacred space that the Sadducees apparently had in the first century, they do give their own answer to the question: what does it mean to be holy?[81]

77. Geva, 'Twenty-Five Years of Excavations',pp. 12–14.
78. Examples of the debates in the Mishnah between Sadducees and Pharisees concern the Day of Atonement and the proper procedure for the burning of the ashes of the red heifer. See Bowker, *Jesus and the Pharisees*, p. 18.
79. J. Riches, *Jesus and the Transformation of Judaism* (London: Darton, Longman & Todd, 1980), p. 83.
80. Goodman, *Ruling Class*, p. 79.
81. Borg, *Conflict, Holiness and Politics*, p. 71.

Pharisees: The 'Who' and 'Where' of Purity

The Pharisees were a group with a special interest in non-priestly purity, in particular eating ordinary food in ritual purity. Jacob Neusner understands the Pharisees as primarily a table-fellowship group before 70 CE, a picture which matches with the gospel evidence on the Pharisees.[82] They applied priestly laws concerning purity to their ordinary meals following their abandonment of politics during the time of Hillel.[83] Sanders argues against Neusner, and thinks the Pharisees had no desire to live 'on par' with the priesthood;[84] everyone was interested in purity and the Pharisees were not special enforcers of the law, did not think their laws were required for everyone, and did not exclude anyone based on their practice (or non-practice) of purity.[85] In *Jesus and Judaism*, Sanders says, 'Purity laws which govern everyone did not affect table fellowship, but access to the Temple'.[86]

Geographically, although E. P. Sanders suggests that Pharisees 'did not leave Jerusalem and continued to believe in the sacrificial system, in which the priests speak for God',[87] the evidence in the gospels suggests that Pharisees were also present in Galilee.[88] Pharisees in the Gospel of Mark are located in Galilee and debate issues such as fasting, observance of the Sabbath, divorce, eating with 'sinners' and hand washing (i.e. Mk 2.16, 18, 24; 3.2; 7.1; 10.2).[89] Though Jose-

---

82. Neusner's oft quoted statistics state that 67% of the legal pericopae of the rabbinic traditions about the Pharisees before 70 deal with dietary laws. J. Neusner, *The Rabbinic Traditions about the Pharisees Before 70, Part III: Conclusions* (Leiden: E. J. Brill, 1971), pp. 78–89, 304, 318. J. Neusner, 'Mr. Sanders' Pharisees and Mine: A Response to E. P. Sanders' *Jewish Law From Jesus to the Mishnah*', *SJT* 44 (1993), pp. 73–95. Also, *From Politics to Piety: The Emergence of Pharisaic Judaism* (Englewood Cliffs, NJ: Prentice-Hall, 1973), pp. 66–7.

83. Neusner, *Politics to Piety*, p. 14. Hillel is thought to be roughly a contemporary of Jesus, living sometime ca. 50 BCE to 10 CE.

84. Sanders, *Practice and Belief*, pp. 438–40.

85. Sanders, *Jesus*, pp. 182–99.

86. Sanders, *Jesus*, p. 186. See also M. Hengel and R. Deines, 'E. P. Sanders' "Common Judaism", Jesus, and the Pharisees', *JTS* 46 (1995), pp. 1–40. They believe that Sanders has underestimated the Pharisees for their influence on Jewish society and 'as a consequence of this maginalizing of the Pharisees, there emerges what might be called a "Sadducean tendency" in Sanders' presentation of "common Judaism" as a religion of the temple and priesthood' (p. 4).

87. Sanders, *Jesus*, p. 273.

88. See J. Marcus, *Mark 1–8: A New Translation with Introduction and Commentary* (New York: Doubleday, 2000), pp. 519–23.

89. Marcus, *Mark 1–8*, p. 520.

3. *Embodied Sacred Space: Purity in the Land* 83

phus discusses Pharisees in the context of Jerusalem (*Life* 189-98, 191-92), he himself claims to have been a Pharisee (*Life* 10-12) and spent considerable time in Galilee. Purity also had a broader meaning relating to God's holiness and the holiness of the land which could, in the Pharisaic vision, be put in place within communities throughout the land.[90] Spatially, the Pharisees may have found it necessary to (or easier to) enforce their vision for Israel outside of the temple. In any case, they were well established before the destruction of the temple.[91] They do more than simply transfer purity from the temple and priests to communities in the land and laity.[92] What the Pharisees add as their own 'twist' on purity regulations is the ability of qualified lay persons to interpret the laws even in disagreement with priests. Rather than simply being more 'thorough' or 'enthusiastic' about purity, the Pharisees may have actually had some influence with the people regarding forms of purity where a general concern already existed in the society.[93] In light of the archaeological evidence in particular, 'the "acting like a priest" theory cannot fully explain the comprehensive phenomenon of non-priestly purity'.[94] And the Pharisees do not have to consider themselves as replacing the priests to have their own authority with regard to interpretation of the law.[95] As Eyal Regev suggests, the Pharisees may have paid particular attention to bodily purity in competition at a social level with the Sadducees and also to distinguish themselves from the masses, or the people of the land.[96] In terms of Kunin's oppositional model of sacred space, the Pharisees' influence was mainly in operation at the level of the largest category of sacred space, the opposition between Israel and the nations. But within this category, they distinguish themselves from the people of the land, and place

90. Certainly Josephus says that the Pharisees were influential among the populous (e.g. *Ant.* 13.298).

91. See Bowker, *Jesus and the Pharisees*. In Bowker's view, the Pharisees and Sadducees were initially concerned with keeping purity within geographical boundaries (pp. 21–3).

92. J. Marcus, *Mark 1–8*, pp. 519–23. Though they did extend the purity laws to lay people in their expansion of the 'traditions of the elders'.

93. M. Goodman, 'A Note on Josephus, the Pharisees and Ancestral Tradition', *JJS* 1.1 (Spring 1999), pp. 17–20. Shaye Cohen, *From the Maccabees to the Mishnah* (Philadelphia: Westminster Press, 1987), p. 171.

94. Regev, 'Non-Priestly Purity', p. 237.

95. See D. R. DeLacey, 'In Search of a Pharisee', *TynBul* 43.2 (1992), pp. 353–72. He says, 'It is perfectly reasonable to suppose that they [the Pharisees] strove for a purity analogous to, but neither identical to nor a replacement for, that of the priests' (pp. 362–3).

96. Regev, 'The Idea of Non-Priestly Purity', pp. 192–9.

themselves in competition with the priests through their interpretation of the law (as in *m. Hag* 2.7, regarding *midras* uncleanness).

However, the law could be emphasized even outside of the land, so in this sense one might ask if the strategy of the Pharisees shows a 'diasporification' of the land (i.e., distinctive practices distinguishing Jews regardless of their location). One principle that emerges in rabbinic Judaism is that the law could be observed outside the land, but only perfectly observed inside the land, where additional commandments related to the land apply.[97] Still, though the Mishnah discusses the land at various points, no single view emerges. Charles Primus detects a difference between views of the sanctity of the land in a rabbinic debate (*m. Hallah* 2.1) as to whether a dough-offering is required if the dough is made from produce exported from the land to another location.[98] In the first view, the land has a special holiness that may be transferred (by people, objects) to locations outside the land. The sanctity of life in the land is 'infectious' and moves across boundaries.[99] In the second view, holiness is contained within borders and sacred space has meaning which is specific to different areas.[100] Though it is not possible to take these views as going back to the earlier Pharisees, we see that these issues were important ones to grapple with.

In another example from the Mishnah, the land is famously described in terms of concentric circles of holiness emanating from the holy of holies in the temple (*m. Kelim* 1.6-9). The rabbis understand world order in terms of a temple system, even though their own situation is quite different from the ideal:

> The spatial and social categories are no longer fully congruent: Jews live both in the Land of Israel and abroad (most in fact living abroad); the Land of Israel is inhabited by both Jews and gentiles (who do not live under Jewish jurisdiction)... The specific problems raised in the Mishnah deal with defining *who* must observe these agricultural laws (social taxonomy) and *where* they must be observed (spatial taxonomy) now that the boundaries have been violated and the categories confused.[101]

This situation of non-congruity of spatial and social categories existed prior to the destruction of Jerusalem, and the issues of 'who' and

---

97. Richard Sarason, 'The Significance of the Land of Israel in the Mishnah', in L. A. Hoffman (ed.), *The Land of Israel: Jewish Perspectives* (Notre Dame, IN: University of Notre Dame Press, 1986), pp. 109–36 (126).

98. C. Primus, 'The Borders of Judaism: The Land of Israel in Early Rabbinic Judaism', in L. A. Hoffman (ed.), *The Land of Israel: Jewish Perspectives* (Notre Dame, IN: University of Notre Dame Press, 1986), pp. 97–108 (104).

99. Primus, 'Borders', pp. 103–07.

100. Primus, 'Borders', pp. 103–07; on defining sacred space, p. 106.

101. Sarason, 'Significance of the Land', p. 117.

'where' with regard to purity would also have been relevant in an earlier time. If the meaning of 'the land' at the time of the Pharisees had not yet been 'relativized to social categories',[102] we should connect their concern with purity to the desire to keep the sanctity of the land.[103] In *m. Kelim* 1.6-9 there is a hierarchy established from priests to Pharisees to *amme ha aretz*, but even the lowest have 'their own sort of purity'.[104] The Gentiles are not mentioned, and may be presumed to be outside the category of the sacred. Yet, DeLacey comments: 'It is noteworthy that there is no discussion of how the presence of an *am ha aretz* home or a Roman pigsty would affect the holiness of the land'.[105] The fact that such issues are not considered shows something of the need to deal with the realities of lived life and to do so in such a way as to be able to succeed in their social context.[106] The focus on separation between Israel and the nations (e.g., Lev. 18; 20) is perhaps more judiciously approached in the hierarchical scale of the rabbis.

Whether between Israel and the nations, *amme ha aretz* and Pharisees, or Pharisees and priests, social boundaries were established through an emphasis on ritual purity. Marcus Borg describes a purity society in the first century:

> I conclude that a 'quest for holiness' or a 'quest for purity' (phrases which I use as synonyms) was the dominant cultural dynamic in the Jewish homeland in the first century. It created a social world ordered as a purity system, one with sharp social boundaries.[107]

Beliefs about purity relate to the social and political situation of the Pharisees (and Sadducees) and have practical implications for *where* holiness is located and *who* is properly holy. Though the Pharisees distinguish themselves from both the priests and *am ha aretz* over purity issues, they uphold the boundary and include them all within the category Israel.

Interpretation of Purity Laws 2: Qumran, Samaritans and John the Baptist

The purity practices of the Qumran community, the Samaritans and John the Baptist should also be related to the purity 'trends' current within

---

102. Sarason, 'Significance of the Land', p. 117.
103. Regev, 'Non-Priestly Purity', p. 243.
104. Regev, 'Non-Priestly Purity', p. 243.
105. DeLacey, 'Pharisee', p. 371.
106. Zealots, for instance, may have argued that the presence of a Roman pigsty did indeed affect the holiness of the land.
107. M. Borg, *Conflict, Holiness and Politics*, p. 8.

Second Temple Jewish sectarianism within the land.[108] In a way that is not true for the Pharisees, each of these groups appears to show a distance from the temple, yet at some level an interest in ritual purity is maintained. Qumran and the Samaritans have each (in different ways) separated themselves from the Jerusalem temple. John is a different sort of figure, but he locates himself in the wilderness, baptizing in the Jordan, which is comparable to ritual immersion.

Qumran: Purity Confined to the Community

According to the conventions of Leviticus, all Israelites would have the possibility of purifying themselves and distinguishing themselves from 'the nations'. An interesting shift occurs at Qumran where even some other Jews could be considered outsiders and impure.[109] Even if this refers to a certain group of Jews that the community consider themselves to be in disagreement with, there is still the possibility that merely being part of Israel was not enough to be included in the widest category of sacred space. The *Rule of the Community* has this to say about the one who does not enter the community:

> He will not become clean by the acts of atonement, nor shall he be purified by the cleansing waters, nor shall he be made holy by the seas or rivers, nor shall he be purified by all the water of the ablutions. Defiled, defiled shall he be all the days he spurns the decrees of God, without allowing himself to be taught by the Community of his counsel. (1QS iii.4-6)

Such a statement indicates that even proper practice of the law – ritual bathing – would not purify the person or persons who did not follow the Community's interpretation of the law. In a sense, the 'normal' possibilities for moving from impurity to purity in Leviticus were 'blocked' for those outside the boundary. We could imagine a modified chart from the one presented earlier.

---

108. See Cohen, *From the Maccabees*, p. 171: 'Jewish sectarianism was a phenomenon restricted to the mother country. Alienation from the temple and priests was required if sectarianism was to have a focus, and outside the land of Israel that focus did not exist, because all Jews were equally distant from the holy land and from contact with the sacred. All the sources that speak about the Pharisees, Sadducees, Essenes, and other sects, place them exclusively in the land of Israel, for the most part in Judea'.

109. For a different view see P. R. Davies, 'Space and Sects in the Qumran Scrolls', in D. M. Gunn and P. M. McNutt (eds.), *'Imagining' Biblical Worlds: Studies in Spatial, Social and Historical Constructs in Honor of James W. Flanagan* (Sheffield: Sheffield Academic Press, 2002), pp. 81–98. He views the *Community Rule* as representing a group who apply negative distinctions to members of their 'parent' sect, represented by the *Damascus Document* (p. 93).

3. Embodied Sacred Space: Purity in the Land

```
Holy (qadosh)
    Desecrate/Desanctify (hillel/hiqdish)
Holy (qadosh)                           Pure/Common (tahor/hol)
    Sanctify (qiddesh)                      Pollute (timme)
    (anointment, commandment)           Pure/Common (tahor/hol)                    Impure (tame)
                                            Purify (tiher)
                                            (ablution, sacrifice)
                                            BLOCKED
```

According to this ideology, purity and impurity are still understood to be possible states of the body. There are still certain practices which are associated with purity (i.e., bathing). However, an important change has occurred in that it is impossible for some to become purified by the normal ritual performance. Thus, the major distinction is not between those who are part of Israel and practice the law and those who are not/do not, but between those who follow the community rule and others who cannot be purified. As John Riches puts it:

> Now for Qumran the situation has clearly changed in that there is no longer a clear distinction between Jew and Gentile, between those who do the Law and those who do not. The experience of the community is rather of a situation of conflict with those who observe the law in a different way from themselves.[110]

Whereas the Pharisees gave their own interpretation of purity within wider society within the land, the Qumran community applies strict rules for the purity of their own community.

Archaeological evidence shows that *miqvaot* were in use by the desert community. Notably, they are located near the room where the communal meal was likely to have taken place. A pantry was discovered at the site which contained 'more than one thousand vessels for eating adjacent to a large room'[111] which was most likely the dining room. There are references to the practice of bathing prior to communal meals in *Community Rule* (i.e. 1QS v.13-14) and the *Damascus Document* (CD xi.21-22). The common meal itself is described in 1QS vi.2-5, 16-17, 22, 24-25 as well as other places (vi.4-5, vii.19-20, viii.17). The hierarchy within the community is reinforced by participation in the central common meal. Only those who are clean may participate

---

110. See Riches, *Jesus*, p. 124.
111. T. S. Beall, 'The Essenes', in L. H. Schiffman and J. C. VanderKam (eds), *Encyclopedia of the Dead Sea Scrolls* (2 vols.; Oxford: Oxford University Press, 2000), vol. 1, pp. 262–9 (266).

in this meal and initiates must undergo a one-year period where they do not share in the 'pure food' of the community (i.e. 1QS v.16, 24-25). Discussing the rendering of food impure, Harrington contrasts Qumran's emphasis on impure persons (who are expelled for defiling food or possessions) with the rabbis emphasis on whether or not the food itself is impure.[112]

The severity of the attitude found at Qumran is rightly emphasized. The spatial boundaries of inside and outside the community are justified by application of the terminology of purity and impurity. Those who do not conform are punished with strict consequences and physical removal from the space of the community. The language of purity excludes outsiders and even designates them as sinful.[113]

Though new 'innovations' relating to purity were based on Scripture, they could also go beyond Scripture. For instance, Qumran documents describe the practice of avoiding contact with excrement. Latrines had to be removed from the living area (11Q19 xlvi.13-16 and 1QM vii.3-7).[114] Though Deuteronomy describes a practice of going outside the war camp to dig a hole for excrement due to the holiness of the camp (Deut. 23.12-14), this practice is not part of the laws for purity in Leviticus or Numbers for the people generally (only in context of the war camp).[115] Certainly, it does not have direct bearing for the priests and their duties in the temple. But it does say something about how the community marks off space as holy. The practice, if it was followed, shows the strict establishment of purity within the borders of the community. It goes beyond the 'normal' considerations of bodily contagion in Leviticus and reinforces boundaries for the community.

112. H. Harrington, *The Impurity Systems of Qumran and the Rabbis: Biblical Foundations* (Atlanta, GA: Scholars Press, 1993), p. 63.

113. M. Himmelfarb, 'Impurity and Sin in 4QD, 1QS, and 4Q512', *DSD* 8.1 (2001), pp. 9–37. Himmelfarb emphasizes the dualistic and evocative use of purity terminology in 1QS, though purity laws in particular are not dealt with in the document: 'Still, although it does not concern itself with purity laws, 1QS does use the language of purity, primarily in highly rhetorical passages that represent those outside the community as sinful and impure, in contrast to those who join the community and are cleansed of their sin and impurity' (p. 30). The connection between impurity and sin is significant. In Himmelfarb's estimation, it is 'evocative' and 'poetic' rather than halakhic (p. 37).

114. If the evidence of Josephus concerning the Essenes is to be considered here, he states that they washed after this 'natural function' as if they had become unclean and refrained from even going to stool on the Sabbath (*War* 2.147-149).

115. Harrington discusses this practice, concluding that it was within reason to assume that the sectarians both bathed and washed their clothes after contamination from excrement (*Impurity Systems*, pp. 100–103).

3. Embodied Sacred Space: Purity in the Land

An interesting passage at the beginning of the Damascus Document gives a view on the boundaries of the land. The author speaks of a time after the Teacher of Righteousness has been raised up when Israel (of the last generations – CD i.12) strayed at the arrival of 'the scoffer' (i.14):

> This is the time about which it has been written: [Hos. 4.16] <Like a stray heifer, so has Israel strayed> when 'the scoffer' arose, who scattered the waters of lies over Israel and made them veer off into a wilderness without path, flattening the everlasting heights, diverging from the tracks of justice and *removing the boundary with which the very first had marked their inheritance, so that the curses of his covenant would adhere to them*, to deliver them up to the sword carrying out the vengeance of the covenant (CD i.13-18, emphasis added).

In this passage, 'the scoffer' is blamed for the removing of the boundary of inheritance allowing curses instead of blessing to fall upon the nation. Has Israel now become the wilderness? The community itself is located on the 'wrong side' of the Jordan, that is, within the land. If the real danger is being vomited out of Qumran rather than the land (e.g. the strict regulations for initiates), are boundaries now only properly maintained within the community? Purity practices are carried out in the space of the community, not in the space of the land.

Also in the Damascus Document, the community appear to consider themselves a remnant (cf. CD ii.11-12). In the *Rule of the Community*, they have a role in atoning for the land and judging wickedness (1QS v.6; viii.10, ix.3-6) based on an interpretation of Isa. 28.16 which says: 'Thus says the Lord Yahweh, behold I lay in Zion a foundation stone, a tested stone, a precious cornerstone, a sure foundation'.[116] In the *War Scroll* (i.2-3), the 'exiled of the desert' will wage war on the army of Belial. The passage (1 QM i-ii) may perhaps show a view of the land from outside where 'wicked foreigners and renegade Jews' dwell in the land. If so, according to Davies, this would be 'a radical redrafting of the geography of the holy land' with the community separate from the holiness of the temple and constituting a 'holy of holies' (atoning for the land) within their own group.[117] This may show an eschatological view where the members of the Qumran community interpret their position in the 'Jerusalem wilderness' as connected to Isa. 40.3, thereby using a 'passage that apparently fired Jewish hopes for an apocalyptic holy war that would begin in the Judean wilderness and climax in the liberation of Zion'.[118]

---

116. R. J. McKelvey, *The New Temple: The Church in the New Testament* (Oxford: Oxford University Press, 1969), pp. 46–52.
117. P. R. Davies, 'Space and Sects', p. 94.
118. J. Marcus, *The Way of the Lord: Christological Exegesis of the Old Testament in the Gospel of Mark* (Louisville, KY: Westminster/John Knox Press, 1992), p. 23.

Following on from this, we should re-examine other eschatological beliefs of the sectarians, particularly their view of themselves existing as a 'temporary temple' until such a time as the future temple would be established.[119] Observance of the law is a point of conflict for the community tied to their separation from the temple and temple leadership. We have already examined Qumran's plans for a future temple and their requirement that sectarians refrain from contact with the current temple.[120] The requirement to bathe before participating in the community meal could perhaps be likened to pilgrims wishing to gain access to the temple precincts and using *miqvaot* outside the Hulda gates on the southern sector of the temple walls.[121] Thus, the method of marking off space where the sacred is encountered (maintaining purity by bathing in *miqvaot*) is not wholly dissimilar to the Jerusalem temple, though those of the Qumran community have consciously separated themselves (the 'true' sons of Zadok) from the temple leadership and the temple in Jerusalem. The community prepares the way in the desert, expecting the eschatological event (war) at the end of times, and taking on the model of the wilderness camp for their own community.[122]

For Qumran, the emphasis has moved away from the distinction (i.e., in Leviticus) between Jew and Gentile. It is those outside the community itself who are considered impure. The Prince of Lights and the Angel of Darkness rule over and influence humankind. If the spirit of deceit (1QS iii.20-21) had led many *in Israel* astray and 'the scoffer' had caused the boundary of the inheritance of the nation to be removed, then the understanding of identity at Qumran was strongly connected to their belief that they were assisted by the Angel of Truth and could be pure. Whereas Leviticus establishes by purity (holiness and separation) the boundaries of the land for the nation, the Qumran community may judge that at least for the present time, that boundary has been removed and holiness is only truly affected within the community itself, acting as the 'temporary temple'.

119. Harrington, *Impurity Systems,* pp. 52–3.
120. L. Schiffman, *The Halakhah at Qumran* (Leiden: E. J. Brill, 1975), p. 128.
121. L. I. Levine, 'Archaeological Discoveries from the Greco-Roman Era', in H. Shanks (ed.), *Recent Archaeology in the Land of Israel* (trans. A. Finkelstein; Washington, DC: Biblical Archaeology Society, 1984), pp. 75–87 (82).
122. F. Schmidt, *How the Temple Thinks: Identity and Social Cohesion in Ancient Judaism* (trans. J. E. Crowley; Sheffield: Sheffield Academic Press, 2001). Schmidt holds, as we have discussed in the previous chapter, that the camp in the wilderness and the return to the wilderness are key for Qumran. 'It is in this origin that the Community finds its principal model for thinking about holiness, purity and perfection outside of and without the Jerusalem Temple' (p. 149).

The community at Qumran deliberately take themselves out of the current priestly system and make their own rules and rituals for living. They see themselves as a temporary temple in the wilderness, waiting for their establishment in the future temple. The ideology of holiness we encountered in Leviticus has been modified by interpretation at Qumran, so that belonging to Israel does not guarantee the ability to become purified. The community draws a boundary of the sacred between itself and those outside their rule. Even within their own community, purity demands reinforce the hierarchy between junior and senior members of the community.

The Holy Land of Samaria?

A brief note on Samaritan practice of ritual purity reveals something of a common practice of purity with other parts of the land. Despite hostilities between Samaritans and Jews, there were striking similarities between these two groups. Regarding purity practices, it would appear that the Samaritans also used *miqvaot* from at least the first century CE.[123] In Magan's estimation, the Samaritans observed 'ritual purification in *miqva'ot* identical to those in and around Jerusalem in the Second Temple period'.[124] This supports a strong halakhic link between Samaritans and Jews despite their exclusive attitudes toward one other.[125] Bóid supposes that this indicates that a common tradition of interpretation of the law predates the division between Jews and Samaritans, pointing to a time when all Israel could have included both Jews and Samaritans.[126] The practice of purity was not the point of conflict between Jews and Samaritans.[127] However, at least in part, the distinctiveness of the Samaritans may be viewed as related to their understanding of geography and sacred space (see John 4).[128] Both

---

123. R. Pummer, *The Samaritans* (Leiden: E. J. Brill, 1987), p. 38.
124. Y. Magen, 'Qedumim – A Samaritan Site of the Roman-Byzantine Period', in F. Manns and E. Alliata (eds), *Early Christianity in Context: Monuments and Documents* (Jerusalem: Franciscan Printing Press, 1993), p. 177.
125. See I. R. M. M. Bóid, *Principles of Samaritan Halachah* (Leiden: E. J. Brill, 1989), pp. 327-47.
126. Bóid, *Principles of Samaritan Halachah*, p. 328.
127. See, for instance, R. J. Coggins, *Samaritans and Jews: The Origins of Samaritanism Reconsidered* (Oxford: Blackwell, 1975), particularly the section on Samaritan practice and belief, pp. 131-8.
128. R. Coggins, 'Jewish Local Patriotism: The Samaritan Problem', in Siân Jones and Sarah Pearce (eds), *Jewish Local Patriotism and Self-Identification in the Graeco-Roman Period* (Sheffield: Sheffield Academic Press, 1998), pp. 66-78. See also Coggins, *Samaritans and Jews*, p. 135.

Jews and Samaritans interpreted the Pentateuch as a sacred text. Both were interested in purity and ritual bathing.[129]

One possibility is that Samaria was thought of as part of the land just as much as Judea and Galilee at this time. Josephus includes Samaria within the land along with Judea, Galilee and Perea in *War* 3.35-40. Says Coggins:

> On this point of the extent of the 'promised land', it may well be that any Jewish writer trying to be loyal to the biblical tradition would feel obliged to include in his own description the whole area once occupied by the kingdoms of Israel and Judah.[130]

The Samaritans occupied one small area and probably did not aspire to attain the entire land.[131] Perhaps they endeavoured to keep their one 'part' of the land pure. Another possibility is that they understand their practice of purity more exclusively in terms of local patriotism.[132] In the end, lack of evidence for Samaritan beliefs in this period makes it impossible to connect their practice of non-priestly purity to a wider cosmology or worldview. Nonetheless, though Gerizim may be in mind in an eschatological sense in the first century, Samaritans were not concerned with imminent sacrifices, either in Gerizim or Jerusalem.

John's Baptism of Repentance in the Jordan

Among the various interpretations of purity in the Second Temple period, an important figure for consideration is John the Baptist. Though there are certainly similarities between John's practice of baptism and the general practices of ritual immersion, the most analogous group to John is Qumran.[133] The strongest similarities between John and Qumran in

---

129. See Bóid on 'details and principles', where uncleanness and the practices for restoring cleanness for women, men, sexual intercourse and contact with Gentiles are outlined (pp. 285–304).

130. Coggins, *Samaritans and Jews*, p. 258.

131. J. M. Cohen, *A Samaritan Chronicle: A Source-Critical Analysis of the Life and Times of the Great Samaritan Reformer, Baba Rabbah* (Leiden: E. J. Brill, 1981). Baba Rabbah, of the fourth century CE, is described in Chronicle II (dating perhaps to the ninth century or later, though traditions may be older – see p. 198) as dividing the land among the Samaritans (*Sam. Chron.* 10.14). Earlier (*Sam. Chron.* 10.1), Baba limits his division to 'the recognized areas of Samaritan habitation' (p. 181). On Chronicle II, see also S. Isser, 'Jesus in the Samaritan Chronicles', *JJS* 32 (1981), pp. 166–94.

132. This connection is made by Coggins, 'Jewish Local Patriotism', p. 74.

133. Two articles in one volume explore this connection. See Stephen J. Phann, 'The Essene Yearly Renewal Ceremony and the Baptism of Repentance' (pp. 337–52) and James H. Charlesworth, 'John the Baptizer and Qumran Barriers in Light of the

3. Embodied Sacred Space: Purity in the Land

the sources (*Ant.* 18.116-119; the Gospels) lie in exegesis, location and immersion. That is, they both offer apocalyptic interpretations of Isa. 40.3, they both locate themselves in the desert, near the Jordan river, and they both prescribe immersion.[134] A major difference between the two is that John's baptism appears to be open to all (Mk 1.5; Mt. 3.5; Lk. 3.3) whereas Qumran restricts their purity observance to the community alone. Mark says, 'people from the whole Judean countryside and all the people of Jerusalem were going out to him, and were baptised by him in the river Jordan, confessing their sins' (Mk 1.5). As Charlesworth points out, John does not follow the strict dualism and condemnation of the Sons of Darkness such as is found in 1QS.[135] He is, however, 'on the way towards creating a special group within Judaism'.[136] However, John's appeal to centurions in Lk. 3.14 and the Q statement about children of Abraham being raised from stones (Mt. 3.9//Lk. 3.8) raises questions about whether John challenges the boundary between Israel and the nations. John has disciples (Mt. 9.14) and teaches them to fast and pray (Lk. 11.1). There are also indications of judgement for those who do not repent (i.e. Mt. 3.7-12; Lk. 3.7-10, 17). John's baptism is a characteristic feature of his message, though what seems to be missing is a spatial restriction of purity for John (as for Qumran to the community) or a reinforcement of boundary through social separation and distinctions between insiders and outsiders.

Still, John's baptism should be seen as related to the purity concerns of wider first-century society. In Leviticus, sin offerings involve sacrifice, not immersion (Leviticus 4–6). As Taylor points out, some prophetic traditions emphasized aspects of behaviour over sacrifice (i.e. Hos. 6.6),[137]

Rule of the Community' (pp. 353–75), in D. W. Parry and E. Ulrich (eds), *The Provo International Conference on the Dead Sea Scrolls: Technological Innovations, New Texts, and Reformulated Issues* (Leiden: E. J. Brill, 1999). See also J. Taylor, *John the Baptist within Second Temple Judaism: A Historical Study* (London: SPCK, 1997), pp. 15–48.

134. See Charlesworth, 'John the Baptizer', pp. 356–7.

135. Charlesworth, 'John the Baptizer', pp. 361–6. Though his analysis is perhaps too imaginative when he offers John's reactions to various passages found in the *Rule of the Community*. Cf. R. L. Webb, *John the Baptizer and Prophet: A Socio-Historical Study* (Sheffield: Sheffield Academic Press, 1991). He argues that there is nonetheless a sharp distinction in John between two groups of people – the repentant and the unrepentant (p. 197).

136. G. Theissen, *A Theory of Primitive Christian Religion* (trans. J. Bowden; London: SCM Press, 1999), p. 33.

137. Taylor, *John the Baptist*, p. 109. Taylor cites the best examples of this 'attested notion' that 'atonement was made by repentance and righteous conduct rather than by the sacrifice of an animal' (in addition to Hos. 6.6, she suggests Ps. 51.16-17;

but this is not necessarily related to forgiveness of sins. In any case, for John, baptism and repentance are linked (βάπτισμα μετανοίας – Mk 1.4; Lk. 3.3; cf. Mt. 3.11), emphasizing righteousness over sacrifice, and introducing a new ritual practice. Therefore, we could 'chart' the different connections:

Leviticus	sin offering (sacrifice)	Priest offers atonement for the sin on behalf of the person; they are forgiven (i.e. Lev. 4.26, 35; 5.10, 16, etc.)
John the Baptist	baptism of repentance	for forgiveness of sins

John's ritual is different from either Levitical law or a prophetic emphasis on mercy over sacrifice. John's rite could also be depicted as part of the movement from purity to impurity (to purity):

```
Holy (qadosh)
        Desecrate/Desanctify (hillel/hiqdish)
Holy (qadosh)                     Pure/Common (tahor/hol)
    Sanctify (qiddesh)                          Pollute (timme)
    (anointment, commandment)    Pure/Common (tahor/hol)              Impure (tame)
                                  Purify (tiher)
                                  (ablution, sacrifice)
                                  NEW RITUAL – βάπτισμα μετανοίας
```

Probably not enough is known about John to say whether his new rite qualifies (cf. 1QS iii.4-6 where purification may be restricted to those who follow the rule of the community[138]), adds to, or replaces the 'normal' means of purification.[139] Though Gruenwald has argued too strongly for replacement, he rightly points out that John's activity is a 'radical step in a different direction' from the 'normal' temple requirements.[140] John

---

1 Sam. 15.22; Prov. 15.8). However, what God prefers in these instances varies radically, from mercy and knowledge of God (Hosea) to a broken spirit and contrite heart (Psalms) to obedience to the Lord (Samuel) to prayer of the righteous (Proverbs; compared to sacrifice of the wicked). Are these *means* of atonement and remission of sin or a way of showing comparative importance?

138. Note also the connection (poetic, not halakhic) between sin and impurity at Qumran in Himmelfarb, 'Impurity and Sin', pp. 36–7.

139. Taylor takes the view that John considers the practice of immersion to be ineffective without righteousness (*John the Baptist*, p. 110). See also J. G. Dunn, 'Jesus and Purity: An Ongoing Debate', *NTS* 48 (2002), pp. 449–67. 'John's preaching gives no indication that a sacrifice or act of atonement was necessary' (p. 459).

140. Ithamar Gruenwald, 'From Priesthood to Messianism: The Anti-Priestly Polemic

3. *Embodied Sacred Space: Purity in the Land*

requires the performance of ritual (baptism) to go along with repentance, though without the priests as mediators.[141] Even though John does not mention the temple or sacrifice, it is a significant and provocative action to suggest a new ritual for forgiveness which does not involve temple or priests.[142] In the context of a social situation where immersion was an important part of Jewish identity and could be practiced throughout the land without the aid of a priest, John's choice of baptism seems somehow appropriate.[143] He does not choose a *miqveh*, but the Jordan. This element of the location of the baptism is also significant in understanding the meaning of the action with regard to land and sacred space.

In the foundational stories of the Hebrew Bible, Israel crossed two bodies of water on their way from Egypt to the promised land: one was the Red Sea, which they crossed to go into the wilderness under Moses' leadership (Exod. 14.1-31); the other was the Jordan river which they crossed to enter the land under Joshua's leadership (Josh. 3.1-17).[144] It is precisely the imagery of Israel under Moses and Joshua which is evoked by Josephus' sign-prophets (*Ant.* 18.85-7; 20.97-99, 167-72, 188; *War* 2.259; 6.285-86; Acts 21.38).[145] They take up the story of exodus and entry into the land, and enact their vision in the physical space they have made meaningful to their followers (until they are stopped or killed). Theudas in particular (*Ant.* 20.97-99) is valuable for comparison with

---

and the Messianic Factor', in I. Gruenwald (ed.), *Messiah and Christos: Studies in the Jewish Origins of Christianity, Presented to David Flusser on the Occasion of His 75th Birthday* (Tübingen: Mohr Siebeck, 1992), pp. 75–93. He believes that John 'replaces the altar with the Jordan River' (p. 90).

141. I. Gruenwald, 'From Priesthood', p. 90.

142. Compare Dunn, who hypothesizes that John may have played the role of priest in baptising. Dunn, 'Jesus and Purity', p. 459. It is interesting, however, that biblical law indicates self-immersion, whereas John is himself the subject of the verb βαπτίζω.

143. John's baptism is not associated with the purity of food, sexual conduct, leprosy, menstruation, etc. Though we may not know *all* the reasons for immersing in the first century, John's rite stands out as distinctive. Morna Hooker points out the connections between sin and uncleanness in the psalms and prophets, suggesting John's baptism as a moral cleansing. ' "Wash yourselves; make yourselves clean" thundered Isaiah, and his words were not simply a demand to his hearers to remove the blood that dripped from their hands' (M. Hooker, *The Signs of a Prophet: The Prophetic Actions of Jesus* [London: SCM Press, 1997], pp. 9–13 [12]).

144. Interestingly, in context of our discussion of John's *baptism*, the crossing of the sea under Moses is described in 1 Cor. 10.2 using the verb βαπτίζω: they are baptized 'in the cloud and in the sea'.

145. See the chart offered by Scot McKnight, 'Jesus and Prophetic Actions', *BBR* 10.2 (2000), pp. 197–232 (215–16).

John; he understands himself as a prophet, brings people to the Jordan and promises them that he will divide it and they will cross over. Fadus kills and captures them, beheading Theudas. The figures mentioned in *Ant.* 20.167-68 and 20.188 gather followers in the wilderness. In comparison, what can we make of John, gathering people in the wilderness and baptizing in the Jordan?

The Q saying about Abraham (Mt. 3.9//Lk. 3.8) indicates that kinship is undermined as a boundary marker within the message of John. However, the significance of this saying in the setting of the Jordan river has not been fully appreciated. In Luke's view, the axe is at the root of the trees and soldiers (i.e., Gentiles who have no relation to Abraham) may be accepted to receive baptism of repentance. Even the very phrase 'we have Abraham as our ancestor' (Mt. 3.9; Lk. 3.8) is reminiscent of the Abrahamic promise, 'to your descendants I will give this land' (Gen. 15.18). It is not unreasonable that 'we have Abraham as our ancestor' could indicate 'we are entitled to the promise of Abraham – the land'. Taylor points out the Elisha/Elijah imagery in this passage, comparable to 2 Kgs 2.6-15, where Elisha succeeds Elijah at the Jordan and both are able to part the Jordan.[146] In Ezekiel 36, a passage Raymond Brown considers a crucial eschatological text of the first century, the people are brought into the land in the great eschatological moment and they are sprinkled with 'clean water' (Ezek. 36.24-27).[147] The symbols are spatial. They suggest a new entry into the land. John's message is eschatological, pointing to the coming of the stronger one.[148] Like Jesus and the sign-prophets, John may be considered a kind of millenarian prophet. The image of John (and Jesus) going out to the wilderness and poised at the banks of the Jordan is evocative of Joshua as he leads the people into the promised land (Joshua 4) and gives a portrait of eschatological expectation against a very particular backdrop, strikingly not evoking the system of the temple (cf. *War* 6.285-86; *Ant.* 20.169-72), and drawing on the imagery of entry into the land.

In terms of social space, John should be considered to offer a new ritual – baptism of repentance – in a society where there was a wide concern with keeping purity within spatial boundaries for the sacred (i.e., temple, land). His action is provocative and threatening to those concerned with the interpretation and regulation of 'normal' purity requirements (i.e., Pharisees, Sadducees, cf. Mt. 3.7). In terms of sacred space, John offers

---

146. Taylor, *John the Baptist*, p. 281.
147. R. E. Brown, *The Death of the Messiah: From Gethsemane to the Grave* (2 vols.; London: Doubleday, 1994), vol. 2, p. 1140. See also Hooker, *Signs*, p. 12.
148. See Hooker, *Signs*, pp. 9–13.

a highly symbolic appropriation.[149] The mythic history taking place in the wilderness and leading to entry into the land are recalled in his eschatological call to repentance.

Rejection of Purity, Rejection of Land? Jesus and Ritual Purity

Having gathered considerable contemporary resources around the time of Jesus, these may be put to the test in comparison with the 'controversial' text of Mk 7.15. This is a text about the practice of non-priestly purity in everyday meals. The saying should not be dismissed as inauthentic without attempting to understand it within a comprehensive, plausible picture of Jesus.

Much of the discussion of Jesus and purity revolves around the saying in Mk 7.15.[150] The context of this saying is a debate between Jesus and the Pharisees over why the followers of Jesus do not wash their hands before eating. In v. 15, Jesus says, 'There is nothing outside a person which by going in can defile, but the things coming out from a person are what make them unclean'. In Matthew, we find, 'It is not what goes into the mouth that defiles, but what comes out of a mouth, this defiles a

---

149. Once again, Lefebvre tells us that representational spaces draw on symbols and myths of the past. They are 'alive' and 'speak' with passion and are not necessarily complimentary to the dominant appropriations of space in society. See Lefebvre, *Production*, pp. 42, 116–17.

150. See B. Chilton, 'A Generative Exegesis of Mark 7.1-23', in B. Chilton and C. Evans (eds), *Jesus in Context: Temple, Purity and Restoration* (Leiden: E. J. Brill, 1997), pp. 297–317; J. Riches, *Transformation*, pp. 112, 128–44. J. D. G. Dunn, *Jesus, Paul and the Law: Studies in Mark and Galatians* (London: SPCK, 1990), pp. 37–60; J. D. G. Dunn, 'Jesus and Ritual Purity: A Study of the Tradition History of Mark 7.15', in *À Cause de L'Évangile* (Paris: Éditions du Cerf, 1985), pp. 251–76. Dunn, 'Jesus and Purity'; Heikki Räisänen, 'Jesus and the Food Laws: Reflections on Mark 7.15', *JSNT* 16 (1982), pp. 79–100; S. Bryan, *Jesus and Israel's Traditions of Judgement and Restoration* (Cambridge: Cambridge University Press, 2002), pp. 164–8. S. McKnight, 'A Parting Within the Way: Jesus and James on Israel and Purity', in B. Chilton and C. A. Evans (eds), *James the Just and Christian Origins* (Leiden: E. J. Brill, 1999), pp. 83–129 (83–98); T. Kazen, *Jesus and Purity*, pp. 60–88. J. G. Crossley, *The Date of Mark's Gospel: Insight from the Law in Earliest Christianity* (London: T&T Clark, 2004), ch. 7; R. Booth, *Jesus and the Laws of Purity: Tradition History and Legal History in Mark 7* (Sheffield: JSOT Press, 1986), pp. 219–21; P. J. Tomson, 'Purity Laws as Viewed by the Church Fathers and by the Early Followers of Jesus', in M. J. H. M. Poorthuis and J. Schwartz (eds), *Purity and Holiness: The Heritage of Leviticus* (Leiden: E. J. Brill, 2000), pp. 85–6; E. Ottenheijm, 'Impurity Between Intention and Deed: Purity Disputes in First Century Judaism and in the New Testament', in M. J. H. M. Poorthuis and J. Schwartz (eds), *Purity and Holiness: The Heritage of Leviticus* (Leiden: E. J. Brill, 2000), pp. 129–48.

person' (15.11).[151] The saying is also preserved in the *Gospel of Thomas* (14). If authentic, this statement goes against Jewish dietary laws, both written and oral (rabbinic).[152] Whilst it is possible to make a distinction between a situation wherein food becomes defiled (e.g., eating ordinary food with unwashed hands) and eating unclean foods (e.g., pork),[153] this does not deny the force of the statement which indicates that nothing which is eaten can make the body impure.[154]

The issues of eating with Gentiles and whether or not to eat pork or meat sacrificed to idols were matters of concern for early Christians (e.g., Gal. 2.11-18; Acts 11.3; cf. Acts 10.14-15; Rom. 14.14). It may therefore seem strange that the saying in Mark and Matthew was not used to support an 'open' attitude towards food laws for purity. However, as Dunn notes, it is not the normal practice of Paul to cite the Jesus tradition to support an argument,[155] and it is by no means inconceivable to suppose that when Paul remarks on his conviction that in the Lord Jesus nothing is unclean (Rom. 14.14) and 'everything is clean' (Rom. 14.20) that he meant to evoke 'that whole train of thought which Jesus' words on purity had sparked off'.[156] In this sense, the saying fits with the second aspect of the plausibility criteria, namely that there is a continuing theological tradition or 'trend' which began with Jesus' attitude towards purity and continued in the early church.[157]

Taking a strikingly different stance, Bruce Chilton separates Mk 7.15 from its context and calls it 'an instrument to bridge diverse practices

---

151. Dunn, 'Jesus and Ritual Purity', p. 273. He believes that Matthew's version of the saying in 15.11 is the more authentic version of an early tradition going back to Jesus.

152. Riches, *Transformation*, pp. 136–7.

153. Kazen, *Jesus and Purity*, p. 61. Cf. Dunn, 'Jesus and Purity', p. 463.

154. Probably Jesus and his disciples were known for eating with unwashed hands, and not for eating unclean foods such as pork. We agree with Bryan (*Jesus and Israel's Traditions*, p. 165) that Jesus and the Pharisees were not debating whether it was allowed to eat pork, 'still less whether one's hands should be washed before doing so!' Still, the statement in Mk 7.15 and Mt. 15.11 must be reckoned with in the whole context of Jesus' attitude towards purity and not dismissed as 'only' referring to handwashing.

155. Dunn, 'Jesus and Ritual Purity', p. 272. As Dunn elsewhere notes, Peter's declaration that he has never eaten anything unclean is the most difficult to deal with ('Jesus and Purity', p. 463).

156. Dunn, 'Jesus and Ritual Purity', p. 273. See also Bryan, *Israel's Traditions*, p. 165.

157. G. Theissen and D. Winter, *The Quest for the Plausible Jesus: The Question of Criteria* (trans. M. E. Boring; Louisville, KY: Westminster/John Knox Press, 2002), p. 211.

3. Embodied Sacred Space: Purity in the Land 99

of purity'.[158] Jesus does not deny external purity; he only insists that purity begins from the inside and radiates out.[159] The account of the cleansing of a leper in which Jesus tells the man to show himself to the priest as commanded in the law (Mk 1.40-44; Mt. 8.2-4; Lk. 5.12-14) is especially important to Chilton. He believes it shows that Jesus makes judgements on matters of purity. This would make sense in the context of Leviticus, where in chs 13–14, the priest has a vital role in determining whether a leper may be declared clean. However, if Jesus takes the priest's role here, why is there a need for the priest to certify the man's newly cleansed status? Further, the confirmation of the cleansing is said to be a testimony to (or against – εἰς) the priests (1.44). This one piece of evidence concerning the leper is not enough to judge Jesus' attitude toward purity, as in fact Mk 7.15 on its own is insufficient.

Taking into account Theissen and Winter's plausibility criterion, the leper fits with the stronger of the categories because the account *resists* early Christian tendencies (i.e. the statements in Acts and Paul, though obviously there was controversy), rather than showing persistence of the idea, as in Mark 7.[160] What is needed, however, is not a decision about individual authenticity but an overall picture of Jesus which is able to make sense of his relationship to first-century purity. There are good reasons to doubt the picture suggested by Chilton:

> Jesus and his circle appear to have been keenly concerned with purity as such, in a manner similar to the Pharisees'; purity was generally a focus of discussion and controversy within early Judaism... the formal categorization of Jesus as a Pharisee is not unwarranted.[161]

In the Gospels, Jesus is depicted as healing the sick and exorcizing demons. Regarding healing, Jesus puts himself into contact with people who would normally (according to the law) be impure, and also transmit that impurity to others – lepers (Mk 1.40-45; 14.3; Mt. 11.5; 26.6; Lk. 7.11-19) and the woman with the flow of blood (Mk 5.25-34; Mt. 9.20-22; Lk. 8.43-48). Jesus also comes into contact with corpses (cf. Numbers 19), particularly in the story of Jairus' daughter in Mk 5.21-24 and 35–43. The girl is explicitly said to be dead (5.35) and the text is clear that Jesus touches her, taking her hand to heal her (5.41). Also, in Lk. 7.11-17, Jesus raises the son of a widow in

---

158. Chilton, 'A Generative Exegesis', p. 302.
159. Chilton, 'A Generative Exegesis', p. 303.
160. Theissen and Winter, *Plausible Jesus*, p. 211. Mark 7 and parallels must fit with the 'persistence' aspect, which Theissen and Winter consider to be the weaker of the two.
161. Chilton, 'A Generative Exegesis', p. 305.

Nain. The parable of the Good Samaritan is also noteworthy in that it contains a 'near' or 'seeming' corpse (Lk. 10.30-35).[162]

As noted by Bryan, the 'almost exclusive' use of purity language by Jesus is in designation of 'unclean' or 'evil spirits' (e.g. Mk 1.23-27; 5.1-34; Mt. 12.43-45; Lk. 11.24-26).[163] Purity (and impurity) language may certainly identify insiders and outsiders and establish boundaries between people and places. For Jesus, the language of impurity does not condemn individual humans but is associated with spirits. These spirits are embodied in various individuals, though they may be cast out through the power of God. Therefore, the embodied impurity of an unclean spirit is not a fixed state. Those who are cured may come back to be in their 'right mind' (e.g. Mk 5.15). In the Beelzebul controversy (Mk 3.23-26 and parallels), the antithesis to the Kingdom of God is the Kingdom of Satan.[164] Jesus, says Marcus, 'came to view himself as the effective opponent of Satan, the Stronger One whose exorcisms testified to his role as the spearhead of the inbreaking age of God's dominion' in the manner of a prophetic figure.[165] The battle over impurity is waged against Satanic forces.

What implication does this have for the land? It is interesting that in Mark, Jesus drives a 'legion' of demons from a man who lives among the tombs into a herd of pigs in the 'country of the Gadarenes' (Mk 5.1 – in the Decapolis, east of the Jordan[166]). Impurity abounds in this description. Joel Marcus notes the associations between unclean spirits and unclean space:

> Some of the story's elements, however, seem to reflect an origin in a chauvinistic Jewish environment; it implicitly links unclean spirits with what are for Jews unclean places (graveyards), unclean people (Gentiles) and unclean animals (pigs).[167]

---

162. For an extensive treatment of each of these issues for Jesus in relation to defilement through contact, see Kazen, *Jesus and Purity*, pp. 89–198. On Samaritan impurity, see Bryan, *Israel's Traditions*, pp. 172–88.

163. Bryan, *Israel's Traditions*, p. 160. See also McKnight, 'A Parting Within the Way', pp. 95–6. McKnight sees Jesus' exorcisms (and contact with the woman with the flow of blood – Mark 5.24-34) as 'purifications of unclean Israelites' (p. 96).

164. See Joel Marcus, 'The Beelzebul Controversy and the Eschatologies of Jesus', in B. Chilton and C. A. Evans (eds), *Authenticating the Activities of Jesus* (Leiden: E. J. Brill, 1999), pp. 247–77.

165. Marcus, 'Beelzebul Controversy', p. 266.

166. See Marcus, *Mark 1–8*, pp. 341–2.

167. Marcus, *Mark 1–8*, p. 347. Marcus notes that the story may not originate with Jesus: 'Mark himself is probably responsible for some of the loose ends in the present form of the tale, though most of it is pre-Markan' (p. 347).

3. Embodied Sacred Space: Purity in the Land

Even if this story is not entirely 'authentic', it shows the strong association of uncleanness with spirits. These unclean spirits, seemingly, could go wherever they will. If they are cast out, there was no guarantee that they will not return. Matthew 12.43-45 and Lk. 11.24-26 show an unusually striking and visual depiction of how an unclean spirit moves about:

> When the unclean spirit has gone out of a person, it wanders through waterless regions looking for a resting place, but it finds none. Then it says, 'I will return to my house from which I came'. When it comes, it finds it empty, swept, and put in order. Then it goes and brings along seven other spirits more evil than itself, and they enter and live there; and the last state of that person is worse than the first. So will it be also with this evil generation.

This could be compared to *Jubilees* and *1 Enoch* where the demonic spirits roam the earth (e.g., *1 En.* 16.1; *Jub.* 50.5[168]). If Jesus was intending to cast demons out of the land to purify it, they would be able to come back. Demons in this description have no respect for staying outside of boundaries. This may indeed have 'the effect of diminishing the significance of the land and its borders'.[169]

Jesus also practices table fellowship with 'sinners' in the Gospels. Unlike the Pharisees who were concerned with the practice of ritual purity in the land and placed themselves closest to the priests in relationship to the sacred, Jesus is consistently unconcerned with the purity of his companions at meals (e.g. Mk 2.15-16; Mt. 9.10; Lk. 5.30). At Qumran, participation in the sacred meal of associates was done with strict attention to purity. For Jesus, impurity is associated with the demonic realm and sinners are welcomed at table. Jesus does not engage in halakhic debate over the finer points of non-priestly purity like the Pharisees.[170] Rather, he emphasizes the importance of the love commandment over adherence to purity laws.[171] The principle of love of enemies (Mt. 5.44; Lk. 6.27) is crucial and is very different from Qumran, where Moses and the prophets' commands are interpreted as loving everything which one

---

168. *Jubilees* 50.5 says, 'jubilees will pass until Israel is purified from all the sin of fornication, and defilement, and uncleanness, and sin and error. And they will dwell in confidence in the land. And then it will not have any Satan or evil (one). And the land will be purified from that time and forever'.

169. J. K. Riches, *Conflicting Mythologies: Identity Formation in the Gospels of Mark and Matthew* (Edinburgh: T&T Clark, 2000), p. 59. Cf. Bryan, *Israel's Traditions*, pp. 185–8.

170. Tomson, 'Church Fathers', p. 86.

171. This is the (convincing) argument of Richard Bauckham in his article, 'The Scrupulous Priest and the Good Samaritan: Jesus' Parabolic Interpretation of the Law of Moses', *NTS* 44 (1998), pp. 475–89.

accepts and hating everything that one rejects, 'in order to keep oneself at a distance from all evil'. (1QS i.3-6). The command to love God, neighbour, and even enemies shows the distinctiveness of the teaching of Jesus.[172]

Jesus, unlike John, did not introduce a new ritual for purity and contact with the divine. Though he participates in John's baptism, he does not baptize others himself.[173] Jesus and his disciples are never depicted as immersing for ritual purity. This is, of course, an argument from silence and should not be given great importance. However, in *Papyrus Oxyrhynchyus* 840 Jesus and his disciples specifically do not perform the required immersions before entering the temple.[174] They walk into a pure place without performing the necessary ritual. This may give further support to the view that Jesus rejected the practice of ritual purity.

All this should be seen in light of the itinerant mission of Jesus. As we noted about purity in society, it was not portable (e.g., *miqvoat*), but located and related to a concern for the holiness of the land.[175] As Jesus and his disciples wander through grain fields on the Sabbath, they eat the heads of grain. The circumstances are compared to when David ate holy bread with his companions because they were hungry (Mk 2.23-27). This is not the purity of the Pharisees. It does not emphasize new halakhic interpretations, or attempt to define who is pure and who is less pure, or *where* is pure and where is less pure. It is not the purity of the Sadducees. There is no focus on the temple and its holiness. It is not the purity of Qumran. Enemies are not condemned as defiled, but included in the commandment to love. It is not even the purity of John. There is no emphasis on the ritual practice of sacred space. A compre-

---

172. And, as Schottroff has argued, loving enemies does not necessitate the denial that enemies do, in fact, exist and can be entirely hostile at that. See L. Schottroff, 'Non-Violence and the Love of One's Enemies', in L. Schottroff (ed.), *Essays on the Love Commandment* (trans. R. H. Fuller and I. Fuller; Philadelphia, PA: Fortress, 1978), pp. 9–39. Speaking of Mt. 5.44-45, she says: 'It does not encourage doubt about the hostility of the enemy of the unrighteousness of the unrighteous on whom God sends sun and rain. What the commandment requires is that we should love our enemies even though they truly are our enemies' (p. 24).

173. Cf. Taylor, *John the Baptist*, pp. 294–9. Marcus argues that Jesus gains a new understanding at his baptism: 'Jesus' conviction of eschatological advent and of his own unique role within that advent came to him at the time of his baptism by John, when he saw Satan thrown down from heaven (Lk. 10.18) and arrived at the conclusion that the dominion of the Devil was now being replaced by the dominion of God' ('Beelzebul Controversy', p. 267).

174. See the translation and discussion of the text in Kazen, *Jesus and Purity*, pp. 256–60.

175. See Borg, *Conflict, Holiness and Politics*, pp. 71–7.

3. Embodied Sacred Space: Purity in the Land

hensive picture of Jesus does indeed suggest that he may have actually rejected notions of purity. It is possible that the notion of purity, with its opposition between Israel and the nations was not useful to the sort of mission he embarked upon.[176] Purity distinguishes and separates. Jesus does not keep a small, spatially restricted pure community. He travels throughout the towns and villages of Galilee healing, exorcizing and welcoming 'sinners'.

As an itinerant preacher, it is worth asking whether the practice of purity was practically possible for Jesus and his group, being reliant on others for shelter and food. Not only are there statements such as Mk 7.15 and Jesus' lack of regard for contact contagion, but an emphasis on love of God, neighbour and enemy suggests that Jesus' attitude was distinctly different from those of other Jewish groups in society on matters of purity. Unlike the present order, the alternative ideal space of the 'kingdom' was not substantiated by the laws of purity; these rules did not define participation and identity.

To connect this chapter to the previous chapter, a rejection of purity as a boundary marker fits with Jesus' lack of focus on the temple in his mission. We do not have evidence that Jesus had worked out a detailed vision of the future including the temple; we are lacking evidence to suggest that Jesus believed that God's action in the future would be brought about through proper adherence to the rules of non-priestly purity. Purity structures such as *miqvaot* marked off the space of the land and enabled pure bodies to exist within Israel, yet they were fixed and relate to the largest spatial category for the sacred of all Israel. Jesus' group is itinerant and focused on a new definition of the kingdom as the household of God.[177] As with the temple, Jesus' attitude to purity practice is strikingly different from other Jewish groups, and his major association of impurity is with 'unclean spirits'. Jesus does not emphasize bodily purity, and this points to a different understanding of purity for Jesus, associated more directly with the impurity of spirits and less with the strict maintenance of group boundaries through ritual practices. But it does not necessarily follow that for the eschatological (millenarian) prophet, rejection of purity means rejection of the land. The subject for our next chapter – the Twelve – indicates a powerful, and spatial, symbol which must be considered if we want to sketch a comprehensive picture of Jesus in relationship to land.

---

176. Riches, *Transformation*, pp. 143–4.
177. Halvor Moxnes, *Putting Jesus in His Place: A Radical Vision of Household and Kingdom* (Louisville, KY: Westminster/John Knox Press, 2003).

Chapter 4

IMAGINED SPACE: JESUS' GROUP OF TWELVE

Only in lived experience is the religious meaning of sacred place realized. This is, I believe, as true for Jesus' notion of 'the kingdom' as it is for Mecca or Lourdes, or the Temple Mount in Jerusalem. Even though the great diversity of sacred spaces is recognized in scholarship, less attention is paid to the meaning of heaven or 'the kingdom' as sacred space. Douglas Davies comments,

> It is very easy to discuss sacred places that can be located on ancient or modern maps, but it is much more difficult to talk about those 'places' that are often described as though they exist in a physical way but which belong essentially to the world of faith and certainly cannot be visited today. The Garden of Eden and Heaven might be two obvious examples.[1]

Jesus' ideas about 'the kingdom' are not indicative of an arcadian myth of return to paradise and the Eden of the past.[2] Rather, they point forward, to a future in which God reigns supreme and the suffering of the present is removed, reversed to place the 'least of these' at the top of the pile. There is no sense of visiting this kingdom, but there is the sense that it will be the experienced reality of believers in the future. As emphasized at the beginning of this study, even an imagined place of the future is not reducible to mere symbolic, or religious, language, but also relates to social experience and is connected to practice.

In discussion of Jesus' group of twelve, we enter into the realm of imagined, or mythical, representational spaces. These types of spaces may overlay 'actual' social experience and offer an alternative vision of the world. The Twelve reveal not so much who may participate in the kingdom (else women would be excluded, which they clearly are not), as what the kingdom will look like. They recall the promises of the past

---

1. D. Davies, 'Christianity', in J. Holm (ed.), *Sacred Place* (London: Pinter, 1994), p. 33.
2. Richard Harris, *Paradise: A Cultural Guide* (Singapore: Times Academic Press, 1996), p. 33.

4. Imagined Space: Jesus' Group of Twelve

and evoke a twelve-tribe constitution of Israel. It is worth looking at how 'twelve' may function symbolically.

Twelve is a clearly a significant number in Jewish tradition.[3] In various texts we find twelve sons of Jacob (Gen. 35.22; 42.13, 32), twelve tribes of Israel (Gen. 49.28; Ezek. 47.13), twelve leaders of Israel (Gen. 17.20; 25.16 – twelve princes, sons of Ishmael; Num. 1.44; 34.18; Josh. 3.12; 4.4; 1 Kgs 4.7). There are various objects which are twelve in number such as twelve stones (Exod. 15.27; Josh. 4.3, 8, 20), twelve springs (Exod. 15.27; Num. 33.9), twelve loaves (Lev. 24.5), twelve staffs (Num. 17.2). There are offerings such as twelve oxen (Num. 7.3), twelve silver plates, twelve silver basins and twelve gold dishes (Num. 7.84), twelve bulls (Num. 7.87; 29.17; Ezra 8.35), twelve rams (Num. 7.87), twelve male lambs, twelve male goats (Num. 7.87; 1 Esd. 7.8; Ezra 6.17). Twice we find tearing into twelve pieces – once of the prophet Ahijah's new garment (1 Kgs 11.30) and another horrific example where a woman is cut into twelve pieces (Judg. 19.29). There is mention of twelve towns (Josh. 21.7), twelve lions (1 Kgs 10.20; 2 Chr. 9.19), twelve priests (Ezra 8.24) and twelve prophets (Sir. 49.10).

In Christian tradition, the number twelve (perhaps proportionately no less frequently) occurs as well. There we find twelve disciples (Mt. 10.1; [20.17]), twelve apostles (Mt. 10.2; Rev. 21.14), 'the Twelve' (Mk 3.16; 4.10; 9.35; 10.32; 11.11; 14.10, 20, 43; Mt. 26.14, 20; Lk. 8.1; 9.1; 18.31; 22.3, 47; Jn 6.67, 70, 71; Acts 6.2; 1 Cor. 15.5), twelve thrones (Mt. 19.28), twelve tribes (Mt. 19.28; Lk. 22.30; Jas. 1.1; Rev. 21.12), twelve baskets (Mk 6.43; Mt. 14.20; Lk. 9.17; Jn 6.13); twelve legions of angels (Mt. 26.53), twelve patriarchs (Acts 7.8), twelve thousand 'sealed servants of God' from each of the twelve tribes (Rev. 7.3-8), twelve stars (Rev. 12.1), twelve gates (Rev. 21.12, 21), twelve pearls (Rev. 21.12) and twelve kinds of fruit (Rev. 22.2).

The 'story of twelve' in Jewish tradition begins with the twelve sons of Jacob (Gen. 35.22; 42.13, 32) who 'are' the twelve tribes of Israel (Gen. 49.28). These twelve tribes, upon entering the land, each receive an inheritance in Israel (Josh. 13.7–19.48). As we can plainly observe from the above list, there are numerous instances where 'twelve' is used in other texts besides these 'foundational' ones. 'Twelve' becomes part of the terminology that might be used when speaking about Israel or some aspect of national life (e.g., leaders and their roles, offerings). It could potentially serve as quite a 'loaded' indicator, in that it could recall

---

3. Scot McKnight offers a similar listing of 'twelves' in the Hebrew Bible. S. McKnight, 'Jesus and the Twelve', *BBR* 11.2 (2001), pp. 203–31 (214–15).

the 'story of twelve' (or 'map of twelve') without actually relating it. Like the Table of Nations in Genesis, the division of land in Joshua among the twelve tribes is also a way to construct the world, to map a sacred geography showing all Israel in their proper place.[4] Speaking about twelve tribes evokes twelve territories, one for each tribe.

Even so (as with the land itself), we should be careful not to limit the spatial implications of twelve tribes/twelve territories to some particular physical location. When looking at biblical texts relating to the tribes, entering the discussion is not predicated by an ability to place locations on a map, or to identify a particular territory. Rather, symbolism and meaning may be found at different levels: historical, social and spatial.[5] In different social and historical circumstances, the twelve tribes/twelve territories in Judaism indicate a locative worldview. Upon initial observation, it seems that Jesus' use of 'twelve' *could have* locative implications. For this reason, the calling of twelve disciples by Jesus in the Gospels is of particular importance to our discussion of Jesus and land.

The action of calling twelve disciples evokes a new spatial vision which includes the land. And yet, we have not seen a particular focus on the boundaries of sacred space for Jesus, either through a positive interest in the temple, or by an emphasis on ritual purity. What is the significance of the Twelve for the theme of land? Prior to engaging with this question, the symbolic meaning of the Twelve must be examined. Firstly, the theme of twelve will be set within biblical tradition. This will be useful to answer the question: if the Twelve evoke a particular model, what is that model? Secondly, the theme must be set within the context of the first century in order to illuminate what Jesus' calling of twelve disciples amounts to as a symbolic action.

Twelve Tribes and the Land in Judaism

Our survey in the previous section, noted some of the 'twelves' found in Jewish tradition. The twelve sons of Jacob were a kind of 'point of origin' for further uses of the number twelve. The portrayal of the twelve tribes in the Hebrew Scriptures and beyond is of importance to

---

4. Besides the Joshua text (13.7–19.48) of the division of the land, see also Ezekiel 48.1-35 as well as Jonathan Z. Smith's comments on this as an exercise in social mapping J. Z. Smith, *To Take Place: Toward Theory in Ritual* (Chicago: University of Chicago Press, 1987).

5. See J. Flanagan, 'The Trialectics of Biblical Studies', online: http://www.cwru.edu/10296748/affil/GAIR/papers/2001 papers/flanagan1.html (accessed 6 November 2006). Flanagan argues for a theory of spatiality which incorporates historical, social and spatial aspects of human existence.

our study, and in this section we will be able to elaborate on the twelve tribes in various ways. Of particular interest will be the geographical associations between the twelve tribes and the land (of Israel). Once we have drawn out the implications here for the territorial dimension of the twelve tribes, we may look at some examples of uses of the number twelve where the eponymous ancestors are not listed, but relevance to the twelve tribes and the land still apply. A further area of investigation will then be to investigate the twelve representative leaders from the tribes (or phylarchs) under Moses. Specifically, we will focus on the role of these figures in governing and dividing the land. Finally, we will examine the twelve tribes in the context of Jewish eschatology, focusing in particular on the future vision of tribal distribution of Ezekiel 48. Throughout these subsections, we will keep in mind the question that Sanders wants to put forward in his discussion of the actions of Jesus: what is the range of meanings and do they converge?[6] Put another way, does the symbol of twelve consistently imply a connection to the land or is it possible to think of twelve tribes as detached from some notion of territory? If the range of meanings for twelve in these various aspects does converge towards a land-based understanding, then we must consider Jesus' calling of a group of twelve in light of that meaning.

Twelve Tribes and Land:
Keeping the Number of Territories Consistent

One of the ways we know of the twelve tribes is through maternal relationship: In the book of Genesis (29.32–30.24 and 35.17-18), Rachel, Leah, Bilhah and Zilpah variously give birth to twelve sons who are given appropriate names by Rachel and Leah (Rachel naming her own sons and her servant Bilhah's sons and Leah naming her own and Zilpah's). Descendants from these twelve men are said to constitute tribal associations. Thus, we know the twelve tribes by kinship. Another way the tribes are known is by their placement. Each tribe has a place in the land according to Joshua 13–19. Zecharia Kallai discusses aspects of what she calls 'The Twelve-Tribe Systems of Israel'.[7] Genealogy and geography are the two major lines along which descriptions of the twelve tribes 'work' in various texts where they are mentioned. A basic tribal framework is modified in various lists of the tribes.[8] Different descriptions may emphasize one aspect (genealogical or geographical), or the

---

6. Sanders, *Jesus and Judaism* (Philadelphia: Fortress Press, 1985), p. 9.
7. Z. Kallai, 'The Twelve-Tribe Systems of Israel', *VT* 47 (1997), pp. 53–90.
8. Kallai, 'Twelve-Tribe Systems', pp. 56–8.

other. Modifications are made with a particular interest in maintaining twelve units.

In Genesis 48, Joseph brings his two sons, Manasseh and Ephraim, to his father Isaac for blessing. After some disagreement between Isaac and Joseph over which hand should be on the head of which son (48.13-20), Isaac blesses them and says this to Joseph:

> I am about to die, but God will be with you and will bring you again into the land of your ancestors. I now give you one portion more than to your brothers. (48.21-22)

So, it is explained that Joseph will have two portions in the land, and those will be for his two sons who now have the same status as Israel's other sons:

> Therefore your two sons, who were born to you in the land of Egypt before I came to you in Egypt, are now mine; Ephraim and Manasseh will be mine, just as Reuben and Simeon are. (Gen. 48.5)

In the next chapter, Jacob blesses his sons, but Ephraim and Manasseh receive no mention. Kallai notes that they 'figure separately only in *lists of a geographical nature that refer to the settling of the land*'.[9] Among such lists (Gen. 46.8-25; Num. 1.5-16; 1.20-46; 2.3-32; 7.12-73; 10.14-28; 13.1-16; 26.3-55; 34.16-29; Deut. 33.4-29; Joshua 13–19; 21.4-40; Judg. 1.1-36; Ezek. 48.1-29; 1 Chron. 12.24-38; 27.16-22), most do not include Levi at all, or mention the Levites in order to state that they have a distinct place or function apart from the other tribes (Num. 1.5-16; 1.20-46; 2.3-32; 7.12-73; 10.14-28; 13.1-16; 26.3-55; 34.16-29; Joshua 13–19; 21.4-40; Judg. 1.1-35; Ezek. 48.1-29) The Levites are not to have any allotment or inheritance in Israel (e.g., Deut. 10.9; 18.1; 12.12). The Lord (Num. 18.20-21; Josh. 13.29; 18.7), tithes and offerings (Num. 18.23-24; Josh. 13.8), towns and the pasture lands of towns (Num. 35.2; Josh. 14.3-4; 1 Chron. 6.64), or cities/houses in cities (Num. 35.2-7, including 6 cities of refuge plus 42 other cities for a total of 48; Lev. 25.32-33; Josh. 21; Ezek. 45.5) are to be the inheritance of the Levites. They are not to have a territory as the other tribes. However, instead of having eleven territories with the Levites maintaining a special function and no territory, the narratives keep the number of territories at twelve, as with the inclusion of Ephraim and Manasseh.

Therefore, a principle that seems fixed in various descriptions is a concern to keep twelve as the necessary number of tribes – a whole

---

9. Kallai, 'Twelve-Tribe Systems', p. 62, emphasis added.

4. *Imagined Space: Jesus' Group of Twelve*

with twelve units. So, for instance in an example where Levi is included in the list of tribes, along with Joseph, Ephraim and Manasseh (Deut. 33.6-25), Simeon is omitted in order to keep to the framework of twelve. Again, in 1 Chron. 12.24-38, Levi, Ephraim and half-Manasseh all 'count' individually. To accommodate the number twelve, Reuben, Gad and (the other) half-Manasseh of the Transjordan are listed together as one group (1 Chron. 12.37).[10] In 1 Chron. 27.16-22, Gad and Asher are missing from the list of tribal leaders. The two halves of Manasseh each have their own representative and Levi and Aaron each have one as well (Zadok is the representative for Aaron). This makes for a total of thirteen leaders, but perhaps the joining of Aaron with Levi is intended to highlight Zadok, and so it may be that there is no break in the framework of twelve. The exclusion of Gad and Asher suggests that the number twelve could still be in mind here.[11]

The most important aspect of this brief examination is that both the number of territories and the number of tribes is symbolically fixed at twelve. There are twelve tribes because there are twelve original sons of Israel. The descendants of these twelve actually constitute the tribes in the way they are presented. It is never said that Levi ceases to be a tribe. In fact, quite arguably, Levi has the most important role as a tribe. The work of the Levites is the most crucial to the cult, their duties the most documented, their genealogy explicitly connected to their status. Levi remains a tribe throughout, but a tribe without a territory. Still, there are twelve territories.

When Joshua distributes the tribes in the land, nine and a half are placed on the west side of the Jordan river and two and a half have their inheritance on the east side. The Levites have cities, not territories, and it is Ephraim and Manasseh who maintain the number of territories at twelve. The sons of Joseph, they were raised to the same status of the brothers of Joseph by Jacob's blessing (Gen. 48.5). This status is for portions in the land (Gen. 48.21-22) and not for status in the group of twelve patriarchs, sons of Jacob (Genesis 49). Ephraim and Manasseh are considered to be tribes (of Joseph?), but they never take away the tribal status of Levi and

---

10. See Kallai, 'Twelve-Tribe Systems', p. 85.
11. According to Kallai, Gad and Asher are excluded so as 'not to breach the frame of twelve' ('Twelve-Tribe Systems', p. 86). She says, 'The only question is whether Levi and Aaron, or the half-tribes of Manasseh, are counted as one. Only with the exclusion of one of them is the total of twelve attainable' (p. 86). Perhaps neither can be joined. In the passage, thirteen chiefs are specifically listed. However, the lack of inclusion of Gad and Asher (and Joseph) does seem to suggest that somehow 'space' has been made in this list.

do not increase the number of tribes to thirteen. As a further illustration of the insistence on twelve as the number of territories, in the division of the land Manasseh is split into to two halves on either side of the Jordan. Manasseh is never considered to be two territories, but always one territory in two halves. Again, the number twelve is maintained. The named tribes and named territories coincide.[12] All twelve tribes are in the land. All the land is included in the promise to Abraham: 'to your offspring I will give this land' (Gen. 12.7).

Twelve Objects and Land: Unity and Disunity

An extremely difficult passage in Judges makes symbolic use of the twelve-tribe configuration of Israel. This 'text of terror' shows an unnamed concubine raped, tortured and then cut into twelve pieces by her master and sent 'throughout all the territory of Israel' (Judg. 19.29). Though an appalling depiction, it is apparently meant to show the terrible state of the tribes, reflecting 'a time when leaders were lacking, God seldom appeared, and chaos reigned among the Israelite tribes'.[13] The Levite who owned the woman says in explanation for his action, 'Then I took my concubine and cut her into pieces, and sent her throughout the whole extent of Israel's territory; for they have committed a vile outrage in Israel. So now, you Israelites, all of you, give your advice and counsel here' (Judg. 20.6-7). Clearly, this violent image is meant as a symbolic 'message' to all Israel, depicting tensions between tribes.[14] The crime against the woman is blamed on the tribe of Benjamin (without condemnation of the Levite's final act of mutilating the woman) and leads to division and a battle between Benjamin and the rest of the tribes (Judg. 20.1-48).

A text in 1 Kings shows Ahijah tearing his garment into twelve pieces (1 Kgs 11.30). Jeroboam is to take ten pieces, for, according to Ahijah, God has said, 'I am about to tear the kingdom from the hand of Solomon, and will give you ten tribes. One tribe will remain his, for the sake of my servant David and for the sake of Jerusalem, the city

12. See R. D. Nelson, *Joshua: A Commentary* (OTL; Louisville, KY: Westminster/ John Knox Press, 1997), p. 176.

13. P. Trible, *Texts of Terror: Literary-Feminist Readings of Biblical Narratives* (Philadelphia: Fortress Press, 1984), p. 65.

14. Cf. D. A. Knight, 'Joshua 22 and the Ideology of Space', in D. M. Gunn and P. M. McNutt (eds), *'Imagining' Biblical Worlds: Studies in Spatial, Social and Historical Constructs in Honor of James W. Flanagan* (London: Sheffield Academic Press, 2002), pp. 51–63. He shows the indications 'of suspicions or antipathy persisting between east and west [eastern and western tribes]' in Joshua 22 and Judg. 12.1-6 (p. 59).

that I have chosen out of all the tribes of Israel' (1 Kgs 11.31-32). An irrecoverable division between the tribes (the kingdoms of Israel and Judah) is symbolized by the tearing and distribution of a garment torn in twelve pieces. The symbolic import of the number twelve in relationship to the nation was so strong that it could be used quite graphically to show division and rupture from the ideal model of a unified Israel. We might also note more subtle tensions such as in the separation of two and a half tribes to exist on the eastern side of the Jordan as well as the notion of the ten lost tribes.

A *positive* symbolic action involving twelve representatives of the twelve tribes occurs in the beginning of Joshua. When Joshua and the Israelites cross over the Jordan and into the land, twelve leaders from the tribes place twelve stones in the middle of the river and then set them up at Gilgal (Joshua 4) as a memorial. In this liturgical set of events, the significance of the participation of the totality of the tribes as they enter the land is implicit throughout. The people are told by Joshua that when their children ask what the stones mean, they are to say, 'Israel crossed over the Jordan here on dry ground' (Josh. 4.22, cf. 4.7). The twelve representatives from the tribes who gather the twelve stones portray through ritual all Israel's crossing. 'Twelves' can hold a very strong place in liturgy such as that depicted at Gilgal and in the actions of the priests on behalf of the people. Even the use of twelve (i.e., twelve bulls, twelve loaves of bread) in sacrifices and offerings are a sign which depicts solidarity among Israelites and their obedience to God in the land, their participation in the covenant.[15] Twelve in such instances serves to show the people as a whole, although a whole in twelve parts. This contrasts dramatically with the horrific cutting of the woman and the tearing of Ahijah's cloth. Thus, 'twelve' can work symbolically in a positive or negative capacity. When used to depict unity for the people, it relates particularly to Israel located within the land, with the twelve tribes together. Boundaries (of the land, crossing the Jordan, etc.) are also important.

Twelve Leaders and Land: A Territorial Governing Role?

The first chapter of the book of Numbers describes in detail the first census of Israel and the institution of twelve leaders, one for each tribe. Moses is commanded to take the census of the whole congregation (Num. 1.2) along with 'a man from each tribe', the 'head of his ancestral

---

15. See for example Leviticus 18 and 24.5-9 where the twelve loaves of choice bread are set before the Lord in a holy place every sabbath day 'as a commitment of the people of Israel, as a covenant forever' (Lev. 24.8).

house'. (Num. 1.4). Moses and the twelve leaders function together for this activity. Each leader is named and listed according to their tribe. In the second chapter of Numbers, the leaders of the tribes are listed again in the order of placement of each of tribe in the camp. Three tribes are to camp in each cardinal direction around the centred Levites, who care for the tent of meeting (Num. 2.3-32 – Levites, 2.17). These twelve tribal leaders under Moses feature quite prominently in the book of Numbers. Besides their role in the census, they also participate in a ceremony after Moses sets up the tabernacle by presenting offerings (Num. 7.1-78). A second census takes place for the new generation of Israelites who are to enter the land (Num. 26.1-55). The leaders are not specifically mentioned in this text, but it recalls the first census and it is taken by Moses and Eleazer the priest (Num. 26.1-3) who are elsewhere mentioned along with the leaders (Num. 27.2; 31.13; cf. Josh. 14.1). The census, taken 'by the Jordan, opposite Jericho' (Num. 26.3), determines the size of the tribes and therefore the size of their inheritance in the land:

> The Lord spoke to Moses saying, 'To these the land shall be apportioned for inheritance according to the number of names. To a large tribe you shall give a large inheritance and to a small tribe you shall give a small inheritance; every tribe shall be given its inheritance according to its enrolment'. (Num. 26.52-54)

Also in conjunction with entering and apportioning the land, we find that the leaders of the twelve tribes are involved. They are sent to spy out the land:

> Send men to spy out the land of Canaan, which I am giving to the sons of Israel; from each of their ancestral tribes you shall send a man, every one a leader among them. (Num. 13.1)

They are assigned roles for the apportioning of inheritances:

> The Lord spoke to Moses, saying: These are the names of the men who shall apportion the land to you for inheritance: the priest Eleazar and Joshua son of Nun. You shall take one leader of every tribe to apportion the land for inheritance. (Num. 34.26)

In the book of Joshua as well, the tribal leaders figure alongside Joshua and Eleazer in the apportioning of the land (Joshua 13–19). Here, one tribal representative is to be taken from each tribe (Josh. 3.12). In Numbers and Joshua, the roles of the twelve tribal leaders are to do with the organization of the tribes in preparation for entering the land, as well as for entry into the land and distribution of the twelve territories once they enter it.

Like the symbolic representation of twelve objects, twelve leaders can also emphasize the notion of 'all Israel together'. In Exodus 24 (concerning the ceremony of the blood of the covenant) we see an almost indistinguishable line between the ceremonial participation of the twelve leaders and the whole people. Not unlike the Joshua story of crossing the Jordan, representative leaders from the people participate in the ceremonial events. Moses speaks to 'the people' and 'all the people answer him in one voice' through the twelve leaders. Moses builds an altar in the same passage and sets up 'twelve pillars, corresponding to the twelve tribes of Israel' (Exod. 24.4). Although elders, young men of the people, and the chief men of the people have particular roles, the distinction between them and 'all the people' is somewhat obscured. Similarly, participation in sacrifices and offerings is on behalf of the people. In the story of Moses' return from his meeting with YHWH in Exodus 34, the 'leaders of the congregation' as well as 'all the Israelites' are said to witness his shining countenance (vv. 30-32) once he has come down from Mount Sinai. What the leaders do and see is closely related to what the people do and see.

The key elements of the function of the tribal leaders in Numbers and Joshua are their association with Moses and Joshua and their governance of the tribes in preparation for entering the land and in distributing the land for the tribes. Exodus also has the tribal leaders functioning alongside Moses. The tribal leaders are notable for their roles of governance in relationship to the land in twelve tribes.

Twelve Tribes, Land and Eschatological Expectations

Outside of the Hexateuch, Ezekiel 45–48 shows a new allotment of the land of Israel. Here, twelve tribal leaders are also found:

> And my princes shall no longer oppress my people; but they shall let the house of Israel have the land according to their tribes. (Ezek. 45.8)

The entire section of Ezekiel 40–48 contains various 'maps' of ideal sacred space for Israel and the priests of the nation. Jonathan Smith makes the assertion that 'of all the texts preserved within the biblical canon, it is, perhaps, the most articulate in offering a coherent ideology of place: of temple and city, with focus on the temple'.[16] Indeed, there is a very clear emphasis on the holy city and the temple, but there is also the unambiguous notion that the fulfilment of the promise to Abraham is the inheritance of the twelve tribes in chs 47–48.[17] The land is given boundaries to the north, south, east and west (Ezek. 47.15-20) and it is

16. Smith, *To Take Place*, p. 48.
17. Smith, *To Take Place*, p. 66.

to be divided among the twelve tribes of Israel (Ezek. 47.13) according to the promise to Abraham: 'You shall divide [the land] equally. I swore to give it to your ancestors, and this land shall fall to you as your inheritance'. The return from exile is like a new exodus. So, Wilken:

> Everything that Ezekiel says about the temple and the city is inseparable from his final section on the 'allotment of the land'. Indeed he portrays the return and restoration as a new Exodus; just as the land was apportioned to the tribes when the land was first conquered, so in the return from exile there will be a new appropriation of the land patterned on the allotment of the land at the time of Joshua.[18]

It is striking that resident aliens are to be given an inheritance as well as the twelve tribes (Ezek. 47.22-23). Aliens were respected and given place according to the old pattern (Exod. 22.21; 23.9; Josh. 8.35 and in particular Josh. 20.9), though perhaps, as Brueggeman suggests, this indicates a new graciousness.[19] If so, the text might indicate a loosening of the largest boundary of the sacred. Kallai notes that the description is based on Num. 34.3-12 and states, 'Ezekiel's future land of Israel therefore fully conforms to the promised land, with no hold outside its borders and none missing within'.[20] This future dimension of the description is worthy of emphasis. Ezekiel's description takes the core element of twelve tribes and twelve territories and incorporates it into his vision of a future, ideal land for Israel, centred on the temple. He sees that future as entailing all Israel in the land, the fulfilment of the Abrahamic promise, and the restoration of twelve tribes.

In later Jewish works, the notion of Israel restored to twelve tribes at the end times may be found. The work referred to as the *Testaments of the Twelve Patriarchs* is significant to our understanding of the symbolic use of the twelve tribes, though the dating of this document is less than certain. Charlesworth's edition of the pseudpigrapha places the *Testaments* in the 2nd century BCE, but Robert Kugler's analysis of various scholars' positions on the dating leads him to the conviction (along with de Jonge) that it is actually a Christian text which may serve also to 'testify' to Jews.[21] Even if Kugler and others are right to say that there is no *recoverable* Jewish text within the *Testament of the Twelve*

---

18. R. L. Wilken, *The Land Called Holy: Palestine in Christian History and Thought* (New Haven: Yale University Press, 1992), p. 13.

19. Walter Brueggeman, *The Land; Place as Gift, Promise, and Challenge in Biblical Faith* (Philadelphia: Fortress Press, 1977), p. 143.

20. Kallai, 'Twelve-Tribe System', p. 79.

21. R. L. Kugler, *The Testaments of the Twelve Patriarchs* (Sheffield: Sheffield Acedemic Press, 2001), p. 38.

4. *Imagined Space: Jesus' Group of Twelve*

Patriarchs, it is still of interest to our discussion because of the themes it contains and the continued interest in these themes in Christian circles.

The *Testament* as a whole shows a twelve-tribe model, and the text is made up of the discourses of the sons of Jacob just prior to their deaths. There is a strong eschatological element to the work and the figures of Levi (priestly) and Judah (kingly) play prominent roles in the time of redemption for Israel (*T. Reu.* 6.8; *T. Sim.* 7.1; *T. Jos.* 9.11; *T. Jud.* 25.1 and various references in *T. Naph.* 5.1-5, 6.7, 8.2). In the *Testament of Asher*, there is a warning issued which is worth quoting at length:

> For I know that you will sin and be delivered into the hands of your enemies; your land shall be made desolate and your sanctuary wholly polluted. You will be scattered to the four corners of the earth; in the dispersion you shall be regarded as worthless, like useless water, until such time as the Most High visits the earth... He will save Israel and all the nations. Tell these things, my children, to your children, so that they will not disobey him. For I know that you will be thoroughly disobedient, that you will be thoroughly irreligious, heeding not God's law but human commandments, being corrupted by evil. For this reason, you will be scattered like Dan. and Gad, my brothers, you shall not know your own lands, tribe or language. But he will gather you in faith through his compassion and on account of Abraham, Isaac, and Jacob. (*T. Ash.* 7.2-7)

Within the entire work of the *Testaments of the Twelve Patriarchs*, we find various beliefs. As in this quotation, we see both the notion of dispersion as well as regathering *into the land*. In the *Testament of Benjamin*, at the conclusion of the book, we find the idea that when the Lord's salvation is revealed, the patriarchs will be raised, 'each of us over our tribe' (10.7). All Israel will be gathered (10.11) and the 'light of knowledge will mount up in Israel for her salvation, seizing them like a wolf among them, and gathering the gentiles'. (11.2). There is concern both with the land as a whole (*T. Benj.* 10.5-11) as well as with the temple (*T. Levi* 14.34; *T. Sim.* 7.2, *T. Jud.* 22.3; 25.5; *T. Benj.* 9.5). The vision of the dead being raised reminds us of Ezekiel's great eschatological vision in which the dead are raised and Israel is brought into her own land (Ezek. 37.12). Thus, the *Testaments of the Twelve Patriarchs* shows us some of the range of beliefs regarding the eschaton and the judgement and relates them specifically to a model of the twelve tribes and the patriarchs, though here the temple is also included.

In another example of the use of the model of the twelve tribes at the end times, there is reference to them in the *Testament of Abraham*. The 'Commander-in-Chief' Michael shows Abraham three judgements. The first is by Abel, who sits on a throne, judging the righteous and sinners of the 'entire creation' (*T. Ab.* 13.3). At the second judgement, every person is judged by the twelve tribes of Israel (*T. Ab.* 13.6). The final judgement is by 'the Master God of all' (*T. Ab.* 13.7) and completes the 'three tribunals' of judgement (*T. Ab.* 13.8). The universal nature of this judgement is striking: it is decidedly for the entire creation and not just Israel. As Collins notes, the theme of judgement is 'introduced already in the overview of the earth' in ch. 10.[22] There is no limitation made to Israel. Humanity is judged in terms of individual deeds. The notion that the twelve tribes have a role in judgement, even of the whole earth, alerts us to the imaginative connection in the future scenario made between the theme of judgement and the twelve tribes. Could the twelve tribes mentioned here indicate the twelve tribal leaders? Possibly. Does the notion that all people (not just Israelites) are judged by the twelve tribes nullify the connection between the twelve tribes and the land of Israel? Not by any necessity.

In this section, we have seen examples where thought about an ideal Israel could be conceived of in twelve tribes and including roles for the twelve leaders of the tribes as well. The gathering of the Gentiles is part of the beliefs found in the *Testaments of the Twelve Patriarchs*. The example of the *Testament of Abraham* shows the twelve tribes involved in future judgement. These 'future' ideas about the twelve tribes are not unrelated to other aspects of geography and tribal order. Core elements include: twelve tribes and twelve territories and twelve indicating the unity of Israel; the land-based functions of the tribal leaders are present in readings of the future for Israel. As we have seen, however, these core elements are connected to other ideas that are also reworked in various ways, and these could include a loosening of the boundary between Jews and Gentiles: the largest spatial category of sacred/profane between Israel and the nations.

The Authenticity of a Group of Twelve

The action of creating a group of twelve is not dissimilar to some of the land-centred themes of Josephus' sign-prophets (e.g., Theudas – *Ant.* 20.97-99; the Egyptian – *Ant.* 20.169-172, *War* 2.261, Acts 21.38). If Jesus institutes a group of twelve leaders intending that they should have some ruling role in God's kingdom (i.e. Mt. 19.28, Lk. 22.30), then this reinforces the suggestion that the symbolic use of twelve is also associated with a landed vision of the world. The similarity of the action of calling the Twelve with the actions of the sign-prophets brings

---

22. J. J. Collins, *The Apocalyptic Imagination: An Introduction to Jewish Apocalyptic Literature* (Grand Rapids, MI: Eerdmans, 2nd edn., 1998), p. 253.

to the fore questions as to what sort of eschatology 'the Twelve' might indicate.

This said, not all agree that the Twelve should be placed with Jesus. There have been various scholars who have argued that a group of twelve fits more readily with the early church and had its origin there.[23] This question, along with the question of whether or not the Twelve implies an imminent eschatology, are the two major points of debate with regard to the historicity and importance of the Twelve. Within these debates, I argue that there is a tendency to under-evaluate the group of the Twelve as a whole, especially with regard to Jewish hopes regarding land.[24]

The major extended passages that deal with the Twelve in the gospel traditions are those of the choosing of the Twelve (Mk 3.13-16; Mt. 10.1-4; Lk. 6.12-16; see also Acts 1.13) and the commissioning of the Twelve (Mk 6.6b-13; Lk. 9.1-6; cf. Mt. 10.5-23). Also of importance is a saying in Matthew and Luke about the Twelve sitting on thrones to rule the tribes (Mt. 19.28; Lk. 22.30). In the traditions about Judas, the designation that he is one of 'the Twelve' acts almost as an identity marker (to show shock or horror) in many places where he is mentioned (i.e. Mt. 26.14, 47; Mk 14.10, 20, 43; Lk. 22.3, 47; see also Jn 6.70, 71). These texts may be read in consideration of the historical, social *and* spatial importance of Jesus' group of twelve.

Before moving on to discuss the possible importance of a group of twelve for Jesus with regard to land, we must consider in more detail whether it is plausible that this group should be placed with Jesus.[25]

---

23. Among these are P. Vielhauer, 'Gottesreich und Menschensohn in der Verkündigung Jesu', in W. Schneemelcher (ed.), *Festschrift für Gunther Dehn, zum 75 Geburtstag am 18 April 1957* (Neukirchen: Verlag der Buchhandlung des Erziehungsvereins, 1957), pp. 51–79; and W. Schmithals, *Das Evangelium nach Markus* (2 vols.; Gütersloh: Gerd Mohn, 2nd edn, 1986), vol. 2. More recently, the argument against the historicity of the Twelve has been made by A. van Aarde, 'The Historicity of the Circle of the Twelve: All Roads Lead to Jerusalem', in *Hervormde Teologiese Studies* 55.4 (1999), pp. 795–826.

24. J. P. Meier, 'The Circle of the Twelve: Did it Exist During Jesus' Public Ministry?', *JBL* 116.4 (1997), pp. 635–72. E. P. Sanders holds that the twelve probably do go back to Jesus and not the early church (Sanders, *Jesus*, pp. 98–106). Also, J. P. Meier goes to great lengths to demonstrate that the Twelve did exist and are a firm part of the early tradition. However, though he raises the question of the significance of the Twelve for the eschatology of Jesus at the start of his investigation, he leaves the question un-addressed at the end for 'further work' (Meier, 'Circle of the Twelve', p. 672).

25. G. Theissen and D. Winter, *The Quest for the Plausible Jesus: The Question of Criteria* (trans. M. E. Boring; Louisville, KY: Westminster/John Knox Press, 2002), pp. 191–212.

There are those who regard the Twelve as one of the most solid and early aspects of the traditions about Jesus,[26] but even so, there are also those who would regard the Twelve as a firmly post-Easter group.[27] We will begin with those who question the authenticity of the Twelve and then outline the major reasons for accepting the Twelve as a group with a strong connection to Jesus.

Since the Gospels took their form in a time when early Christianity was emerging and distinguishing itself from Judaism, the question of whether new material could have been invented by the early church to suit some purpose or practice is a legitimate one. It is not outside of the realm of possibility that the early church invented a group of twelve apostles and placed them in the context of Jesus' ministry.[28] If this were so, what purpose would the group serve? John Dominic Crossan thinks that the Twelve were instituted after the death of Jesus in connection with Peter's mission to the Jews. Thus, in 1 Cor. 15.5-11 (a major and early text), we find:

> He appeared to Cephas, then to the twelve. Then he appeared to more than five hundred brothers and sisters at one time, most of whom are still alive, though some have died. Then he appeared to James, then to all the apostles. Last of all, as to one untimely born, he appeared also to me. For I am the least of the apostles, unfit to be called an apostle, because I persecuted the church of God. But by the grace of God I am what I am, and his grace toward me has not been in vain. On the contrary, I worked harder than any of them – though it was not I, but the grace of God that is with me. Whether then it was I or they, so we proclaim and so you have come to believe.

Here, Crossan sees a clear distinction between Peter (Cephas) and the Twelve and James and the apostles. Paul counts himself as one of the apostles, and therefore this group must be distinct from the twelve. First Corinthians, written prior to the Gospels, no doubt provides early evidence for a group known as the Twelve. However, questions arise when this is pushed further to say that the group was only in place after the death of Jesus. Crossan says that there are 'whole sections of early

---

26. Meier ('Circle of the Twelve', pp. 635–72) goes into more detail than most regarding the authenticity of the Twelve. In summary, he contends that the Twelve do go back to Jesus because of: (1) multiple attestation from different sources, i.e. from Mark, John, Paul (1 Cor. 15.3-5), Luke (Jude instead of Thaddeus in Lk. 6.16, Acts 1.13), and 'Q' (Mt. 19.28//Lk. 22.30); (2) embarrassment over Judas' membership in the Twelve when he hands Jesus over to the authorities; and (3) the lack of prominence of the Twelve in the early church.

27. See n. 23 above.

28. The question is – is it probable?

Christianity' that never heard of the institution of the Twelve.[29] However, 'different and independent early Christian traditions' knew about Judas. Based on these two premises, Crossan concludes that Judas is 'early' and a 'historical follower of Jesus who betrayed him', but the Twelve are a later institution of the early church, associated with Peter.[30]

In his argument, Crossan also states that the Twelve are new Christian patriarchs intended to replace the ancient Jewish patriarchs.[31] Van Aarde also makes a similar assertion:

> This group [the Jesus faction in Jerusalem, pre-70 CE] idealized their movement by thinking about it as the 'eschatological Israel' and referring to the 'first' disciples as 'the twelve'. This designation is *clearly analogous* to 'the twelve patriarchs' referred to in the Hebrew scriptures.[32]

At first glance, this suggestion is entirely relevant in light of the earlier discussion of the twelve rulers in biblical tradition. However, we encounter here the unfortunate frustration with both Crossan and van Aarde that neither has offered any specific support for (or against) this assertion. Why, we would have to ask according to the suggestion of analogy to the patriarchs, would the creation of twelve Christian patriarchs be particularly relevant and important in the early church? Crossan and van Aarde ultimately leave us with more questions than answers as to why the Twelve *must* belong to the time after the death of Jesus and not before. Though we can agree that 1 Cor. 15.5 is an important and early piece of evidence for the existence of the Twelve, we cannot accept that it establishes the Twelve as a group which came into existence after the death of Jesus.

In arguing for the authenticity of the group of the Twelve, E. P. Sanders views the 1 Corinthians text as a strong and early piece of evidence for the group's existence. The fact that some manuscripts have 'eleven' instead of 'twelve' indicates, for Sanders, that the Twelve were originally in mind, since scribes would not correct 'eleven' to make it 'twelve' if they knew about Judas. The correction is made with the death of Judas in mind.[33] The 'second bit of firm evidence' for Sanders

---

29. Crossan, *Who Killed Jesus?: Exposing the Roots of Anti-Semitism in the Gospel Story of the Death of Jesus* (San Francisco: HarperSanFrancisco, 1996), p. 75.
30. Crossan, *Who Killed Jesus?*, p. 75.
31. Crossan, *Who Killed Jesus?*, p. 75. See also van Aarde who says about the 'pillars' of Gal. 2.9 – 'This group idealized their movement by thinking about it as the 'eschatological Israel' and referring to the 'first' disciples as 'the Twelve'. This designation is clearly analogous to 'the twelve patriarchs' referred to in the Hebrew Scriptures' (van Aarde, 'Historicity of the Circle', p. 801).
32. Van Aarde, 'Historicity of the Circle', p. 801, emphasis added.
33. Sanders, *Jesus*, p. 98.

is Mt. 19.28. By a similar mode of reasoning, he says that Judas would not have been included in a group judging Israel (an elevated position of leadership) when his betrayal was known. For Sanders, the mention of the Twelve in 1 Corinthians, as well as Mt. 19.28 and the 'fact' of a disciple who betrayed, are solid and early tradition because they would not be invented after a tradition that Judas *as one of the Twelve* betrayed Jesus.[34] Meier also latches on to this detail, which fits a criterion of embarrassment over Judas as one of the Twelve. He finds 'no cogent reason why the early church should have gone out of its way to invent such a troubling tradition as Jesus' betrayal by Judas, one of his chosen Twelve'.[35] It would be illogical to invent such a tradition. Rather, the early church found themselves in a position of having to explain the fact of Judas by using Hebrew Scriptures to 'soften' the reality of Judas' betrayal as one of the Twelve. Meier is correct to point out that the invention of the Twelve would demand a very strange tradition history, for it would exalt their status, while Judas' membership in the group would appear to run counter to that purpose.[36] The different evangelists do seem to explain away the 'embarrassing' detail of Judas in different ways (e.g., the use of Zech. 11.12 in Mt. 26.15 and Psalm 41 in Mk 14). So, the idea that there were actually two difficult 'facts' facing the early church – the existence of the Twelve and betrayal by one of them – makes it less probable that one of them was invented (or both, as Vielhauer would have it).

It would seem that there was a strong tradition that Jesus chose twelve, as evidenced by the inclusion in each of the synoptic evangelists of lists giving the names of the individual members of that group of twelve. It is impossible to establish the accuracy of any particular list of twelve, and in fact the differences suggest that it is the number twelve which is important, rather than individual names.[37] Mark and Matthew included

---

34. This argument ends up being quite speculative in that Sanders has to accept one 'historical fact' (betrayal by one of Jesus' disciples) in order to argue for the authenticity of another 'fact' (the concept of the number twelve, going back to Jesus). Sanders admits that this is a 'problem', saying, 'The betrayal argues for the authenticity of the twelve unless the betrayal itself is inauthentic'. (Sanders, *Jesus*, p. 99). Though this rather speculative way of arguing the point (of authenticity) engages with those who think the Twelve is the invention of the early church, there are perhaps clearer and more persuasive way of asserting that the Twelve are part of the earliest traditions going back to Jesus than relying on a speculative chronology.

35. Meier, 'Circle of the Twelve', p. 665.

36. Meier, 'Circle of the Twelve', p. 667.

37. Meye's older study of the historicity of the Twelve emphasizes the fact that all three synoptic evangelists have given a list of the Twelve, even though the lists are

Thaddeus, and Luke includes Jude of James. The lists are preserved in a precise manner,[38] whether or not they show that there were actually twelve men around Jesus. It may be that the group was symbolic, though we refrain from saying that it is merely symbolic.

Apart from their importance during Jesus' ministry, the Twelve seem to have had a limited period of influence in the early church. Richard Bauckham identifies the Twelve as the leaders of the early church in Jerusalem. Until around 44 CE, they had leadership roles in the Jerusalem church, as in Acts where the Twelve are the 'only category of Christian leaders' in Acts before 11.30.[39] Peter is the major figure associated with the twelve (Acts 1.15, 5.1-11, 15, 29), and the Twelve come to be replaced in the Jerusalem church by James and the elders. If Luke's presentation of the leadership of the Twelve ending with persecution by Agrippa (Acts 12.1-17) is even approximately accurate, the group would have had to form very quickly and also lose its leadership role in a very short amount of time (not much more than ten years). The Twelve actually lose and do not gain significance in the early church after the death of Jesus. The notion that they were invented, as well as a tradition that one of them betrayed Jesus, is unlikely.

There is good textual evidence for Jesus' calling a group of twelve, including an early mention of the group in 1 Corinthians and an apparent conflict in the tradition where there is a need to explain both the existence of the Twelve and that Judas, as one of the Twelve, betrayed Jesus. Though Crossan and others think that these traditions were invented after the death of Jesus, this must remain only a possibility and not a probability. The weight of the evidence is with the argument that the Twelve as a group do in fact go back to Jesus.

The Twelve and Eschatology

Now that we have identified reasonable evidence in favour of placing the Twelve as a group going back to Jesus, what is the eschatological significance of the group? Bauckham certainly assigns the Twelve an eschatological role:

---

not uniform. Robert P. Meye, *Jesus and the Twelve: Discipleship and Revelation in Mark's Gospel* (Grand Rapids: Eerdmans, 1968), p. 201.

38. Meier, 'Circle of the Twelve', p. 648.

39. R. Bauckham, 'James and the Jerusalem Church', in R. Bauckham (ed.), *The Book of Acts in Its Palestinian Setting*, volume 4 of B. W. Winter (ed.), *The Book of Acts in Its First Century Setting* (Grand Rapids, MI: Eerdmans, 1995), pp. 415–80 (428).

> Though Luke does not give much impression of the (by this time, rather antiquated) eschatological ideas of the early community, we can take it as certain that the Twelve, the phylarchs of the eschatological Israel (Mt. 19.28; Lk. 22.29-30), would have taken up residence in Jerusalem precisely because of their and its eschatological roles.[40]

However, is the meaning of the Twelve necessarily connected to the temple? Do they merely 'indicate that Jesus saw his mission as having to do with "Israel"'?[41] Do they indicate the restoration of Israel and the gathering of the twelve tribes?[42] What is the meaning of this group within Jesus' message of the kingdom?

There are three main texts which have direct relevance to the Twelve and eschatology. The most important one is Mt. 19.28, which is also found with minor differences in Lk. 22.30, where Jesus says that the Twelve will sit on twelve thrones to judge the tribes. Also in connection with the eschatological scenario of Mt. 19.28//Lk. 22.30 is Mk 10.45 where the sons of Zebedee seek to sit at Jesus' right and left in the kingdom. Matthew 8.11-12//Luke 13.28-29 indicates a gathering from east and west in the kingdom. Examination of these texts will provide a better understanding of what sort of eschatological vision might fit with the notion of twelve disciples.

Twelve Thrones, Twelve Tribes: Matthew 19.28//Luke 22.30

Though the wording and context of the saying concerning the Twelve judging the twelve tribes of Israel is slightly different in Matthew and Luke, they both present a similar picture of the future role of the Twelve. The Matthean text reads:

> Jesus said to them, 'Truly I tell you, at the renewal of all things (ἐν τῇ παλιγγενεσίᾳ), when the son of man is seated on the throne of his glory, you who have followed me will also sit on twelve thrones (ἐπὶ δώδεκα θρόνους) judging (κρίνοντες) the twelve tribes of Israel (τὰς δώδεκα φυλὰς τοῦ Ἰσραήλ).

Luke does not have the term *palingenesia* and only speaks of twelve tribes but does not use the phrase 'twelve thrones', but only 'thrones':

> So that you may eat and drink at my table in my kingdom, and you will sit on thrones judging the twelve tribes of Israel (ἐπὶ θρόνων τὰς δώδεκα φυλὰς κρίνοντες τοῦ Ἰσραήλ).

40. Bauckham, 'James', p. 439.
41. Borg, *Jesus*, p. 76.
42. Sanders, *Jesus*, p. 104.

4. *Imagined Space: Jesus' Group of Twelve*

The content of these statements gives a primary role to the Twelve in the kingdom. Since they did not, in fact, constitute a prominent group in the early church, this lends support to the authenticity of this Q tradition. A further consideration is whether the differences in Matthew's and Luke's versions of the saying and contexts add anything to the discussion. Do we have any clues as to the locality of this scenario?

For Davies, the context in Luke (an argument among the disciples over who is the greatest) points to the fact that the kingdom is a 'new kind of kingdom – in another dimension of existence'.[43] It is true, as Davies says, that Lk. 22.24-30 places Jesus and his followers in opposition to the 'kings of the Gentiles' and the 'ones having authority over them' in v. 25. Jesus is among them as one who serves (22.27) and his followers are to be like servants as well (22.26) in contrast with the kings who lord their position over the Gentiles and the rulers who take the name of benefactors (22.25). However, even if this new kind of kingdom, which is compared with the rulers of the Gentiles, indicates another dimension, this need not diminish the significance of the image of the land in the text; 'another dimension of existence' could of course be modelled symbolically on the land. Whatever the location of the kingdom, it has a different set of leadership criteria, and is characterized by table fellowship. The fact that Luke does not speak of twelve thrones in particular (Lk. 22.30) does not establish that the saying is meant to be broad and symbolic *as opposed to* specific and literal (though indeed it is symbolic).[44] The element of twelve tribes is present and this is specific enough on its own to indicate that the thrones will be the same number as the disciples and the tribes. Further, 'twelve' may also be considered to apply to the thrones as well.

Davies regards the Matthean context differently. Here, he allows that the '*palingenesia*' (Mt. 19.28) may be a 'rebirth', that is, 'not a wholly new order, but a renewing of the existing order'.[45] In this order there could be a restored Israel with twelve tribes. For emphasis, we quote Davies:

> In this view, the clear distinction drawn by Luke between This Age and
> The Age to Come is blurred by Matthew: his *palingenesia* ushers in this

---

43. W. D. Davies, *The Gospel and the Land: Early Christianity and Jewish Territorial Doctrine* (Berkley: University of California Press, 1974; repr., Sheffield: JSOT Press, 1994), p. 363. While the context in Luke does speak of serving in contrast to the behaviour of Gentile authorities (22.25-6) as well as the conferral of a kingdom (22.29), to say that this indicates 'another dimension of existence' seems to push the text too far.
44. Cf. Davies, *Gospel and the Land*, p. 363.
45. Davies, *Gospel and the Land*, p. 363.

world in a renewed form, in which 'eternal life' is to be enjoyed. These verses, then, point to a perspective which looked forward to a *temporal* restoration.[46]

The inheritance of eternal life that Davies speaks about is mentioned in Mt. 19.29 and is part of the reward for the disciples who have left everything to follow Jesus. The itinerant followers of Jesus are contrasted with the rich young man who was not willing to leave behind his possessions for discipleship (Mt. 19.16-21). The man wanted to know what to do to receive eternal life (19.16). The disciples are to inherit eternal life (19.29). And, not only that, but they are to take the roles of rulers of the tribes (19.28) and receive houses, family and fields (19.29) according to their decision to leave everything.

For Matthew, then, the future roles of the disciples are part of their reward. For Luke, this is presumably the case as well, though the emphasis is not on discipleship as leaving everything but as taking on the characteristic of a servant. There are connections with the kingdom (Lk. 22.30), the son of man coming in his glory (Mt. 19.28), eternal life (Mt. 19.29) and the *palingenesia* (Mt. 19.28), but do these connections mean that the renewal takes place in 'another dimension of existence' which is somehow separate from the land? To begin to answer these questions, we turn to the meaning of 'in the *palingenesia*'.

In the Palingenesia

Though Davies accurately notes that Mt. 19.12 contains 'no specific reference to the land on which the restored Israel is to dwell',[47] there is an implicit reference to the land in the notion of the twelve and the twelve tribes. The phrase, ἐν τῇ παλιγγενεσίᾳ, is key to an analysis of the text. As Davies himself is aware, Josephus uses the term *palengenesia* on one occasion.[48] It reads as follows:

> When they heard it, they returned thanks to God for giving them back the land of their fathers, and gave themselves up to drinking and revelry, and spent seven days in feasting and celebrating the recovery and rebirth of their native land (τὴν ἀνάκτησιν καὶ παλιγγενεσίαν τῆς πατρίδος ἑορτάζοντες). (*Ant.* 11.66)

---

46. Davies, *Gospel and the Land*, p. 363, emphasis added. His example from the *Psalms of Solomon* is found at 17.28: 'And he shall gather together a holy people, whom he shall lead in righteousness, and he shall judge the tribes of the people that has been sanctified by the Lord his God'.

47. Davies, *Gospel and the Land*, p. 365.

48. In fact, this is Josephus' only use of the term, and Matthew's use in 19.28 is one of only two occurrences of the term in the New Testament (the other being Titus 3.5).

Here, Josephus is referring to the return of the Jewish exiles to Jerusalem. There is no doubt in this particular passage that the land referred to is the land of Israel. The term *palingenesia* in itself cannot be taken to indicate a particular type of renewal, but must be read in context to determine what kind of renewal is taking place. The term has a rich history in Hellenistic tradition and is used by Philo to indicate the soul's journey toward immortality.[49] It is certainly possible that it could say something about renewal in the context of return to the land of Israel.

In the context of Mt. 19.28 where this term is used, the 'renewal' takes place in the future (the Twelve are not now ruling over the tribes, but will take on that role), and the very association with the Twelve and a tribal organization of God's people is a strong indication that this renewal has something to do with the promise to Abraham of the land and the gathering of the tribes. However, the promises may have been modified and adapted so that we cannot exclude the possibility that beliefs regarding eternal life or immortality are in view here. Though we cannot pinpoint the exact nature of this renewal, it is part of the future which God's action will bring about.

The future setting of the renewal envisioned need not exclude the possibility that the setting is (or is modelled on) the land of Israel. There are other examples that we could give where an eschatological or future judgement takes place in the land of Israel. First, in Daniel 7, we find thrones being put in place and the Ancient One taking his throne (Dan. 7.9). One like the son of man comes, is presented to the Ancient One, and is given an everlasting kingdom (Dan. 7.9-14). In the interpretation of the dream, holy ones of the most high receive and possess the kingdom.

We might also compare the Dream Visions of *1 Enoch*. Towards the end of the final vision which describes a 'messianic kingdom', we see that 'a throne was erected in a pleasant land'. (*1 En.* 90.20). A few lines later, the Lord's judgement takes place (*1 En.* 90.24-25). Although Allison has emphasized that κρίνω should be taken in the sense of ruling rather than condemnation,[50] it may not be inappropriate in an eschatological context to think of ruling in the sense of judgement as well (cf. Mt. 25.31-46,

---

49. Fred W. Burnett, 'Philo on Immortality: A Thematic Study of Philo's Concept of παλιγγενεσία', *CBQ* 46 (1984): 447-70 (447).

50. D. C. Allison, *Jesus of Nazareth, Millenarian Prophet* (Minneapolis: Fortress Press, 1998), p. 142. He says that the sense is 'ruling' rather than 'condemning' and that the primary role is governance of Israel. See also W. D. Davies and D. C. Allison, *A Critical and Exegetical Commentary on the Gospel According to Saint Matthew* (3 vols.; Edinburgh: T&T Clark, 1988–1997), vol. 3, pp. 55-56.

where Matthew does not use κρίνω specifically, though the scene is one of judgement. Note also that this passage refers to the Son of Man and a throne in v. 31 as in Mt. 19.28.) The kingdoms of Daniel 7 are not described in any kind of geographical fashion and the 'pleasant land' of *1 Enoch* does not give any indication of the extent or location of said land. Still, it is likely that their referents are Israel and the land of Israel. Unlike the 'judgements' in Daniel and *1 Enoch*, the saying about the Twelve judging the twelve tribes from twelve thrones does seem to paint a similar, yet notably different picture. For, where the kingdom of the 'son of man' in Daniel 7 and the pleasant land in *1 Enoch* are probably more generally meant to refer to the land of Israel, the Twelve judging the twelve tribes indicates their restoration more specifically. In light of the similarities of these future visions of judgement, we are all the more drawn to undertake to flesh out what Jesus might have in mind with this particular model of restored Israel. The eschatological glimpse of the future role of the twelve connects them clearly with twelve tribes of a restored Israel.

Thus, though this is an eschatological portrait, we do not need to assume that it is a landless portrait. Even though the land is not specifically mentioned, we saw in Josephus that *palingenesia* can have geographical associations for the land and the mention of the twelve tribes also can recall twelve territories. The tribes, after all, each were to have their own *place* in the land (Josh. 13–19). Though Davies is not unjustified in pointing out the lack of an explicit reference to the land, there does seem to be a sense in Mt. 19.28 and Lk. 22.30 that the eschaton has a spatial aspect to it and that spatial conception seems to most naturally entail the envisioning of a restored Israel in twelve tribes in the land.

Before moving on, attention may be drawn to an interesting argument made by William Horbury who says 'there is a strong possibility that Mt. 19.28 arose during the ministry, yet is inauthentic'.[51] He accepts that the Twelve go back to Jesus and that Jesus specifically chose the model of the Twelve, yet, for the group themselves, Mt. 19.28//Lk. 22.30 may 'represent the messianic fervour of the disciples and their associates, fanned perhaps by the princely model and the circumstances of the Galilaean mission'.[52] Yet, even in this case, Jesus deliberately accepted and used an eschatologically charged model of the Twelve. And, the very model of the Twelve itself could imply the eschatological roles of the Twelve that they are to fulfil in Mt. 19.28//Lk. 22.30.

---

51. W. Horbury, 'The Twelve and the Phylarchs', *NTS* 32.4 (1986), pp. 503–27 (525).

52. Horbury, 'Phylarchs', p. 525.

4. *Imagined Space: Jesus' Group of Twelve*

Ultimately, W. D. Davies rejects the notion that Mt. 19.28 might indicate a temporal restoration in his discussion of 'Jesus and the Land', finding it 'unlikely, in view of Mk 10.35ff'.[53] In view of the fact that this position was later completely reversed in Davies and Allison's commentary on the gospel of Matthew,[54] we might reconsider the idea in *The Gospel and the Land* of a temporal restoration of Israel with twelve tribes and twelve thrones in light of Davies and Allison's altered position (where this logion is attributed to Jesus) and in light of Mk 10.35. We will begin by looking at the content of the Markan text:

> James and John, the sons of Zebedee, came forward to him and said to him, 'Teacher, we want you to do for us whatever we ask of you'. And he said to them, 'What is it you want me to do for you?' And they said to him, 'Grant us to sit, one at your right hand and one at your left, in your glory (ἐν τῇ δόξῃ σου)'. (Mk 10.35-37)

Jesus denies their request saying,

> To sit at my right hand or at my left is not mine to grant, but it is for those for whom it has been prepared'. When the ten heard this, they began to be angry with James and John. (Mk 10.40-41)

The reason for Davies' initial rejection of Mt. 19.28//Lk. 22.30 was that the content of that saying contradicted this Markan text where Jesus is unwilling or unable to give special places to the disciples. We accept the revised position of Davies and Allison that this text actually confirms the picture in Mt. 19.28 (par. Lk. 22.30) and note the particular points that they share in common: (a) It 'implies that Jesus has the authority to assign places in the eschatological kingdom' and (b) it also assumes 'that his followers will be next to him'.[55] James and John are not to be given the places of honour, but they and the ten (= twelve) are presumed to be part of the eschatological picture of this particular scene.

What is important about this text for our discussion is that the eschatological picture is very similar to the one we have just examined in Mt. 19.28 and Lk. 22.30.[56] As the disciples sat on thrones in Matthew and Luke, so in Mark, James and John request to sit at Jesus' right and left in his glory. Jesus is also the central figure in both texts. We could

---

53. Davies, *Gospel and the Land*, p. 365.
54. Davies and Allison, *Critical and Exegetical Commentary*, p. 58. Rather discreetly, the reversal is made saying, 'One of us has, on another occasion, found this last objection [that Mk 10.35-45 contradicts Mt. 19.28//Lk. 22.30] telling. On further reflection, however, it is problematic' (p. 58).
55. Davies and Allison, *Critical and Exegetical Commentary*, p. 58.
56. Davies and Allison, *Critical and Exegetical Commentary*, p. 58.

perhaps say that in Mark, the sons of Zebedee wish to draw the social hierarchy in the kingdom as follows:

Jesus – James and John – the Ten (v. 41)

Although Jesus allows that some may be great among them (vv. 43-44), it seems that though the unity of the Twelve is kept in this passage through the denial of the request.

Once again, there is nothing in this context which necessitates a landless scenario. Though the Twelve are not to model themselves on Gentile rulers (Mk 10.42), they are all apparently expecting future places of honour. As in the Lukan argument between the disciples over who is the greatest, the text in Mark does not give the impression that for Jesus and the Twelve, 'what is governed' is of a completely different nature from the domains of Gentile rulers, only that their behaviour is to be radically different from those leaders. The phrase, in your glory (ἐν τῇ δόξῃ σου) used in v. 37 reminds us that elsewhere in Mark glory is associated with the coming of the Son of Man (Mk 8.38, 13.26). Apparently, at least for Mark, the coming of Jesus in his glory is associated with roles for the Twelve and with God's action for the nation of Israel in Danielic fashion (compare Mk 8.38 and 13.26-27 with Dan. 7.13). We note once again that even though it is a description of the disciples' future roles and places in the kingdom, this does not mean that there is an otherworldly setting for the disciple's desired leadership roles. The similarities between Mt. 19.28, Lk. 22.30 and Mk 10.35-45 confirm the eschatological scenario we have described. It is one in which the disciples are to have particular roles and honour that they do not presently have, and one that fits with the descriptions of future judgement of Israel such as we find in Daniel and *1 Enoch*.

Matthew 8.11-12//Luke 13.28-29

In what we have seen so far, the Twelve are associated with the future judgement of the twelve tribes (Mt. 19.28//Lk. 22.30), and Mk 10.35-41 confirms this eschatological scenario as it assigns the Twelve along with Jesus to positions of authority. None of these texts excludes the possibility of the land as an eschatological spatial model. Rather, a renewal of Israel, in particular Israel in twelve tribes, seems to be indicated. Another text which relates to the discussion at hand is Mt. 8.11-12//Lk. 13.28-29. This text speaks of a gathering from east and west to dine with Abraham in the kingdom.

> I tell you, many will come from east and west and will eat with Abraham, Isaac and Jacob in the kingdom of heaven, while the sons (υἱοί) of the kingdom will be thrown out into the outer darkness where there will be weeping and gnashing of teeth. (Mt. 8.11-12)

> There will be weeping and gnashing of teeth when you see Abraham and Isaac and Jacob and all the prophets in the kingdom of God, and yourselves thrown out. Then they will come (ἥξουσιν) from east and west, from north and south, and will eat in the kingdom of God. (Lk. 13.28-29)

There are two aspects of this text which are of particular interest to our discussion: one is the identification of the 'many' who come from east and west (and north and south in Luke); and second, the identification of those who are thrown out of the kingdom. Scholarly discussions on this matter have to do with whether or not Gentiles are meant to be included in the kingdom according to the statement. Once again, comparative Jewish texts show diversity rather than one single view, and yet the gathering normally centres on the land. The directions 'from east and west' imply gathering into a specific place. Another question concerns what it might mean to eat with Abraham, Isaac and Jacob in the kingdom. The mention of Abraham, Isaac and Jacob in this passage is also associated with Jesus' practice of eating with 'sinners'.

Gathering

We have already noted that the twelve are part of the eschatological vision of Jesus, and indicate that he thought in terms of a restoration of the tribes.[57] Dale Allison emphasizes the point that gathering from the east and west meant *gathering to Palestine and Zion*.[58] The notion that Israel is the centre in these 'gathering' passages can be seen in several examples. *Baruch* 4.36-7 indicates that the gathering is to Jerusalem:

> Look to the east, O Jerusalem, and see the joy that is coming to you from God. Look, your children are coming, whom you sent away; they are coming, gathered from east and west, at the word of the Holy One, rejoicing in the glory of God.

Psalms of Solomon also has Jerusalem as the place where those gathered from east and west come together:

---

57. Allison, *Millenarian Prophet*, pp. 101–2. See also Bart Ehrman, *Jesus: Apocalyptic Prophet of the New Millennium* (Oxford: Oxford University Press, 1999), pp. 186–7.
58. Allsion, *Millenarian Prophet*, p. 144.

> Stand on a high place, Jerusalem, and look at your children brought together from the east and west by the Lord. From the north they come in the joy of their God; from distant islands God has brought them. (*Pss. Sol.* 11.2-3)

It is to Israel (Isa. 43.1) that the declaration of Isaiah 43 is addressed:

> Do not fear, for I am with you; I will bring your offspring from the east, and from the west I will gather you; I will say to the north, 'Give them up', and to the south, 'Do not withhold; bring my sons from far away and my daughters from the end of the earth'. (43.5-6)

These are some of the clearest examples where gathering from the east and west is specifically stated to be a gathering to Israel and Jerusalem.

The theme of gathering is a fairly common one and though the directions that the gathered come from are not always specifically mentioned, gathering is commonly associated with Israel and may also be associated with the tribes.[59] There are also texts in which the nations have some role in the gathering or assembly. Take the eighth chapter of Zechariah, for instance. In 8.7-8, we find the following:

> Thus says the Lord of hosts: I will save my people from the east country and from the west country; and I will bring them to live in Jerusalem. They will be my people and I will be their God.

Then, later in the chapter, in 8.22, the nations are drawn to Zion as well:

> Many peoples and mighty nations will come to seek the Lord of hosts in Jerusalem, and to entreat the favour of the Lord.

The people of Israel and the nations both come to Jerusalem. The people of Israel are restored from their dispersed locations to live in Jerusalem in the land (Zech. 8.8-13). The nations seek the favour of Israel's God (Zech 8.21-22) because they have heard that God is with the Jews (Zech 8.23).

There are other instances where the gathering of Israel is connected to the nations. In the Isaiah 43 passage quoted above (Isa. 43.5), the offspring of Israel were gathered from the east and west. In the same description, the nations are gathered as well, serving in some capacity as witnesses (Isa. 43.9). Elsewhere in Isaiah, we find a description of the gathering of a remnant by Yahweh:

> He will raise a sign for the nations, and will assemble the outcasts of Israel, and gather the dispersed of Judah from the four corners of the earth. (Isa. 11.12)

---

59. Micah 2.12 sees Jacob and 'the survivors of Israel gathered. The tribes of Jacob are gathered in Sir. 36.1. *Sibylline Oracles* describes 'the gathering together' and mentions ten tribes (*Sib. Or.* 2.165-173).

The nations are not part of the gathering in this instance, but witness the assembly of Israel. To give just one more example of the close associations between the gathering of Israel and the gathering of the nations, we turn to the book of Tobit. Chapter 13 includes this description:

> A bright light will shine to all the ends of the earth; many nations will come to you [Jerusalem – Tob. 13.9] from far away, the inhabitants of the remotest parts of the earth to your holy name, bearing gifts in their hands for the King of heaven. (Tob. 13.11)

The story of Tobit, told from the viewpoint of the Diaspora, is particularly concerned with the gathering of Israel into the land. Tobit commends the children of God to acknowledge God before the nations (Tob. 13.3). Then God will gather them out of the nations where they have been scattered (Tob. 13.5). They will return to the land: 'They will go to Jerusalem and live in safety forever in the land of Abraham, and it will be given over to them' (Tob. 14.7). The 'nations' come to Jerusalem bearing gifts (Tob. 13.11), but it is the children of Israel who go to Jerusalem and *live* in the land as inhabitants.

Another place where the nations are portrayed as giving gifts is mentioned in *Psalms of Solomon*. The author implores the raising of Israel's king, the son of David (*Pss. Sol.* 17.21) who is to accomplish Israel's redemption in this manner:

> He will bring together a holy people whom he will lead in righteousness. He will judge the tribes of the people that have been made holy by the Lord their God. (*Pss. Sol.* 17.23)

> He will distribute them in their tribes upon the land; the sojourner and the foreigner will no longer dwell beside them. He will judge peoples and nations in the wisdom of his righteousness. And he will have gentile nations serving him under his yoke and he will glorify the Lord in a place visible from the whole earth. And he will cleanse Jerusalem to reach a sanctification as she has from the beginning so that nations will come from the ends of the earth to see his glory, bringing as gifts her children who had become quite weak, and to see the glory of the Lord with which God has glorified her. (*Pss. Sol.* 17.28-31)

Here we see again that there is a role for the nations in the gathering scenario. This scene, however, has the particular feature that the gathering specifically involves the tribes having places in the land. There is also the important idea of the judgement of the tribes. We can compare also the Wisdom of Sirach where the tribes are gathered and have their inheritance 'as in the beginning' (Sir. 36.13, 16).

We see that gathering may be used to speak of the gathering of God's people to Israel and it may also be used to speak of the Gentiles who witness the gathering or even come themselves to Jerusalem as in Tob. 13.11 and Zech. 8.22. There are, however, distinctions between these two groups. The nations can be gathered, but the gathering which is from the cardinal directions seems to apply particularly to Israel.[60] This is not to say that there are two types of gathering, only that the particular language of east and west (and sometimes north and south) seems to be used exclusively for Israel, scattered abroad. The nations seem not to be at home in the land, but come as witnesses or gift-bearers, acknowledging what God does for Israel to restore her and to gather her in Jerusalem. Tobit can speak of the time when he was in his own country, referring to the land of Israel (Tob. 1.4), and this is the sense that we get from looking at the evidence: a time is anticipated when Israel will be gathered to her own country from the Diaspora and the Gentiles will be part of the recognition of their restoration to their land. The traditional associations with 'east and west' seem to be with the gathering of the Jewish Diaspora to Israel and Jerusalem.[61] A role for the nations seems to be part of the traditional associations with the gathering of the Jewish Diaspora. The gathering can also be thought of as a gathering of the tribes in the land (*Pss. Sol.* 17.23, 28; Sir. 36.13, 16).

While this is all of interest to our topic and important to establish, we need to ask if it helps us at all to better understand the Q logion where east and west language is used. Are the traditional associations the correct ones to apply when reading this passage? Joachim Jeremias and others since have seen this passage as reflecting Jesus' belief that the Gentiles would be part of the gathering in the eschaton, based largely on the context of the saying in Matthew of the healing of the centurion's servant.[62] We have already seen that it is primarily the gathering of the Diaspora and not the Gentiles which is traditionally associated with this particular language. However, we want to consider the possibility that it is precisely the traditional associations of the gathering that are being modified in a saying like this one.

In partial concurrence, but ultimately in contrast with Allison, N. T. Wright views the vision of those who come from east and west as related

---

60. As far as we have been able to investigate, we agree with Allison when he states, 'Although "east and west" is common in prophetic texts about the restoration of Jews to their land, my research has not turned up a single text in which the expression refers to an eschatological ingathering of Gentiles' (*Millenarian Prophet*, pp. 179–80).

61. Allison, *Millenarian Prophet*, p. 180.

62. J. Jeremias, *Jesus' Promise to the Nations* (trans. S. H. Hooke; London: SCM Press, 1967), pp. 55–63.

to the Twelve, but indicating something completely different – that Jesus saw the gathering as an expansion beyond traditional associations to include Gentiles. The Twelve indicate the eschatological reconstitution (restoration) of Israel since the actual tribes themselves had not been in existence for hundreds of years.[63] Yet, for Wright, the restoration was actually taking place presently in Jesus' call of the Twelve to be a 'restored, redefined family'.[64] This restored family was 'in principle open to all, beyond the borders of Israel. Land and family were simultaneously rethought in the promise that the eschatological blessing would reach beyond the traditional confines'.[65] He further states that the symbol of holy land is *subsumed* 'within a different fulfillment of the kingdom, which would embrace the whole creation'.[66] For Wright, what is ultimately important is the openness of the kingdom beyond the normal boundaries, and a belief that the kingdom entails the whole earth.

Where we agree with Wright is where he supposes that eschatological blessing could extend beyond traditional expectations. That is to say, that some of the traditional associations we have identified may not be intended in the calling of twelve disciples and use of 'east and west' language by Jesus. A redefined family is also part of the associations with the Twelve (e.g., Mk 3.31-35). Where we differ with Wright, however, is in saying that the 'borders' of the kingdom are extended to the whole creation. There does seem to be an element of the eschatological description – including the Twelve and 'east and west' language – which is actually quite particular and still evokes the symbolism of the land of Israel.

The matter of whether Gentiles are to be included in the gathering is, in the end, most difficult to decide. Gentile inclusion was certainly important in the context of early Christianity, and there are some indications that it could have been a consideration for Jesus as well (e.g. the story of the Canaanite/Syrophoenician woman). The setting in Matthew of the 'east and west' saying and a saying like Mt. 3.8-10//Lk. 3.8-9 about the children of Abraham could suggest that Jesus thought in terms of a role for Gentiles in the eschatological gathering that was more than that of witnesses or gift-bearers. What is essential in connection with our theme of land is that there is a core locative element in the symbolic use of twelve. Those who are brought in come *to* some place in particular

63. N. T. Wright, *Jesus and the Victory of God* (Minneapolis: Fortress Press, 1996), p. 300.
64. Wright, *Victory*, p. 431.
65. Wright, *Victory*, p. 431.
66. Wright, *Victory*, p. 446.

which is not the entire creation. The connections between the eschatological scenario of Mt. 8.11-12//Lk. 13.28-29, Mt. 19.28//Lk. 22.30 and Mk 10.35-45 indicate that it is a re-distribution among the tribes that is in mind at the gathering from east and west.

The element of Mt. 8.11-12 and Lk. 13.28-29 that is most naturally seen as indicative of change in traditional associations is that of eating with Abraham, Isaac and Jacob. In the saying, this is to be the activity of those who are gathered into the land. There are two connections we might see here. One is with table fellowship and the other is with the resurrection.

The vision of eating with Abraham, Isaac and Jacob can recall Jesus' practice of table fellowship.[67] In the book of *Jubilees*, we find an interesting example that relates to 'future eating' and is included in the blessing of Levi:

> You [Levi] will be joined to the Lord and be the companion of all the sons of Jacob. His table will belong to you, and you will eat (from) it, and in all generations your table will be full, and your food will not be lacking in any age. (*Jub.* 31.16-17)

Levi is also told by his father Isaac that his sons will become 'judges and rulers and leaders for all of the seed of the sons of Jacob' (*Jub.* 31.15). This is not the same as eating with Abraham, Isaac and Jacob, but there is a similar theme, describing the table of the Lord and the sons of Jacob in the future scenario.

At the very least, then, this shows us that it was possible to think of future blessings in terms of an abundant table of God. Jesus seems to have made eating with sinners a focus, and seems not to have been concerned with the practice of non-priestly purity. The mention of Abraham, Isaac and Jacob recalls an ideal time in Israel's history, the time of the patriarchs. Another text connects the patriarchs to the resurrection:

> And as for the dead being raised, have you not read in the book of Moses, in the story about the bush, how God said to him, 'I am the God of Abraham, the God of Isaac, and the God of Jacob'? He is not the God of the dead, but of the living. (Mk 12.26-27)

Abraham is associated with resurrection in another instance in Luke where Lazarus dies and is carried away by the angels to be with 'Father Abraham' (Lk. 16.22). To make even one further connection, in Mk 13.27, the Son of Man sends out angels to 'gather his elect from the four winds, from the ends of the earth to the ends of heaven'. It is

---

67. S. McKnight, *A New Vision for Israel: The Teachings of Jesus in National Context* (Grand Rapids, MI: Eerdmans, 1999), p. 151. See also pp. 47–9 and 150–53.

noteworthy that the eschatological gathering of Israel into the land (in twelve tribes) has been connected for Jesus with a belief in resurrection and the idea of a great future 'eating at table' with God. Such visions need not be defined in detail.

Comparative Aside: Twelve Leaders at Qumran

Another group of twelve may be found among the Dead Sea Scrolls. In the *Rule of the Community*, there is a council made up of twelve men and three priests 'perfect in everything that has been revealed about all the law' (1QS viii.1). The council is further described in these terms:

> When these things exist in Israel the Community council shall be founded on truth, [blank] like an everlasting plantation, a holy house for Israel and the foundation of the holy of holies for Aaron, true witnesses for the judgment and chosen by the will (of God) to atone for the earth and to render the wicked their retribution. (viii.4b-7a)

This text could be compared with the pesher on Psalm 37, which identifies the community with the meek who will receive the inheritance of the land. The twelve that are part of the Qumran community council are designated for atonement and judgement and thus have very distinctive governing roles (compare Mt. 19.28, Lk. 22.30;[68] see also 1QS viii.10). More importantly, however, they are associated with the temple at least through terminology, as the holy of holies is mentioned. Perhaps the council can be understood as a foundation for the holy of holies in a similar way to the community's view of themselves as the temple. Here again, in comparison with Jesus, who did not take the temple as his model, and did not reinforce the boundaries of the sacred with the practice of ritual purity, the council of twelve at Qumran is very different to the twelve disciples. Both may evoke a sense of all Israel in the land, but the content of that vision is quite different.

Jesus' Group of Twelve

The Jewish myth of land is connected to the twelve tribes which make up Israel in such a way that it would be strange to think of 'twelve' used symbolically, apart from a locative vision of the world. In the Gospels, the Twelve are not seen as a governmental ruling body like the Sanhedrin, nor are they assigned a pedigree of tribal descent that makes them

---

68. Note Dale Allison's point that in Mt. 19.28//Lk. 22.30, the verb judging (κρίνω) implies ruling rather than judging in the sense of condemning (*Millenarian Prophet*, p. 142).

suitable for the roles of leaders. They are not given a role in relationship to Jerusalem or the temple cult in the eschatological scenario, and they do not become new or better priests in the coming age. Jesus' group of twelve, rather, evokes a tribal model, and does so in anticipation of God's action on behalf of his people to bring the kingdom. They are not merely the disciples 'par excellence' among a 'small group of devotees, simple Galilean folk'.[69] They are the unlikely rulers of a new age.

Bringing into focus the discussion of the symbol of the Twelve in relationship to the land, we note B. F. Meyer's description of the Twelve as 'a startling sign made up of radically disparate elements' (i.e., Galilean and Judean, Johannite and Zealot, etc.), showing that 'the restoration itself would have a startling character'.[70] Meyer thereby leads us to consider the significance of Jesus' own re-appropriation of the Jewish theme of land in relationship to the calling of the Twelve. Twelve may indicate 'all Israel' and also a 'restoration eschatology' for Jesus with elements of nationalism, but it remains that Jesus seems to give meaning to the symbol of the Twelve within quite a unique and indeed startling network of associations.

We have seen in our discussion of the Twelve that such a model has implications for Jesus' eschatological ideas about the future, and for the spatial content of such beliefs. As symbolic and representational space, the kingdom does not need to conform to the space experienced by Jesus and his followers in Galilean society. We accept that the group of twelve disciples most probably goes back to the time of Jesus and that it tells us something about Jesus' message of the kingdom, by including the Twelve judging the twelve tribes of Israel (Mt. 19.28//Lk. 22.30, see also on Mk 10.35-45). The vision that emerges is one that points to the gathering of Israel into the land (Mt. 8.11-12//Lk. 13.28-29).

The model of the Twelve, so closely associated with a time in Israel's history of unity and 'wholeness' for the nation, could imply a deep sense of attachment to land for Jesus. As John the Baptist in a very dramatic way brought to life the declaration of the way of the Lord in the wilderness, so Jesus has given meaning to the symbol of the Twelve and dramatically depicted the twelve tribes restored to their land in twelve

---

69. G. Vermes, *Jesus the Jew: A Historian's Reading of the Gospels* (Philadelphia: Fortress Press, 1981), p. 30, also pp. 41, 49.

70. B. F. Meyer, *The Aims of Jesus* (London: SCM Press, 1979), p. 154. We are also reminded of Gerd Theissen's description of the followers of Jesus as 'wandering radicals' and 'itinerants' who leave home and family and possessions (G. Theissen, *Social Reality and the Early Christians: Theology, Ethics, and the World of the New Testament* [trans. M. Kohl; Edinburgh: T&T Clark, 1993], pp. 35–55).

followers of no particular pedigree. This defines a new type of restoration, which allows that some 'outside' may dine with the patriarchs, and which is connected to other beliefs such as resurrection.

Apocalyptic understandings of the world are shaped by imaginative perception,[71] and in particular imaginative spatial perception, laying a foundation for action, which may have a very definite effect on the social situation of individuals and groups. Space and time are reconfigured through 'otherworldly' or heavenly descriptions, and 'shift the attention of the reader to the heavenly world, either to seek an explanation of what is happening on earth or to take refuge in an alternative reality freed from worldly problems'.[72] Jesus' announcement of the kingdom presented a new orientation, and this would be no less formative for followers than a 'concrete' place such as the temple. Perhaps we would be wise not to underestimate the importance of (particularly Matthew's) heavenly language in relationship to the kingdom.[73] The group of twelve is a symbolic group, showing something of Jesus' understanding of order and governance in the 'kingdom', yet we need not expect this alternative world to be worked out in detail. The point is that there is a break with the present world of experience. There are close associations between the number twelve and tribal organization of the land, and Jesus' group has implications for the spatial organization of the future kingdom. The future role of the Twelve provides spatial grounding for Jesus' expectations about the future in terms of a new, imagined space, namely God's kingdom. The group of twelve relates to the story of exodus and entry into the promised land and shares most in common with the so-called sign-prophets mentioned by Josephus. It is suggestive of a new gathering into the land. This vision is both subversive and indicative of a new understanding of sacred space which is characterized by itinerancy in the present, yet looks toward the coming of a 'future sacred space' under God's control and with social recourse for those who struggle for livelihood in the present.

We can see that there are places for the Twelve in the kingdom and also for 'those outside' as well as Abraham, Isaac and Jacob. The image is of table fellowship, a celebratory banquet, pointing to the social

---

71. Collins, *Apocalyptic Imagination*, p. 42.
72. J. J. Collins, *Apocalypticism in the Dead Sea Scrolls* (London: Routledge, 1997), p. 130.
73. R. Foster, 'Why on Earth Use "Kingdom of Heaven"? Matthew's Terminology Revisited', *NTS* 48.4 (2002), pp. 487–99. Perhaps in equating 'kingdom', 'kingdom of God' and 'kingdom of heaven', scholars have underestimated the importance of Matthew's heavenly language. Does he mean specifically to ground his audience's identity in the heavenly rather than the earthly realm?

practices of Jesus in his ministry. The sense of 'ruling' for the Twelve again indicates power in a particular realm – one that is not presently within their power to rule. Again, we could compare the sign-prophets, who were powerless groups in the face of Roman power, yet envisioned God's action on their behalf. The tribal imagery points to a 'landed' space, and it might help us to remember again here that, in the second century CE, Justin Martyr and Irenaeus both understood that the future kingdom would be an earthly entity. Though there were other strands of thought, it is helpful to remember that there were important early traditions which thought very much in terms of a firmly 'earthed' kingdom.

Chapter 5

JESUS AND LAND: MILLENARIAN DREAMS OF SPACE

At the end of our study, we may conclude with a positive evaluation of Jesus in relationship to the land. Jesus did recall the land promise and tapped into hopes that God would soon fulfil his promises to the nation. Yet he did this in a very different way from other contemporary groups: the Sadducees, Pharisees, or even the Qumran covenanters. He did so as a prophetic figure, offering a symbolic alternative to the present structures of his society. His vision was not centred on the temple, nor reinforced by the ritual maintenance of the boundaries of purity within the land. It recalled a new tribal arrangement which was open at its borders and promised places for those outside, and for those without status or position. It tapped into deeply held hopes for a new and better world, a new spatial arrangement with God as king. Jesus' message established a new sacred space, and a new relationship between God, people and kingdom. It is not necessary to decide whether the mathematical statement 'kingdom equals land' is true or false; but it is important establish that the message of the kingdom evokes the promises to Abraham and defines a new sacred space with its own symbolic associations and practical implications.

How, we might ask, can Jesus' proclamation of the kingdom be understood as part of a larger process of change to established beliefs? The suggestion that Jesus' message or that of other Second Temple prophetic movements could be compared with millenarian movements or cargo cults is not new.[1] Questions may be raised as to the extent millenarian movements would arise at all without the influence of Christianity. Nevertheless (though perhaps because of this), comparisons can be made which highlight the changes to beliefs brought about through millenarian

---

1. See J. D. Crossan, *The Historical Jesus: The Life of a Mediterranean Jewish Peasant* (San Francisco: HarperSanFrancisco, 1991), pp. 158–67; R. A. Horsley, '"Like One of the Prophets of Old": Two Types of Popular Prophets at the Time of Jesus', *CBQ* 47 (1985), pp. 435–63; D. C. Allison, *Jesus of Nazareth: Millenarian Prophet* (Minneapolis: Fortress Press, 1998), pp. 78–94 (172–216); J. G. Gager, *Kingdom and Community: The Social World of Early Christianity* (Englewood Cliffs, NJ: Prentice-Hall, 1975).

figures. Such changes must also be understood spatially, as 'the' meaning of particular sacred spaces is not static but changes over time and with reinterpretation.² Places are highly significant to symbolic and social change in society,³ and therefore a millenarian figure might be particularly influential in reworking meanings of space in society.⁴ At certain times, more radical changes might be made in symbolic understanding. In relationship to circumstances which are experienced as difficult or oppressive, individuals or groups may begin to question established beliefs and look for solutions to the perceived situation of anomie.

Though there may be many types of responses, one way of resolving such a dilemma is through millenarian dreams. Kenelm Burridge begins his study of millenarian activity with a description of changes to the 'rules' of religion. These, he says, are 'grounded in the interplay between experience, working assumptions, and those more rooted assumptions we call faith'.⁵ We could represent the process he describes in this way:

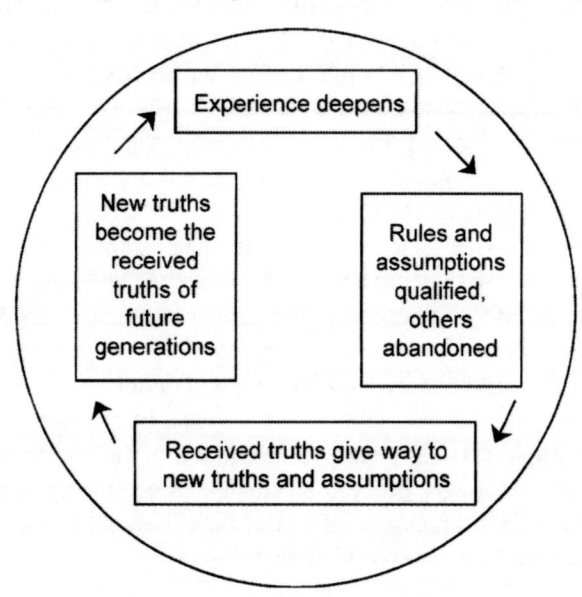

```
        Experience deepens
       ↗                  ↘
New truths              Rules and
become the              assumptions
received                qualified,
truths of               others
future                  abandoned
generations
       ↖                  ↙
        Received truths give way to
        new truths and assumptions
```

2. J. Z. Smith, *Map is Not Territory: Studies in the History of Religions* (Leiden: E. J. Brill, 1978), pp. 138–44.
3. Smith, *Map is Not Territory*, p. 143.
4. See my fuller argument, comparing Jesus and Maori millenarian beliefs. K. Wenell, 'Land as Sacred and Social Space: Some Reflections on the Early Jesus Movement and the *Hauhau* Religion', in L. Lawrence and M. Aguilar (eds), *Anthropology and Biblical Studies: Avenues of Approach* (Leiden: Deo Publishing, 2004), pp. 208–26.
5. K. Burridge, *New Heaven New Earth: A Study of Millenarian Activities* (Oxford: Blackwell, 1980), pp. 6–7.

5. *Jesus and Land: Millenarian Dreams of Space*

A millenarian movement might arise out of difficult circumstances when a charismatic leader finds a receptive audience for the articulation of a new message. Such a process may prove useful in the interpretation of Jesus' beliefs and hopes regarding sacred space, and in particular land.

Richard Harris, in his book *Paradise: A Cultural Guide*, outlines six different categories of paradise, among them the arcadian, the utopian and the millenarian. Of the millenarian 'type', he says:

> Millenarian paradises resemble Utopias in their temporal aspect; that is, they are set in the future as opposed to an Arcadian past. The distinction between the two is in the part played by humans in bringing about their emergence; Utopians strive to construct a better society on earth, while Millenarians more or less confidently and passively – in some cases smugly – await its preordained arrival as part of an inexorable divine plan.[6]

Though it is true that a millenarian attitude places the burden of action on God and is oriented to the future, this does not mean that participants in the meantime will be passive. However, it may mean that their actions do not 'logically' lead toward a conclusion, such as might be found in a utopian vision of a future society brought about through human effort. In fact, it may be that the goal of the millennium is vague and ill-defined. Kenelm Burridge describes a millenarian ideology he observed in Manam Island in 1952. They had a belief in an 'unknownland' located somewhere in the west (no one knew exactly where it was or had been to the location) which entailed 'a state of plenty, a condition of being in which everything would be wholly understood, in which everything would be available to all'.[7] This example reinforces the notion that spaces whose primary location is within the realm of beliefs (mythical places) need not be defined in detail in order to be powerful in their own right. Consideration of rather more vague hopes for the future recalls some of J. J. Collins' views of apocalyptic beliefs, namely that 'their concern does not find its primary expression in the construction of a new world order', yet there is a disjunction between present experience and the future ideal world.[8] An alternative to the present reality is imagined, but it is brought about through divine intervention. However we choose to label Jesus' vision of the kingdom, it fits with this *type* of view of the future.

---

6. R. Harris, *Paradise: A Cultural Guide* (Singapore: Times Academic Press, 1996), p. 33.
7. Burridge, *New Heaven, New Earth*, p. 58.
8. J. J. Collins, 'Temporality and Politics in Jewish Apocalyptic Literature', in C. Rowland and J. Barton (eds), *Apocalyptic in History and Tradition* (London: Sheffield Academic Press, 2002), pp. 26–43 (40).

The kingdom is a sacred space built out of sayings and beliefs. We are not able to develop the picture in focused detail. We can, however, see the importance of social and sacred aspects of space in defining the concept of the kingdom. Perhaps the power of these future hopes was actually stronger because it was not worked out in detail, and urgency fuelled the millenarian movement. Although Jesus puts ideas about sacred space together in new and different ways, the kingdom is not 'merely' symbolic; it shapes social actions, such as how to behave towards one's neighbour or enemy. Jesus articulates something about the kingdom of God (a concept already known to Judaism at the time) which had not previously been articulated. Followers found resonance with this new concept, so much so that they were willing to restructure their social lives in light of new beliefs about God and his power in the world. Jesus' beliefs about land are located within a millenarian vision of the kingdom, and that vision may be set within the context of first-century Jewish society in the land.

Experiences of Land, Beliefs about Land

For Jews living in the land at this time (ca. 63 BCE to 70 CE), their experience was quite different from the experience of Jews living in the Diaspora. Communities of Jews in the Diaspora would have been minority communities, yet their numbers in total were greater than the number of Jews living within the land at this time. Rome established administrative provinces in the land, with the province of Judea including the central holy place of both land and Diaspora for Judaism – the Jerusalem temple. Prior to the first and second Jewish wars, there was some at least nominal political power retained in Jewish hands by the Herodian rulers (though they owed their power to Rome) and there was also a role for the high priest (though again this would have been limited in certain respects, as in the example where the high priests robes were retained). Memories of Maccabean victories and expansion to what may be called biblical proportions were not so far distant.

For Palestine, as was true for the Roman Empire generally, land and the ability to control land were the primary means of wealth.[9] There were a small number of wealthy landowners, normally residing in cities, and these would exercise control over the surrounding countryside through the employment of workers such as tenant farmers and day labourers. The numerous and grand building projects of the Herodians also brought

---

9. J. Pastor, *Land and Economy in Ancient Palestine* (London: Routledge, 1997), pp. 160–69.

changes to the land as workers were employed and people were relocated. In one particular example in Galilee, Josephus relates the changes brought to Tiberias whereby inhabitants, a 'Galilean rabble' were forcibly drafted from the surrounding territory to resettle in the city (*Ant.* 18.37). Clearly, if we look at the social situation for many of the Jewish inhabitants of the land at this time, there were serious difficulties to be faced. Survival would have been a real challenge and retention of territorial land was by no means a given.[10]

There was a close connection between the land and the Jerusalem temple in Jewish notions of sacred space. However, Jesus' attitude (as indeed any other individual or group's attitude) toward the temple should not be read as equal to his attitude toward the land. The temple itself was a contested space in Second Temple Judaism, and different models, especially relating to the tabernacle and first temple, were taken up and sometimes offered positive alternatives to the present temple. The values of different groups may be drawn out in their relationship to the central temple.

Because of the biblical connection between purity and the land, purity practices within Palestine are one of the major areas where we might find examples of ritual relating to the maintenance of land as sacred place. Leviticus says:

> You shall keep all my ordinances, and observe them, so that the land to which I bring you to settle may not vomit you out. You shall not follow the practices of the nations that I am driving out before you... You shall be holy to me; for I the Lord am holy, and I have separated you from the peoples to be mine. (Lev. 20.22-26)

Thus, the conventional associations between purity and land also relate to beliefs about separation from the nations and the holiness of God. Beginning in the Hasmonean period, 'custom-built' structures were developed which allowed for the practice of purity laws relating to bathing (even though the texts themselves do not require a built structure). The number of *miqvaot* in the land by the turn of the era is itself evidence of a heightened interest in purity at this time. The presence of *miqvaot* in towns and villages, in Galilee as well as Judea (and even Samaria), on a Hasmonean farm and the houses of the upper city of Jerusalem suggests that this was more than just the practice of the elite. This practice must relate to more than the temple system. It must also have related to beliefs about keeping the land pure and obeying the law for the sake of the relationship between God, people and land.

---

10. See J. Meggitt, *Paul, Poverty and Survival* (Edinburgh: T&T Clark, 1998).

Jesus' millenarian message must be set within this particular context. His action of calling twelve disciples is most similar to the prophetic figures mentioned by Josephus.[11] Though we do not know a great deal about these figures and Josephus treats them as troublemakers, there are common symbolic features in their actions: they recall various themes of exodus and entry into the land; and their main belief is that God will act to deliver them. The special interest of these figures in the biblical stories of exodus and entry into the land strongly suggests that such themes would have had resonance at a popular level. The eschatological focus of such groups looks for God's immediate action to fulfil his ancient promises. In the Gospels, John's baptism in the Jordan and Jesus' calling of twelve disciples are each symbolic actions of the same kind as Josephus' sign-prophets.

Though our texts do not provide us with 'Jesus' view on land', if the Twelve were truly to rule the twelve tribes, this evokes the fulfilment of the promise to Abraham in terms of land. Again, this may have had particular appeal in light of the social situation in Galilee, where (as described above) land redistribution and tenancy were important issues. We may also relate this to other beliefs such as the love of both neighbour and enemy (this is not the exclusive boundary drawing of Qumran, nor the military fervour of the Zealots), and indeed to the announcement of a kingdom, which Moxnes describes as an 'imagined place' with surprising associations, particularly with house and household. Thereby, 'the overturning of conventions made the kingdom into something that followers of Jesus in a liminal position could identify with'.[12] The homeless followers of Jesus find a home in the expectation of the imagined kingdom as household.[13]

We have seen a great diversity of beliefs, as well as related practices and actions, all of which may be said to be part of defining land as sacred space in the Judaism of the early Roman period. This broad range leads us in quite an opposite direction from Bruce Malina's evaluation of 'the social scientific category of territoriality'. He says:

> A territory is always the outcome of the social interpretation of space. In this sense it is a social construction. It exists essentially in the repertory of symbols that constitutes the collective mind of a given social group.[14]

---

11. See Rebecca Gray's treatment of the sign-prophets in R. Gray, *Prophetic Figures in Late Second Temple Jewish Palestine: The Evidence from Josephus* (Oxford: Oxford University Press, 1993).

12. H. Moxnes, *Putting Jesus in His Place: A Radical Vision of Household and Kingdom* (Louisville, KY: Westminster/John Knox Press, 2003), p. 113.

13. Moxnes, *Putting Jesus in His Place*, p. 124.

14. B. J. Malina, ' "Apocalyptic" and Territoriality', in F. Manns and E. Alliata

5. *Jesus and Land: Millenarian Dreams of Space*

Whilst it is important to emphasize the social aspect of spatiality, there is no 'collective mind' with regard to understanding of space. Rather, 'the same set of cultural symbols may be read to produce interestingly different cosmologies and types of ethos'.[15] The diversity of spatial understandings in our study highlights the role of individuals in shaping the symbolic associations of sacred space. The symbols are changeable and manoeuvrable, and should not be seen as fixed.[16] The capacity for new and different interpretations is vast and our comparative investigation of land in Second Temple Judaism sends a strong warning against taking a single meaning for land for a group (however defined) of a particular historical period. This diversity is characteristic of the time and reminds us of that there is no 'collective mind' when it comes to the interpretation of sacred space. Though land may be a troublesome symbol at times, its strong position in foundational biblical texts means that it is not easily ignored, even though, as Halpern-Amaru points out, it may be dangerous for someone in Josephus' position to allude to the land 'as a vibrant mother country in some future time'.[17] Land, as part of a biblically based understanding of sacred space, was very much alive in Judaism at the time of Jesus. Changes were taking place and would continue to do so. Early Christian chiliastic beliefs looked forward to the restoration of land and temple in the end times, though clearly other strands of Christianity, such as that which John's Gospel (e.g. Jn 4.1-42) may represent, had quite different interpretations of these themes.

The social experience of sacred space was considerably varied for Pharisees, Sadducees, members of the Qumran community or the sign-prophets in the period prior to 70 CE. Each group gives consideration to beliefs about land which are based on the interpretation of biblical texts. These beliefs would have been formative for religious worldview and would have motivated particular actions – whether developing ways of keeping purity laws, establishing boundaries for a community or calling

(eds), *Early Christianity in Context: Monuments and Documents* (Jerusalem: Franciscan Printing Press, 1993), pp. 369–80 (369).

15. J. K. Riches, *Conflicting Mythologies: Identity Formation in the Gospels of Mark and Matthew* (Edinburgh: T&T Clark, 2000), p. 11.

16. The vehicles of interpretation are symbols, which are by their very nature malleable, manoeuvrable, manipulable by those who use them. It is this character of symbols which permits them to be shaped by those who use them. A. P. Cohen, *Self Consciousness: An Alternative Anthropology of Identity* (London: Routledge, 1994), p. 17.

17. B. Halpern-Amaru, *Rewriting the Bible: Land and Covenant in Post-Biblical Literature* (Valley Forge, PA: Trinity Press, 1994), p. 127.

followers to participate in symbolic actions evoking the early history of the nation. Such appropriations of space, and accompanying actions, have meanings which relate to the embodied space of ritual purity, to the contested space of the temple and to understandings of land. They suggest comparisons for understanding the imagined space of the kingdom ruled by the Twelve.

Land, like other manifestations of sacred space, must therefore be treated as both sacred and social. Beliefs are essential to its definition, as are the social aspects without which the space would not continue to 'live' in daily experience. Through actions, these beliefs are grounded in social life. To focus only on *beliefs* about space ignores the sense that sacred space is maintained by humans in social environments. To focus only on the *social* aspects is to overlook the role of sacred space within a wider religious worldview.

Biblical Land and Beyond

As we have seen in our study, apart from their own 'original' contexts, biblical texts have taken on meaning for individuals and groups in context of their own situations and in light of their own experiences. When dealing with texts that have been influential in thinking about sacred space, there are certain dangers involved, and these are in no small part related to the interpretations which have come before us and to our own social situations. A final note to end our study considers the ongoing uses of biblical conceptions of sacred space. Two texts in particular may serve to illustrate some of the difficulties involved with undertaking an investigation of biblical space:

> On that day the Lord made a covenant with Abram saying, 'To your descendants I will give this land from the river of Egypt to the great river, the river Euphrates, the land of the Kenites, the Kenizzites, the Kadmonites, the Hittites, the Perizites, the Rephaim, the Amorites, the Canaanites, the Girgashites, and the Jebusites'. (Gen. 15.18-21)

> Jesus came to them and said, 'All authority in heaven and on earth has been given to me. Go therefore and make disciples of all nations, baptising them in the name of the Father, the Son and the Holy Spirit, and teaching them to obey everything that I have commanded you. And remember, I am with you always, to the end of the age'. (Mt. 28.18-20)

In terms of kinship, the land of others is divinely given to Abraham's descendants in Genesis. By commission, the nations become disciples (subjects?) in Matthew. The first text brings an awareness of the present-day difficulties in Palestine and Israel and role of biblical land claims by some in that context. The second text reminds us that the Bible has been

5. Jesus and Land: Millenarian Dreams of Space 147

influential in shaping Western colonial ideologies, allowing for the subjugation of 'other' peoples in 'other' places.[18]

Because of the ongoing significance of biblical texts in relationship to the land of Israel today, scholarly studies may be intended to support, or even be inspired by, particular political positions and theologies regarding present-day situations.[19] Michael Prior passionately called for moral responsibility among biblical scholars in dealing with texts of conquest in the Bible.[20] Moreover, biblical texts have also served as support for colonial endeavours of many varieties in many places throughout the world. Christian conceptions of space have played a significant role in shaping ideologies which have allowed for the subjugation of other peoples to the superiority of Western might.[21]

Just as colonial and also liberating (post-colonial) appropriations of texts come out of particular social settings, so do the biblical texts themselves. Whether or not it is possible to ever reach an exact description of that social context, it is still worth investigating and comparing roughly contemporary texts. Looking at the above texts from Genesis and Matthew, we can note that these are the 'sort of texts' that attitudes towards space within religious worldviews are made of. Clearly, care and sensitivity are needed in the interpretation of biblical models. As an apocalyptic prophet, Jesus was able to define ideal space in new terms, to set out a picture – a map – of the future. There are important theological, ethical, economic and social issues involved with such an endeavour, and this should be recognized in both ancient and modern contexts for the interpretation of sacred space.

18. See J. L. Berquist, 'Critical Spatiality and the Construction of the Ancient World', in D. M. Gunn and P. M. McNutt (eds), *'Imagining' Biblical Worlds: Studies in Spatial, Social and Historical Constructs in Honor of James W. Flanagan* (London: Sheffield Academic Press, 2002), pp. 14–29.

19. See, for instance, Keith Whitelam on the creation and perpetuation of the notion of 'ancient Israel' by scholarship: K. Whitelam, *The Invention of Ancient Israel: The Silencing of Palestinian History* (London: Routledge, 1996). As an example of the prompting of world events in the investigation of 'land' texts, see the 1991 preface to W. D. Davies, *The Territorial Dimension of Judaism* (Minneapolis; Fortress Press, 1991) wherein he identifies the impact of the Six Day War and the Gulf War on his desire to investigate the theme of land.

20. M. Prior, *The Bible and Colonialism: A Moral Critique* (Sheffield: Sheffield Academic Press, 1997). He is particularly critical of W. D. Davies for not drawing attention to the negative effects of biblical land themes.

21. R. S. Sugirtharajah (ed.), *The Postcolonial Bible* (Sheffield: Sheffield Academic Press, 1998); M. Dube, 'Savior of the World But Not of This World', in R. S. Sugirtharajah (ed.), *The Postcolonial Bible* (Sheffield: Sheffield Academic Press, 1998), pp. 118–35; T. Swanson, 'To Prepare a Place: Johannine Christianity and the Collapse of Ethnic Territory', *JAAR* 62:2 (1994), pp. 241–63.

BIBLIOGRAPHY

Adan-Bayewitz, D., *Common Pottery in Roman Galilee: A Study of Local Trade* (Ramat-Gan, Israel: Bar-Ilan University Press, 1993).

Adan-Bayewitz, D. and I. Perlman, 'The Local Trade of Sepphoris in the Roman Period', *Israel Exploration Journal* 40.2-3 (1990), pp. 153–72.

Alexander, P. S., 'Notes on the "Imago Mundi" of the Book of Jubilees', *Journal of Jewish Studies* 33 (1982), pp. 197–213.

—'Geography and the Bible (Early Jewish)', in D. N. Freedman (ed.), *Anchor Bible Dictionary* (6 vols.; New York: Doubleday, 1992), vol. 2, pp. 977–88.

Alexander, T. D. and S. Gathercole (eds), *Heaven on Earth: The Temple in Biblical Theology* (Carlisle: Paternoster, 2004).

Allison, D. C., *Jesus of Nazareth: Millenarian Prophet* (Minneapolis: Fortress Press, 1998).

Barclay, J. M. G., *Jews in the Mediterranean Diaspora: From Alexander to Trajan (323 BCE–117 CE)* (Berkeley: University of California Press, 1996).

Bauckham, R., 'Jesus' Demonstration in the Temple', in B. Lindars (ed.), *Law and Religion: Essays on the Place of the Law in Israel and Early Christianity* (Cambridge: James Clark & Co, 1988), pp. 72–89.

—'The Parting of the Ways: What Happened and Why', *Studia Theologica* 47.2 (1993), pp. 135–51.

—'James and the Jerusalem Church', in R. Bauckham (ed.), *The Book of Acts in Its Palestinian Setting*, volume 4 of B. W. Winter (ed.), *The Book of Acts in Its First Century Setting* (Grand Rapids, MI: Eerdmans, 1995), pp. 415–80.

—'The Scrupulous Priest and the Good Samaritan: Jesus' Parabolic Interpretation of the Law of Moses', *New Testament Studies* 44 (1998), pp. 475–89.

Beall, T. S., 'The Essenes', in L. H. Schiffman and J. C. VanderKam (eds), *Encyclopedia of the Dead Sea Scrolls* (2 vols.; Oxford: Oxford University Press, 2000), vol. 1, pp. 262–9.

Bedal, L.-A., 'A Pool Complex in Petra's City Center', *Bulletin of the American Schools of Oriental Research* 324 (November 2001), pp. 23–41.

Ben-Dov, M., *In the Shadow of the Temple: The Discovery of Ancient Jerusalem* (trans. I. Friedman; New York: Harper & Row, 1985).

Berquist, J. L., 'Critical Spatiality and the Construction of the Ancient World', in D. M. Gunn and P. M. McNutt (eds), *'Imagining' Biblical Worlds: Studies in Spatial, Social and Historical Constructs in Honor of James W. Flanagan* (London: Sheffield Academic Press, 2002), pp. 14–29.

Betz, O., 'The Essenes', in W. Horbury, W. D. Davies and J. Sturdy (eds), *The Cambridge History of Judaism: The Early Roman Period* (Cambridge: Cambridge University Press, 1999), vol. 3, pp. 444–70.

Black, M., *The Book of Enoch* (Leiden: E. J. Brill, 1985).

Bockmuehl, M., *This Jesus: Martyr, Lord, Messiah* (Edinburgh: T&T Clark, 1994).

Boer, R. T., *Marxist Criticism of the Bible* (London: T&T Clark, 2003).

Bóid, I. R. M. M., *Principles of Samaritan Halachah* (Leiden: E. J. Brill, 1989).
Booth, R. P., *Jesus and the Laws of Purity: Tradition History and Legal History in Mark 7* (Sheffield: JSOT Press, 1986).
Borg, M., *Jesus in Contemporary Scholarship* (Harrisburg, PA: Trinity Press, 1994).
—*Conflict, Holiness and Politics in the Teachings of Jesus* (Harrisburg, PA: Trinity Press, 2nd edn, 1998).
Bowker, J., *Jesus and the Pharisees* (Cambridge: Cambridge University Press, 1973).
Brereton, J., 'Sacred Space', in M. Eliade (ed.), *The Encyclopedia of Religion* (New York: Macmillan, 1987), pp. 526–35.
Brooke, G. J., 'The Ten Temples in the Dead Sea Scrolls', in J. Day (ed.), *Temple and Worship in Biblical Israel: Proceedings of the Oxford Old Testament Seminar* (London: T&T Clark, 2005), pp. 417–34.
Brown, R. E., *The Death of the Messiah: From Gethsemane to the Grave* (2 vols.; London: Doubleday, 1994).
Brueggeman, W., *The Land: Place as Gift, Promise, and Challenge in Biblical Faith* (Philadelphia: Fortress Press, 1977).
Bryan, D., *Cosmos, Chaos and the Kosher Mentality* (Sheffield: Sheffield Academic Press, 1995).
Bryan, S., *Jesus and Israel's Traditions of Judgement and Restoration* (Cambridge: Cambridge University Press, 2002).
Burnett, F. W., 'Philo on Immortality: A Thematic Study of Philo's Concept of παλιγ-γενεσία', *CBQ* 46 (1984), pp. 447–70.
Burridge, K., *New Heaven, New Earth: A Study of Millenarian Activities* (Oxford: Blackwell, 1969).
Charlesworth, J. H., 'John the Baptizer and Qumran Barriers in Light of the Rule of the Community', in D. W. Parry and E. Ulrich (eds), *The Provo International Conference on the Dead Sea Scrolls: Technological Innovations, New Texts, and Reformulated Issues* (Leiden: E. J. Brill, 1999), pp. 353–75.
Chilton, B., 'A Generative Exegesis of Mark 7.1-23', in B. Chilton and C. Evans (eds), *Jesus in Context: Temple, Purity and Restoration* (Leiden: E. J. Brill, 1997), pp. 297–317.
Clarke, K., *Between Geography and History: Hellenistic Constructions of the Roman World* (Oxford: Clarendon Press, 1999).
Coggins, R. J., *Samaritans and Jews: The Origins of Samaritanism Reconsidered* (Oxford: Blackwell, 1975).
—'The Samaritans in Josephus', in L. H. Feldman and G. Hata (eds), *Josephus, Judaism and Christianity* (Detroit, MI: Wayne State University Press, 1987), pp. 257–73.
—'Jewish Local Patriotism: The Samaritan Problem', in S. Jones and S. Pearce (eds), *Jewish Local Patriotism and Self-Identification in the Graeco-Roman Period* (Sheffield: Sheffield Academic Press, 1998), pp. 66–78.
Cohen, A. P., *Self Consciousness: An Alternative Anthropology of Identity* (London: Routledge, 1994).
Cohen, J. M., *A Samaritan Chronicle: A Source-Critical Analysis of the Life and Times of the Great Samaritan Reformer, Baba Rabbah* (Leiden: E. J. Brill, 1981).
Cohen, S. J. D., *From the Maccabees to the Mishnah* (Philadelphia: Westminster Press, 1987).
Collins, J. J., *Apocalypticism in the Dead Sea Scrolls* (London: Routledge, 1997).
—*The Apocalyptic Imagination: An Introduction to Jewish Apocalyptic Literature* (Grand Rapids, MI: Eerdmans, 2nd edn, 1998).

—'Temporality and Politics in Jewish Apocalyptic Literature', in C. Rowland and J. Barton (eds), *Apocalyptic in History and Tradition* (London: Sheffield Academic Press, 2002), pp. 26–43.

Crossan, J. D., *The Historical Jesus: The Life of a Mediterranean Jewish Peasant* (San Francisco: HarperSanFrancisco, 1991).

—*Who Killed Jesus?: Exposing the Roots of Anti-Semitism in the Gospel Story of the Death of Jesus* (San Francisco: HarperSanFrancisco, 1996).

Crossley, J. G., *The Date of Mark's Gospel: Insight from the Law in Earliest Christianity* (London: T&T Clark, 2004).

Davies, D., 'Christianity', in J. Holm (ed.), *Sacred Place* (London: Pinter, 1994), pp. 33–61.

Davies, P. R., 'Space and Sects in the Qumran Scrolls', in D. M. Gunn and P. M. McNutt (eds), *'Imagining' Biblical Worlds: Studies in Spatial, Social and Historical Constructs in Honor of James W. Flanagan* (London: Sheffield Academic Press, 2002), pp. 81–98.

Davies, W. D., *The Territorial Dimension of Judaism* (Minneapolis: Fortress Press, 1991).

—*The Gospel and the Land: Early Christianity and Jewish Territorial Doctrine* (The Biblical Seminar, 25; repr., Sheffield: Sheffield Academic Press, 1994).

Davies, W. D. and D. C. Allison, *A Critical and Exegetical Commentary on the Gospel According to Saint Matthew* (3 vols.; Edinburgh: T&T Clark, 1988–1997).

de Jonge, H., 'The Cleansing of the Temple in Mark 11:15 and Zechariah 14:21', in Christopher Tuckett (ed.), *The Book of Zechariah and its Influence* (Aldershot: Ashgate, 2003), pp. 87–100.

DeLacey, D. R., 'In Search of a Pharisee', *Tyndale Bulletin* 43.2 (1992), pp. 353–72.

Deleuze, G. and F. Guittari, *A Thousand Plateaus: Capitalism and Schizophrenia* (trans. Brian Massumi; London: The Athlone Press, 1988).

Douglas, M., *Purity and Danger: An Analysis of the Concepts of Pollution and Taboo* (London: Routledge, 1966).

—'Sacred Contagion', in J. F. A. Sawyer (ed.), *Reading Leviticus: A Conversation with Mary Douglas* (Sheffield: Sheffield Academic Press, 1996), pp. 86–106.

Dozeman, T. B., 'Masking Moses and Mosaic Authority in Torah', *Journal of Biblical Literature* 119.1 (2000), pp. 21–45.

Dube, M., 'Savior of the World But Not of This World: A Post-Colonial Reading of Spatial Construction in John', in R. S. Sugirtharajah (ed.), *The Postcolonial Bible* (Sheffield: Sheffield Academic Press, 1998), pp. 118–35.

Dunn, J. D. G., 'Jesus and Ritual Purity: A Study of the Tradition History of Mark 7, 15', in F. Refoulé (ed.), *À Cause de L'Évangile* (Paris: Éditions du Cerf, 1985), pp. 251–76.

—*Jesus, Paul and the Law: Studies in Mark and Galatians* (London: SPCK, 1990).

—'Jesus and Purity: An Ongoing Debate', *New Testament Studies* 48 (2002), pp. 449–67.

Edwards, D. R., 'Jotapata', in E. M. Meyers (ed.), *Oxford Encyclopedia of Archaeology in the Near East* (5 vols.; Oxford: Oxford University Press, 1997), vol. 3, pp. 251–2.

Ehrman, B., *Jesus: Apocalyptic Prophet of the New Millennium* (Oxford: Oxford University Press, 1999).

Eliade, M., *The Sacred and the Profane: The Nature of Religion* (trans. W. R. Trask; San Diego, CA: Harcourt, 1959).

Eshel, H. 'A Note on "Miqva'ot" at Sepphoris', in D. R. Edwards and C. T. McCollough (eds), *Archaeology and the Galilee: Texts and Contexts in the Graeco-Roman and Byzantine Periods* (Atlanta: Scholars Press, 1997), pp. 131–3.

—'We Need More Evidence', *Biblical Archaeology Review* 26.4 (July/August 2000), p. 49.

Eshel, H. and E. Meyers, 'The Pools of Sepphoris: Ritual Baths or Bathtubs?', *Biblical Archaeology Review* 26.4 (2000), pp. 42–9.

Evans, C., 'Predictions of the Destruction of the Herodian Temple in the Pseudepigrapha, Qumran Scrolls, and Related Texts', *Journal for the Study of the Pseudepigrapha* 10 (1992), pp. 89–147.

Flanagan, J., 'The Trialectics of Biblical Studies', online: http://www.cwru.edu/10296748/affil/GAIR/papers/2001papers/flanagan1.htm (accessed 6 November 2006).

Foster, R., 'Why on Earth Use "Kingdom of Heaven"? Matthew's Terminology Revisited', *New Testament Studies* 48.4 (2002), pp. 487–99.

Foucault, M., 'Of Other Spaces', *Diacritics* 16.1 (1986), pp. 22–7.

Franxman, T. W., *Genesis and the 'Jewish Antiquities' of Flavius Josephus* (Rome: Biblical Institute Press, 1979).

Freyne, S., *Galilee, Jesus and the Gospels: Literary Approaches and Historical Investigations* (Dublin: Gill and Macmillan, 1988).

—'Archaeology and the Historical Jesus', in J. R. Bartlett (ed.), *Archaeology and Biblical Interpretation* (London: Routledge, 1997), pp. 117–44.

—'Jesus and the Urban Culture of Galilee', in D. Hellholm and T. Fornberg (eds), *Texts and Contexts: Biblical Texts in their Textual and Situational Contexts: Essays in Honour of Lars Hartman* (Oslo: Scandinavian University Press, 1996), pp. 597–622. Reprinted in S. Freyne, *Galilee and Gospel: Collected Essays* (Tübingen: Mohr Siebeck, 2000), pp. 183–207. All page references to Freyne, 1996.

Gager, J. G., *Kingdom and Community: The Social World of Early Christianity* (Englewood Cliffs, NJ: Prentice-Hall, 1975).

Garwood, P., D. Jennings, R. Skeates and J. Toms (eds), *Sacred and Profane: Proceedings of a Conference on Archaeology, Ritual and Religion, Oxford, 1989* (Oxford: Oxford University Committee for Archaeology, 1991).

Gaston, L., *No Stone On Another: Studies in the Significance of the Fall of Jerusalem in the Synoptic Gospels* (Leiden: E. J. Brill, 1970).

Geertz, C., *The Interpretation of Cultures* (New York: Basic Books, 1973).

George, M. 'Tabernacle and Temple Spaces', online: http://www.case.edu/affil/GAIR/Constructions/xtrapapers2000.html (accessed 6 November 2006).

Geva, H., 'Twenty-Five Years of Excavations in Jerusalem, 1967–1992: Achievements and Evaluation', in H. Geva (ed.), *Ancient Jerusalem Revealed* (Jerusalem: Israel Exploration Society, 1994), pp. 1–28.

Goodman, M., *The Ruling Class of Judaea: The Origins of the Jewish Revolt Against Rome A.D. 66–70* (Cambridge: Cambridge University Press, 1987).

—'A Note on Josephus, the Pharisees and Ancestral Tradition', *Journal of Jewish Studies* 50.1 (Spring 1999), pp. 17–20.

—'The Temple in First Century CE Judaism', in J. Day (ed.), *Temple and Worship in Biblical Israel: Proceedings of the Oxford Old Testament Seminar* (London: T&T Clark, 2005), pp. 459–68.

Gray, R., *Prophetic Figures in Late Second Temple Jewish Palestine: The Evidence from Josephus* (Oxford: Oxford University Press, 1993).

Gruenwald, I., 'From Priesthood to Messianism: The Anti-Priestly Polemic and the Messianic Factor', in I. Gruenwald (ed.), *Messiah and Christos: Studies in the Jewish Origins of Christianity Presented to David Flusser on the Occasion of His 75th Birthday* (Tübingen: Mohr Siebeck, 1992), pp. 75–93.

Gunn, D. M. and P. M. McNutt (eds), *'Imagining' Biblical Worlds: Studies in Spatial, Social and Historical Constructs in Honor of James W. Flanagan* (London: Sheffield Academic Press, 2002).

Habel, N., *The Land is Mine: Six Biblical Land Ideologies* (Minneapolis: Fortress Press, 1995).

Halpern-Amaru, B., 'Land Theology in Philo and Josephus', in L. A. Hoffman (ed.), *The Land of Israel: Jewish Perspectives* (Notre Dame, IN: University of Notre Dame Press, 1986), pp. 65–93.

—*Rewriting the Bible: Land and Covenant in Post-Biblical Literature* (Valley Forge, PA: Trinity Press, 1994).

Han, K., *Jerusalem and the Early Jesus Movement: The Q Community's Attitude Toward the Temple* (London: Sheffield Academic Press, 2002).

Harrington, H., *The Impurity Systems of Qumran and the Rabbis: Biblical Foundations* (Atlanta, GA: Scholars Press, 1993).

Harris, R., *Paradise: A Cultural Guide* (Singapore: Times Academic Press, 1996).

Harvey, D., *Spaces of Hope* (Edinburgh: Edinburgh University Press, 2000).

Hengel, M., 'Judaism and Hellenism Revisited', in J. J. Collins and G. Sterling (eds), *Hellenism in the Land of Israel* (Notre Dame, IN: University of Notre Dame Press, 2001), pp. 6–37.

Hengel, M. and R. Deines, 'E. P. Sanders' "Common Judaism", Jesus, and the Pharisees', *Journal of Theological Studies* 46 (1995), pp. 1–70.

Herzog, W., 'The New Testament and the Question of Racial Injustice', *American Baptist Quarterly* 5.1 (1986), pp. 12–32.

Himmelfarb, M., 'Impurity and Sin in 4QD, 1QS, and 4Q512', *Dead Sea Discoveries* 8.1 (2001), pp. 9–37.

Holwerda, D. E., *Jesus and Israel: One Covenant or Two?* (Grand Rapids, MI: Eerdmans, 1995).

Hooker, M., *The Signs of a Prophet: The Prophetic Actions of Jesus* (London: SCM Press, 1997).

Horbury, W., 'The Twelve and the Phylarchs', *New Testament Studies* 32.4 (1986): 503–27.

—'Land, Sanctuary and Worship', in J. Barclay and J. P. Sweet (eds), *Early Christian Thought in its Jewish Context* (Cambridge: Cambridge University Press, 1996), pp. 207–24.

Horsley, R. A., ' "Like One of the Prophets of Old": Two Types of Popular Prophets at the Time of Jesus', *Catholic Biblical Quarterly* 47 (1985), pp. 435–63.

—*Galilee: History, Politics, People* (Valley Forge, PA: Trinity Press, 1995).

Hubert, J., 'Sacred Beliefs and Beliefs of Sacredness', in D. L. Carmichael, J. Hubert, B. Reeves and A. Schanche (eds), *Sacred Sites, Sacred Places* (London: Routledge, 1994), pp. 9–19.

Hurowitz, V. A., 'YHWH's Exalted House – Aspects of the Design and Symbolism of Solomon's Temple', in J. Day (ed.), *Temple and and Worship in Biblical Israel: Proceedings of the Oxford Old Testament Seminar* (London: T&T Clark, 2005), pp. 63–110.

Isser, S., 'Jesus in the Samaritan Chronicles', *Journal of Jewish Studies* 32 (1981), pp. 166–94.

—'The Samaritans and their Sects', in W. Horbury, W. D. Davies and J. Sturdy (eds), *The Cambridge History of Judaism: The Early Roman Period* (Cambridge: Cambridge University Press, 1999), vol. 3, pp. 569–95.

Jenson, P., *Graded Holiness: A Key to the Priestly Conception of the World* (Sheffield: Sheffield Academic Press, 1992).

Jeremias, J., *Jesus' Promise to the Nations* (trans. S. H. Hooke; London: SCM Press, 1967).
Kallai, Z., 'The Twelve-Tribe Systems of Israel', *Vetus Testamentum* 47 (1997), pp. 53–90.
Kampen, J., 'The Significance of the Temple in the Manuscripts of the Damascus Document', in R. A. Kugler and E. M. Schuller (eds), *The Dead Sea Scrolls at Fifty: Proceedings of the 1997 Society of Biblical Literature Qumran Section Meetings* (Atlanta: Scholars Press, 1999), pp. 185–97.
Kazen, T., *Jesus and Purity Halakhah: Was Jesus Indifferent to Impurity?* (Stockholm: Almqvist & Wiksell International, 2002).
Killebrew, A., 'Baths', in E. M. Meyers (ed.), *Oxford Encyclopedia of Archaeology in the Near East* (5 vols; Oxford: Oxford University Press, 1997), vol. 1, pp. 283–5.
Knibb, M., 'Temple and Cult in Apocryphal and Pseudepigraphal Writings from Before the Common Era', in J. Day (ed.), *Temple and Worship in Biblical Israel: Proceedings of the Oxford Old Testament Seminar* (London: T&T Clark, 2005), pp. 401–16.
Knight, D. A., 'Joshua 22 and the Ideology of Space', in D. M. Gunn and P. M. McNutt (eds), *'Imagining' Biblical Worlds: Studies in Spatial, Social and Historical Constructs in Honor of James W. Flanagan* (London: Sheffield Academic Press, 2002), pp. 51–63.
Koester, C. R., *The Dwelling of God: The Tabernacle in the Old Testament, Intertestamental Jewish Literature, and the New Testament* (Washington, DC: The Catholic Biblical Association of America, 1989).
Kugler, R. L., *The Testaments of the Twelve Patriarchs* (Sheffield: Sheffield Academic Press, 2001).
Kunin, S. *God's Place in the World: Sacred Space and Sacred Place in Judaism* (London: Cassell, 1998).
Kuper, H., 'The Language of Sites in the Politics of Space', in S. M. Low and D. Lawrence-Zúñiga (eds), *The Anthropology of Space and Place: Locating Culture* (Oxford: Blackwell, 2003), pp. 247–63: repr. from *American Anthropologist* 74.3 (1972), pp. 411–25.
Laaksonen, J. *Jesus und das Land: das Gelobte Land in der Verkündigung Jesu* (Åbo: Åbo Akademis Förlag, 2002).
Lefebvre, H., *The Production of Space* (trans. D. Nicholson-Smith; Oxford: Blackwell, 1991), translation of *La production de la espace* (Paris: Éditions anthropos, 1974).
Levenson, J. D., *Sinai and Zion: An Entry Into the Jewish Bible* (San Francisco: HarperSanFrancisco, 1985).
Levine, L. I., 'Archaeological Discoveries from the Greco-Roman Era', in H. Shanks (ed.), *Recent Archaeology in the Land of Israel* (trans. A. Finklestein; Washington, DC: Biblical Archaeology Society, 1984), pp. 75–87.
—*Judaism and Hellenism in Antiquity: Conflict or Confluence?* (Peabody, MA: Hendrickson, 1999).
Low, S. M. and D. Lawrence-Zúñiga (eds), *The Anthropology of Space and Place: Locating Culture* (Oxford: Blackwell, 2003).
Magen, Y., 'Mount Gerizim and the Samaritans', in F. Manns and E. Alliata (eds), *Early Christianity in Context: Monuments and Documents* (Jerusalem: Franciscan Printing Press, 1993), pp. 91–148.
—'Qedumim – A Samaritan Site of the Roman-Byzantine Period', in F. Manns and E. Alliata (eds), *Early Christianity in Context: Monuments and Documents* (Jerusalem: Franciscan Printing Press, 1993), pp. 167–80.

—'Ritual Baths (*Miqva'ot*) at Qedumim and the Observance of Ritual Purity Among the Samaritans', in F. Manns and E. Alliata (eds), *Early Christianity in Context: Monuments and Documents* (Jerusalem: Franciscan Printing Press, 1993), pp. 181-92.

—'Jerusalem as a Center of the Stone Vessel Industry During the Second Temple Period', in H. Geva (ed.), *Ancient Jerusalem Revealed* (Jerusalem: Israel Exploration Society, 1994), pp. 244-56.

Maier, J., 'The *Temple Scroll* and Tendencies in the Cultic Architecture of the Second Commonwealth', in L. Schiffman (ed.), *Archaeology and History in the Dead Sea Scrolls: The New York University Conference in Memory of Yigael Yadin* (Sheffield: JSOT Press, 1990), pp. 67-82.

Malina, B. J., '"Apocalyptic" and Territoriality', in F. Manns and E. Alliata (eds), *Early Christianity in Context: Monuments and Documents* (Jerusalem: Franciscan Printing Press, 1993), pp. 369-80.

Marcus, J., *The Way of the Lord: Christological Exegesis of the Old Testament in the Gospel of Mark* (Louisville, KY: Westminster/John Knox Press, 1992).

—'The Beelzebul Controversy and the Eschatologies of Jesus', in B. Chilton and C. A. Evans (eds), *Authenticating the Activities of Jesus* (Leiden: E. J. Brill, 1999), pp. 247-77.

—*Mark 1–8: A New Translation with Introduction and Commentary* (New York: Doubleday, 2000).

McKelvey, R. J., *The New Temple: The Church in the New Testament* (Oxford: Oxford University Press, 1969).

McKnight, S., *A New Vision for Israel: The Teachings of Jesus in National Context* (Grand Rapids, MI: Eerdmans, 1999).

—'A Parting Within the Way: Jesus and James on Israel and Purity', in B. Chilton and C. A. Evans (eds), *James the Just and Christian Origins* (Leiden: E. J. Brill, 1999), pp. 83-129.

—'Jesus and Prophetic Actions', *Bulletin for Biblical Research* 10.2 (2000), pp. 197-232.

—'Jesus and the Twelve', *Bulletin for Biblical Research* 11.2 (2001), pp. 203-31.

McLaren, J. S., *Power and Politics in Palestine: The Jews and the Governing of their Land 100 BC–AD 70* (Sheffield: JSOT Press, 1991).

Meggitt, J., *Paul, Poverty and Survival* (Edinburgh: T&T Clark, 1998).

Meier, J. P., 'The Circle of the Twelve: Did it Exist During Jesus' Public Ministry?', *Journal of Biblical Literature* 116.4 (1997), pp. 635-72.

Mendels, D., *The Rise and Fall of Jewish Nationalism: Jewish and Christian Ethnicity in Ancient Palestine* (Grand Rapids, MI: Eerdmans, 2nd edn, 1997).

Meye, R. P., *Jesus and the Twelve: Discipleship and Revelation in Mark's Gospel* (Grand Rapids, MI: Eerdmans, 1968).

Meyer, B. F., *The Aims of Jesus* (London: SCM Press, 1979).

Meyers, E. M., 'Yes They Are', *Biblical Archaeology Review* 26.4 (July/August, 2000), pp. 46-8.

—'Aspects of Everyday Life in Roman Palestine with Special Reference to Private Domiciles and Ritual Baths', in J. R. Bartlett (ed.), *Jews in the Hellenistic and Roman Cities* (London: Routledge, 2002), pp. 193-220.

Milgrom, J., *Leviticus 1–16: A New Translation with Introduction and Commentary* (New York: Doubleday, 1991).

—'The Dynamics of Purity in the Priestly System', in M. J. H. M. Poorthuis and J. Schwartz (eds), *Purity and Holiness: The Heritage of Leviticus* (Leiden: E. J. Brill, 2000), pp. 29-32.

Millar, A. and J. K. Riches, 'Interpretation: A Theoretical Perspective and Some Applications', *Numen* 28.1 (1981), pp. 29–53.

Molotch, H., 'The Space of Lefebvre', *Theory and Society* 22 (1993), pp. 887–95.

Moxnes, H., *Putting Jesus in His Place: A Radical Vision of Household and Kingdom* (Louisville, KY: Westminster/John Knox Press, 2003).

Nelson, R. D., *Joshua: A Commentary* (OTL; Louisville, KY: Westminster/John Knox Press, 1997).

Netzer, E., *Qedem 13: Greater Herodium* (Monographs of the Institute of Archaeology, The Hebrew University of Jerusalem; Jerusalem: Publications of the Hebrew University of Jerusalem, 1981).

Netzer, N., 'Ancient Ritual Baths (*Miqvaot*) in Jericho', in L. I. Levine (ed.), *The Jerusalem Cathedra: Studies in the History, Archaeology, Geography and Ethnography of the Land of Israel* (3 vols.; Jerusalem: Yad Izhak Ben-Zvi Institute, 1981), vol. 1, pp. 106–19.

Neusner, J., *The Rabbinic Traditions about the Pharisees Before 70, Part III: Conclusions* (Leiden: E. J. Brill, 1971).

—*From Politics to Piety: The Emergence of Pharisaic Judaism* (Englewood Cliffs, NJ: Prentice-Hall, 1973).

—'Mr. Sanders' Pharisees and Mine: A Response to E. P. Sanders' *Jewish Law From Jesus to the Mishnah*', *Scottish Journal of Theology* 44 (1993), pp. 73–95.

Økland, J., *Women in Their Place: Paul and the Corinthian Discourse of Gender and Sanctuary Space* (London: T&T Clark, 2004).

Ottenheijm, E., 'Impurity Between Intention and Deed: Purity Disputes in First Century Judaism and in the New Testament', in M. J. H. M. Poorthuis and J. Schwartz (eds), *Purity and Holiness: The Heritage of Leviticus* (Leiden: E. J. Brill, 2000), pp. 129–47.

Park, C. C., *Sacred Worlds: An Introduction to Geography and Religion* (London: Routledge, 1994).

Pastor, J., *Land and Economy in Ancient Palestine* (London: Routledge, 1997).

Phann, S. J., 'The Essene Yearly Renewal Ceremony and the Baptism of Repentance', in D. W. Parry and E. Ulrich (eds), *The Provo International Conference on the Dead Sea Scrolls: Technological Innovations, New Texts, and Reformulated Issues* (Leiden: E. J. Brill, 1999), pp. 337–52.

Poorthuis, M. and J. Schwartz, 'Purity and Holiness: An Introductory Survey', in M. J. H. M. Poorthuis and J. Schwartz (eds), *Purity and Holiness: The Heritage of Leviticus* (Leiden: E. J. Brill, 2000), pp. 3–26.

Primus, C., 'The Borders of Judaism: The Land of Israel in Early Rabbinic Judaism', in L. A. Hoffman (ed.), *The Land of Israel: Jewish Perspectives* (Notre Dame, IN: University of Notre Dame Press, 1986), pp. 97–108.

Prior, M., *The Bible and Colonialism: A Moral Critique* (Sheffield: Sheffield Academic Press, 1997).

Pummer, R., *The Samaritans* (Leiden: E. J. Brill, 1987).

Rabinow, P. (ed.), *The Foucault Reader* (Harmondsworth: Penguin, 1986).

Räisänen, H., 'Jesus and the Food Laws: Reflections on Mark 7.15', *Journal for the Study of the New Testament* 16 (1982), pp. 79–100.

Rapoport, A., 'Spatial Organization and the Built Environment', in T. Ingold (ed.), *Companion Encyclopedia of Anthropology* (London: Routledge, 1994), pp. 460–502.

Regev, E., 'Non-Priestly Purity and its Religious Aspects According to Historical Sources and Archaeological Findings', in M. J. H. M. Poorthuis and J. Schwartz

(eds), *Purity and Holiness: The Heritage of Leviticus* (Leiden: E. J. Brill, 2000), pp. 223-44a.
—'Pure Individualism: The Idea of Non-Priestly Purity in Ancient Judaism', *Journal for the Study of Judaism in the Persian, Hellenistic and Roman Period* 31.2 (2000), pp. 176-202.
Reich, R., 'The Hot Bath-House (*balneum*), the *Miqweh*, and the Jewish Community in the Second Temple Period', *Journal of Jewish Studies* 39.1 (1988), pp. 102-7.
—'The Synagogue and the *Miqweh* in Eretz-Israel in the Second-Temple, Misnaic, and Talmudic Periods', in D. Urman and P. V. M. Flesher (eds), *Ancient Synagogues: Historical Analysis and Archaeological Discovery* (2 vols.; Leiden: E. J. Brill, 1995), vol. 1, pp. 289-97.
—'Ritual Baths', in E. M. Meyers (ed.) *The Oxford Encyclopedia of Archaeology in the Near East* (5 vols.; Oxford: Oxford University Press, 1997), vol. 4, pp. 430-31.
—'They *Are* Ritual Baths: Immerse Yourself in the Ongoing Sepphoris Mikveh Debate', *Biblical Archaeology Review* 28.2 (March/April 2002), pp. 50-55.
Riches, J. K., *Jesus and the Transformation of Judaism* (London: Darton, Longman & Todd, 1980).
—'Apocalyptic – Strangely Relevant', in W. Horbury (ed.), *Templum Amicitiae: Essays on the Second Temple Presented to Ernst Bammel* (Sheffield: JSOT Press, 1991), pp. 237-63.
—'The Social World of Jesus', *Interpretation* 50 (1996), pp. 383-93.
—*Conflicting Mythologies: Identity Formation in the Gospels of Mark and Matthew* (Edinburgh: T&T Clark, 2000).
Riches, J. and A. Millar, 'Conceptual Change in the Synoptic Tradition', in A. E. Harvey (ed.), *Alternative Approaches to New Testament Study* (London: SPCK, 1985), pp. 37-60.
Salles-Reese, V., *From Viracocha to the Virgin of Copacabana: Representation of the Sacred at Lake Titicaca* (Austin, TX: University of Texas Press, 1997).
Sanders, E. P., *Jesus and Judaism* (Philadelphia: Fortress Press, 1985).
—*Judaism: Practice and Belief 63BCE-66CE* (London: SCM Press, 1992).
Sarason, R. S., 'The Significance of the Land of Israel in the Mishnah', in L. A. Hoffman (ed.), *The Land of Israel: Jewish Perspectives* (Notre Dame, Indiana: University of Notre Dame Press, 1986), pp. 109-36.
Schiffman, L., *The Halakhah at Qumran* (Leiden: E. J. Brill, 1975).
Schmidt, F., *How the Temple Thinks: Identity and Social Cohesion in Ancient Judaism* (trans. J. E. Crowley; Sheffield: Sheffield Academic Press, 2001).
Schmithals, W., *Das Evangelium nach Markus* (2 vols.; Gütersloh: Gerd Mohn, 2nd edn, 1986).
Schottroff, L., 'Non-Violence and the Love of One's Enemies', in L. Schottroff (ed.), *Essays on the Love Commandment* (trans. R. H. Fuller and I. Fuller; Philadelphia, PA: Fortress, 1978), pp. 9-39.
Schwartz, D., 'The Tribes of As. Mos. 4:7-9', *Journal of Biblical Literature* 99.2 (1980), pp. 217-23.
Scott, J. M., *Geography in Early Judaism and Christianity: The Book of Jubilees* (Cambridge: Cambridge University Press, 2002).
Sellers, O. R., 'Coins of the 1960 Excavation at Shechem', *Biblical Archaeologist* 25 (1962), pp. 87-96.
Sheldrake, P., *Spaces for the Sacred: Place, Memory and Identity* (London: SCM Press, 2001).
Shields, R., 'Spatial Stress and Resistance: Social Meanings of Spatialization', in G. Benko

and U. Strohmayer (eds), *Space and Social Theory: Interpreting Modernity and Postmodernity* (Oxford: Blackwell, 1997), pp. 186–202.
Smith, J. Z., *Map is Not Territory: Studies in the History of Religions* (Leiden: E. J. Brill, 1978).
—*To Take Place: Toward Theory in Ritual* (Chicago: Chicago University Press, 1987).
Soja, E., *Postmodern Geographies: The Reassertion of Space in Critical Theory* (London: Verso, 1989).
Sommer, B. D., 'Conflicting Constructions of Divine Presence in the Priestly Tabernacle', *Biblical Interpretation* 9.1 (2001), pp. 41–63.
Stemberger, G., 'The Sadducees – Their History and Doctrines', in W. Horbury, W. D. Davies and J. Sturdy (eds), *The Cambridge History of Judaism: The Early Roman Period* (Cambridge: Cambridge University Press, 1999), pp. 428–43.
Stern, M., 'The Province of Judaea', in S. Safrai and M. Stern (eds), *The Jewish People in the First Century: Historical Geography, Political History, Social, Cultural and Religious Life and Institutions* (2 vols.; Compendia Rerum Iudaicarum ad Novum Testamentum; Assen: Van Gorcum, 1974), vol. 1, pp. 308–76.
—'Aspects of Jewish Society: The Priesthood and Other Classes', in S. Safrai and M. Stern (eds), *The Jewish People in the First Century: Historical Geography, Political History, Social, Cultural and Religious Life and Institutions* (2 vols.; Compendia Rerum Iudaicarum ad Novum Testamentum; Assen: Van Gorcum, 1976), vol. 2, pp. 561–630.
—'Social and Political Realignments in Herodian Judaea', in L. I. Levine (ed.), *The Jerusalem Cathedra: Studies in the History, Archaeology, Geography and Ethnography of the Land of Israel* (3 vols.; Jerusalem: Yad Izhak Ben-Zvi Institute, 1982), vol. 2, pp. 40–62.
Sugirtharajah, R. S. (ed.), *The Postcolonial Bible* (Sheffield: Sheffield Academic Press, 1998).
Swanson, D. D., *The Temple Scroll and the Bible: The Methodology of 11QT* (Leiden: E. J. Brill, 1995).
Swanson, T., 'To Prepare a Place: Johannine Christianity and the Collapse of Ethnic Territory', *Journal of the American Academy of Religion* 62.2 (1994), pp. 241–63.
Tan, K. H., *The Zion Traditions and the Aims of Jesus* (Cambridge: Cambridge University Press, 1997).
Taylor, J., *John the Baptist within Second Temple Judaism: A Historical Study* (London: SPCK, 1997).
Theissen, G. *The First Followers of Jesus: A Sociological Analysis of the Earliest Christianity* (trans. J. Bowden; London: SCM Press, 1978).
—*Social Reality and the Early Christians: Theology, Ethics, and the World of the New Testament* (trans. M. Kohl; Edinburgh: T&T Clark, 1993).
—*A Theory of Primitive Christian Religion* (trans. J. Bowden; London: SCM Press, 1999).
Theissen G. and D. Winter, *The Quest for the Plausible Jesus: The Question of Criteria* (trans. M. E. Boring; Louisville, KY: Westminster/John Knox Press, 2002).
Tigchelaar, E. J. C., 'Eden and Paradise: The Garden Motif in Some Early Jewish Texts (*1 Enoch* and other Texts found at Qumran)', in G. P. Luttikhuizen (ed.), *Paradise Interpreted: Representations of Biblical Paradise in Judaism and Christianity* (Leiden: E. J. Brill, 1999), pp. 37–62.
Tiller, P. A., *A Commentary on the Animal Apocalypse of 1 Enoch* (Atlanta, GA: Scholars Press, 1993).

Tomson, P. J., 'Purity Laws as Viewed by the Church Fathers and by the Early Followers of Jesus', in M. J. H. M. Poorthuis and J. Schwartz (eds), *Purity and Holiness: The Heritage of Leviticus* (Leiden: E. J. Brill, 2000), pp. 73–91.

Trible, P., *Texts of Terror: Literary-Feminist Readings of Biblical Narratives* (Philadelphia: Fortress Press, 1984).

Tromp, J., *The Assumption of Moses: A Critical Edition with Commentary* (Leiden: E. J. Brill, 1993).

Tsuk, T., 'Cisterns' (trans. Ilana Goldberg), in E. M. Meyers (ed.), *Oxford Encyclopedia of Archaeology in the Near East* (5 vols.; Oxford: Oxford University Press, 1997), vol. 2, pp. 12–13.

—'Bringing Water to Sepphoris', in *Biblical Archaeology Review* 26.4 (2000), pp. 35–41.

Tuan, Y.-F., *Space and Place: The Perspective of Experience* (Minneapolis: University of Minnesota Press, 1977).

van Aarde, A., 'The Historicity of the Circle of the Twelve: All Roads Lead to Jerusalem', *Hervormde Teologiese Studies* 55.4 (1999), pp. 795–826.

Van Seters, J., 'Solomon's Temple: Fact and Ideology in Biblical and Near Eastern Historiography', *Catholic Biblical Quarterly* 59 (1997), pp. 45–57.

Vanderhooft, D., 'Dwelling Beneath the Sacred Place: A Proposal for Reading 2 Samuel 7:10', *Journal of Biblical Literature* 118.4 (1999), pp. 625–33.

VanderKam, J., *Enoch: A Man for All Generations* (Columbia, SC: University of South Carolina Press, 1995).

—*From Revelation to Canon: Studies in the Hebrew Bible and Second Temple Literature* (Leiden: E. J. Brill, 2000).

Vermes, G., *Jesus the Jew: A Historian's Reading of the Gospels* (Philadelphia: Fortress Press, 1981).

Vielhauer, P., 'Gottesreich und Menschensohn in der Verkündigung Jesu', in W. Schneemelcher (ed.), *Festschrift für Gunther Dehn, zum 75 Geburtstag am 18 April 1957* (Neukirchen: Verlag der Buchhandlung des Erziehungsvereins, 1957), pp. 51–79.

Walker, P., 'Christians and Jerusalem, Past and Present', in B. Norman (ed.), *The Mountain of the Lord: Israel and the Churches* (London: Council of Christians and Jews, 1996), pp. 107–130.

—'The Land in the New Testament', in P. Johnston and P. Walker (eds), *The Land of Promise: Biblical, Theological and Contemporary Perspectives* (Downers Grove, IL: InterVarsity Press, 2000), pp. 81–120.

Webb, R. L., *John the Baptizer and Prophet: A Socio-Historical Study* (Sheffield: Sheffield Academic Press, 1991).

Wenell, K., 'Land as Sacred and Social Space: Some Reflections on the Early Jesus Movement and the *Hauhau* Religion', in L. Lawrence and M. Aguilar (eds), *Anthropology and Biblical Studies: Avenues of Approach* (Leiden: Deo Publishing, 2004), pp. 208–26.

—'Contested Temple Space and Visionary Kingdom Space in Mark 11–12', *Biblical Interpretation* 15.3 (2007), pp. 291–305.

Whitelam, K., *The Invention of Ancient Israel: The Silencing of Palestinian History* (London: Routledge, 1996).

Wilken, R. L., *The Land Called Holy: Palestine in Christian History and Thought* (New Haven: Yale University Press, 1992).

Wright, N. T., *Jesus and the Victory of God* (Minneapolis, MN: Fortress Press, 1996).

Index

Index Of References

Old Testament

Genesis		22.21	114	11.1-43	69
1	9	23.9	114	11.2-8	63
2–3	10	24	112–13	11.32	69
9.24-25	11	24.4	113	11.33	78
10	8–13	24.18	9	11.36	71
10.5	8	25–31	25	12	70
10.20	8	25–40	38	12.5	69
10.31	8	25.8-9	25	12.15	70
10.32	8	25.8	25	13	70
11	9	25.9	24	13–14	99
12.1	9	25.22	25	14.1-34	69
12.7	9, 110	25.40	24	15	70
15.18-21	146	29.4	71	15.4-15	69
15.18	9, 96	29.38-43	25	15.13	69, 71
17	65	30.10-17	25	15.16-18	69, 70
17.18	9	30.11-16	31	15.19-30	70
17.20	105	30.18-21	71	15.20-24	70, 71
25.16	105	34	113	15.12	78
29.32–30.24	107	34.30-32	113	15.31	70
35.17-18	107	36.8-13	25	16.2	70
35.22	105	36.9-21	25	16.23	70
42.13	105	36.14-18	25	16.27	70
42.32	105	36.35-37	25	17–26	70
46.8-25	108	36.37-38	25	17.15	70
48	108	38.9-13	25	17.16	71
48.5	108, 109	38.9-18	25	18	85, 111
48.13-20	108	40.30-32	71	18.24-30	64, 65, 67
48.21-22	108, 109			19.13-22	70
49	109	Leviticus		20	85
49.28	105	4–6	93	20.22-26	64, 67, 143
		4.26	94		
Exodus		4.35	94	20.23	65
14.1-31	95	5.10	94	22	70
15.17	55	5.16	94	22.4-5	71
15.27	105	6.28	78	22.4-7	70
16.1-36	26	8.1-10	26	24.5-9	111
16.35	26	10.10	66	24.8	111

Leviticus (cont.)		18.1	108	7.10	29
24.5	105	23.12-14	88	7.11	26
25.32-33	108	27.12	35	7.13	27
		33.4-29	108		
Numbers		33.6-25	109	1 Kings	
1	111			4.7-19	28
1.2	111	Joshua		4.7	105
1.3	26	3.1-17	95	4.20-28	28
1.4	112	3.12	112	6	28
1.5-16	108	3.13	105	6.2-20	28
1.20-46	108	4	96, 111	6.14	28
1.44	105	4.4	105	6.16	28
1.47-50	26	4.7	111	6.17	105
2	112	4.22	111	6.19	27
2.3-32	108, 112	8.33	35	6.21	28
2.17	112	8.35	114	6.31-32	28
7.1-48	112	13–19	107, 108,	6.33-35	28
7.2	26		112, 126	8.3-11	28
7.3	105	13.7–19.48	105, 106	10.20	105
7.12-73	108	13.8	108	11.30	105, 110
7.84	105	13.29	108	11.31-32	111
7.87	105	14.1	112	12.25-33	35
10.14-28	108	14.3-4	108		
13.1-6	108	18.1	25	2 Kings	
13.1	112	18.7	108	2.6-15	96
18.20-21	108	19.51	25	17.4	36
18.23-24	108	20.9	114		
19	27, 99	21	108	1 Chronicles	
19.19	71	21.4-40	108	6.64	108
26.1-3	112	21.7	105	12.24-38	108, 109
26.1-55	112	22	110	27.16-22	108, 109
26.3-55	108				
26.3	112	Judges		2 Chronicles	
26.52-54	112	1.1-35	108	9.19	105
27.2	112	1.1-36	108	36.8-9	41
29.17	105	12.1-6	110		
31.13	112	19.29	105, 110	Ezra	
33.9	105	20.1-48	110	2.68	29
34.3-12	114	20.6-7	110	3.2	30
34.16-29	108			3.8-9	30
34.18	105	1 Samuel		3.12	30
34.26	112	1–2	28, 35	5.15	29, 30, 43
35.2-7	108	15.22	94	6.7	29
35.2	108			8.24	105
		2 Samuel		8.35	105
Deuteronomy		6	28		
10.9	108	6.17	25	Psalm	
11.29	35	7	28	37	38
12.1-10	26	7.5-7	25	37.11	1, 19
12.12	108	7.8	27	41	120
				51.16-17	93

Index of References

Proverbs		45–48	113	8.23	130
15.8	94	45.5	108	11.12	120
		45.8	113		
Isaiah		47–48	113	**Apocrypha**	
11.12	130	47.13	105, 114	*1 Esdras*	
28.16	89	47.15-20	113	7.8	105
40.3	89, 93	47.22-23	114		
43.1	130	48.1-29	108	*Tobit*	
43.5-6	130	48.1-35	106	1.4	132
43.5	130			2.9	68
43.9	130	Daniel		13.3	131
56.3-7	47	7	125, 126	13.5	131
56.7	47	7.9-14	125	13.11	131, 132
60.21	38	7.9	125	14.7	131
		7.13	128	36.13	132
Jeremiah				36.16	132
7.3-14	49	Hosea			
7.4	49	6.6	93	*Judith*	
7.10	49			12.6-10	68
7.14	48, 49	Micah			
27.18-22	41	2.12	130	*Sirach*	
				36.1	130
Ezekiel		Zechariah		36.3	131
36	96	2.12	8	36.16	131
36.24-27	96	8.7-8	130	49.10	105
37.12	115	8.8-13	130		
38.12	9, 10	8.21-22	130	*Baruch*	
40–48	38, 113	8.22	130, 132	4.36-37	129

New Testament

Matthew		10.1-4	117	19.29	124
3.5	93	10.1	105	20.1-16	58
3.7-12	93	10.2	105	20.17	105
3.7	96	10.5-23	117	21.12-13	17
3.9	93, 96	11.5	99	24.1-2	17
3.11	94	12.43-45	100, 101	25.31-46	125
5.5	1, 19	14.20	105	25.31	126
5.44-45	102	15.11	18, 98	26.6	99
5.44	101	18.23-35	58	26.14	105, 117
6.6b-13	117	19.12	124	26.15	120
6.19-21	57	19.16-21	124	26.47	117
6.24	57	19.16	124	26.53	105
8.2-4	99	19.28	18, 105, 116, 117, 118, 120, 122–4, 125, 126, 127, 128, 134–6	26.60-61	17
8.11-12	18, 122, 128–9, 134, 136			28.18-20	146
				Mark	
9.10	101			1.4	94
9.14	93			1.5	93
9.20-22	99			1.23-27	100

Mark (cont.)		12.26-27	134	22.25	123
1.40-44	99	13.1-2	17	22.26	123
1.40-45	99	13.2	45	22.27	123
1.44	99	13.26-27	128	22.29-30	122
2.15-16	101	13.26	128	22.30	18, 105,
2.16	82	13.27	134		116, 117,
2.18	82	14	120		118, 122–
2.23-27	102	14.3	99		4, 126,
2.24	82	14.10	105, 117		127, 128,
3.1-2	51	14.20	105, 117		134–6
3.2	82	14.43	105, 117	22.47	105, 117
3.8-10	133	14.56-59	17, 52		
3.13-16	117	14.58	45, 55	John	
3.16	105	15.29	45	2.13-22	17, 52
3.23-26	100			2.20	55
3.31-35	133	Luke		2.25	79
4.10	105	3.3	93, 94	4	91
5.1-34	100	3.7-10	93	4.1-42	145
5.15	100	3.8-9	133	6.13	105
5.21-24	99	3.8	93, 96	6.67	105
5.25-34	99	3.14	93	6.70	105, 117
5.35-43	99	3.17	93	6.71	105, 117
5.35	99	5.12-14	96		
5.41	99	5.30	101	Acts	
6.43	105	6.12-16	117	1.3	118
7	99	6.16	118	1.6	55
7.1	82	6.27	101	1.13	117
7.15	18, 97–	7.11-17	99	1.15	120
	100	7.11-19	99	4.1-22	55
8.38	128	8.1	105	4.1	34
9.35	105	8.43-48	99	5.1-11	121
10.2	82	9.1-6	117	5.15	121
10.32	105	9.1	105	5.16-33	55
10.35-45	127, 128,	9.17	105	5.17	34
	136	10.18	102	5.29	121
10.35-41	128	10.30-35	100	6.2	105
10.35-37	127	11.1	93	6.12-14	17
10.35	127	11.24-26	100	7.8	105
10.40-41	127	12.33-34	57	10.14-15	96
10.41	128	13.28-29	18, 122,	11.3	98
10.42	128		128–9,	11.30	121
10.43-44	128		134, 136	12.1-17	121
10.45	122	16.13	57	21.26-36	55
11.11	105	16.22	134	21.38	95, 116
11.15-18	17	18.31	105		
11.15-19	45	19.45-46	17	Romans	
11.17	49	21.5-6	17	14.14	98
11.24-26	100	22.3	105, 117	14.20	98
12.1-9	58	22.24-30	123		

Index of References

1 Corinthians		Hebrews		12.1	105
10.2	95	1.14	2	21.12	105
15.3-5	118			21.14	105
15.5-11	118	James		21.21	105
15.5	105, 119	1.1	105	22.2	105
Galatians		Revelation			
2.11-18	68, 96	7.3-8	105		

PSEUDEPIGRAPHA

1 Enoch		*Psalms of Solomon*		13.7	116
16.1	101	11.2-3	130	13.8	116
89.36	54	17.21	131		
89.50	52	17.23	131, 132	*Testament of Asher*	
89.73	52, 53, 54	17.28-31	131	7.2-7	115
90.20	125	17.28	124, 132		
90.21	54			*Testament of Benjamin*	
90.24-25	125	*Sibylline Oracles*		9.2	55
90.28-29	53, 54	2.165-173	130	9.5	115
90.29	54			10.5-11	115
91.11-13	53	*Testament of Moses*		10.7	115
		1.6-9	42	10.11	115
		1.7-9	43	11.2	115
2 Baruch		2.1	43		
4.1-7	54	2.2	40	*Testament of Joseph*	
4.3	54, 55	2.4-5	40	9.11	115
4.4	54	2.4	43		
4.5	54	3.1-3	41	*Testament of Judah*	
4.6	55	3.2	43	22.3	115
		3.6-9	40	25.1	115
Jubilees		4.7-8	43	25.5	115
1.17	55, 56	4.9	41		
1.27	55	5.3-6	42	*Testament of Levi*	
8–10	9	6.1	42	14.34	115
5.1-2	10	6.8-9	41		
7.26	10	6.8	42	*Testament of Naphtali*	
8.8-9	10	7.1	42	5.1-5	115
8.19	9, 10	7.6-8	42	6.7	115
10.14	10	10.1	42	8.2	115
10.29	10	10.9-10	42		
10.30-31	10	12.13	43	*Testament of Reuben*	
12.12-14	12			6.8	115
26.61	45	*Testament of Abraham*			
27.39	45	10	116	*Testament of Simeon*	
31.15	134	13.3	115	7.1	115
31.16-17	134	13.6	116	7.2	115
50.5	11, 101				

Other Early Literature

Gospel of Thomas
14	18, 98
47.1-2	57
76.3	57

Papyrus Oxyrhynchyus 840
	102

Philo
Against Flaccus
46	31

Legatio ad Gaium
207-276	34
249	34
333	34

Josephus
The Jewish War
2.49	42
2.147-149	88
2.162-165	81
2.164-5	80
2.165	80
2.185-203	34
2.200	34
2.224	32
2.259	95
2.261	116
2.451	34
2.628	34
3.35-40	92
3.307-315	36
4.147-157	80
5.227	80
6.285-286	95, 96
6.300	44
11.119	34

Antiquities of the Jews
Books 1-4	11
1.121	12
1.122-143	12
1.142	11
1.154-156	12
1.154	12
9.277-279	36
9.288-291	36
11.19-119	35
11.66	124
11.304-347	35
11.340	36
12.257-264	36
13.172-173	81
13.173	80
13.255-256	36
13.288-298	34
13.297	80
15.299-316	34, 80
15.318	80
15.420	33
17.261-262	41
18.11	34
18.16	80
18.29	37
18.37	143
18.55-59	35
18.85-87	95
18.85-89	36
18.87	37
18.88-89	36
18.90-95	32, 81
18.90	32
18.91	32
18.92	32
18.92-93	32
18.93	32
18.93-94	32
18.95	32
18.116-119	93
18.261-304	34
18.271	35
18.272	35
18.403-408	81
20.2	32
20.6-14	32
20.6	81
20.97-99	95, 116
20.106-107	32
20.167-168	96
20.167-172	95
20.169-172	96, 116
20.188	95, 96
20.189-190	33
20.192-193	33
20.193-194	33
20.195-196	33
20.195	33
20.199-200	34

Against Apion
1.7	12
2.198	80

Life of Josephus
10-12	83
189-98	83
191-92	83
429	12

Qumran
1QM
i-ii	89
i.2-3	89
vii.3-7	88

1QpHab
x.1	48

1QS
i.3-6	102
iii.4-6	86, 94
iii.20-21	90
v.6	89
v.13-14	87
v.16	88
v.24-25	88
vi.2-5	87
vi.4-5	87
vi.16-17	87
vi.22	87
vi.24-25	87
vii.5-6	38
vii.10	38
vii.19-20	87
viii.1	135
viii.4b-7a	135
viii.10	89, 135
viii.17	87
ix.3-6	89
ix.4-5	38

CD			4QFlorilegium		m.Kelim	
i.12	89			29	1.6-9	84, 85
i.13-18	89				4.4	78
i.14	89		11Q19		10.1	78
ii.11-12	89		iii-xii	39		
vi.11-14	38		xxx-xxxv	39	**Other Ancient Authors**	
xi.21-22	87		xlvi.13-16	88	Pliny	
					Natural History	
4Q171			**Rabbinic**		5.70	31
ii.9-12	19		m.Hag.			
			2.7	84	Strabo	
4QpNah					*Geography*	
i.11	48		m.Hallah		16.4.21	74
			2.1	84		

INDEX OF AUTHORS

Adan-Bayewitz, D. 78, 79
Adan-Bayewitz, D. and I. Perlman 79
Alexander, P. S. 9, 11
Alexander, T. D. and S. Gathercole
   (eds) 2
Allison, D. C. 45, 125, 129, 132, 135, 139

Barclay, J. M. G. 12, 31
Bauckham, R. 37, 48–9, 101, 121–2
Beall, T. S. 87
Bedal, L.-A. 74
Ben-Dov, M. 78
Berquist, J. L. 13, 147
Betz, O. 38
Black, M. 53
Bockmuehl, M. 47–9
Boer, R. T. 28, 35
Bóid, I. R. M. M. 91, 92
Booth, R. P. 97
Borg, M. 45–6, 76, 79, 81, 85, 102, 122
Bowker, J. 80, 81, 83
Brereton, J. 64
Brooke, G. J. 38
Brown, R. E. 96
Brueggemann, W. 14, 114
Bryan, D. 52, 53
Bryan, S. 21, 47–8, 54, 55, 56, 97, 98,
   100, 101
Burnett, F. W. 125
Burridge, K. 140–1

Charlesworth, J. H. 92, 93
Chilton, B. 97, 98–9
Clarke, K. 13
Coggins, R. J. 36, 91, 92
Cohen, A. P. 145
Cohen, J. M. 92
Cohen, S. J. D. 18, 83, 86
Collins, J. J. 41–2, 48, 53, 59, 116, 137,
   141

Crossan, J. D. 45–6, 119, 139
Crossley, J. G. 97

Davies, D. 104
Davies, P. R. 38, 39–40, 86, 89
Davies, W. D. 1, 7, 123–4, 127, 147
Davies, W. D. and D. C. Allison 125, 127
de Jonge, H. 44
DeLacey, D. R. 83, 85
Deleuze, G. and F. Guittari 59
Douglas, M. 63
Dozeman, T. B. 26
Dube, M. 147
Dunn, J. D. G. 94, 95, 97, 98

Edwards, D. R. 69
Ehrman, B. 129
Eliade, M. 4
Eshel, H. 68, 75
Eshel, H. and E. Meyers 68
Evans, C. 53

Flanagan, J. 106
Foster, R. 137
Foucault, M. 58
Franxman, T. W. 11, 12
Freyne, S. 6, 21, 56–8

Gager, J. G. 14, 139
Garwood, P., D. Jennings, R. Skeates and
   J. Toms (eds) 4
Gaston, L. 53
Geertz, C. 5–6
George, M. 24, 28, 30
Geva, H. 79, 81
Goodman, M. 22, 24, 58, 80, 81, 83
Gray, R. 144
Gruenwald, I. 57, 94–5
Gunn, D. M. and P. M. McNutt (eds) 5

Index of Authors

Habel, N. 7–8, 30, 63, 65
Halpern-Amaru, B. 11, 12, 145
Han, K. 41, 42, 52, 53, 54
Harrington, H. 88, 90
Harris, R. 104, 141
Harvey, D. 58
Hengel, M. 31
Hengel, M. and R. Deines 82
Herzog, W. 65, 79
Himmelfarb, M. 88, 94
Holwerda, D. E. 1
Hooker, M. 51, 95, 96
Horbury, W. 21, 126
Horsley, R. A. 22, 139
Hubert, J. 7, 67
Hurowitz, V. A. 29

Isser, S. 35, 37, 92

Jenson, P. 66
Jeremias, J. 132

Kallai, Z. 107–9, 114
Kampen, J. 37
Kazen, T. 69–70, 97, 98, 100, 102
Killebrew, A. 72–3
Knibb, M. 53
Knight, D. A. 110
Koester, C. R. 25, 26, 43
Kugler, R. L. 114
Kunin, S. D. 8, 24, 27, 28, 31, 61
Kuper, H. 3–4, 23

Laaksonen, J. 7
Lefebvre, H. 14–16, 23, 57, 62, 65, 72, 97
Levenson, J. D. 24
Levine, L. I. 31, 90
Low, S. M. and D. Lawrence-Zúñiga (eds) 23

Magen, Y. 36, 69, 71, 74, 75, 76, 78, 79, 91
Maier, J. 39
Malina, B. J. 144–5
Marcus, J. 82, 83, 89, 100
McKelvey, R. J. 89
McKnight, S. 95, 97, 100, 105, 134
McLaren, J. S. 32, 33, 35

Meggitt, J. 143
Meier, J. P. 117, 118, 120, 121
Mendels, D. 32
Meye, R. P. 120–1
Meyer, B. F. 136
Meyers, E. M. 68, 71, 72
Milgrom, J. 66, 67, 70
Millar, A. and J. K. Riches 6
Molotch, H. 14
Moxnes, H. 103, 144

Nelson, R. D. 110
Netzer, E. 74, 75, 78
Neusner, J. 82

Økland, J. 62
Ottenheijm, E. 97

Park, C. C. 4
Pastor, J. 142
Phann, S. J. 92
Poorthuis, M. and J. Schwartz 62–3
Primus, C. 84
Prior, M. 147
Pummer, R. 36, 91

Rabinow, P. 58
Räisänen, H. 97
Rapoport, A. 7
Regev, E. 69, 70, 73, 76, 78, 83, 85
Reich, R. 68, 71, 73, 75–6
Riches, J. K. 2, 10, 11, 21, 50, 51, 59, 81, 87, 97, 98, 101, 103, 145
Riches, J. and A. Millar 6

Salles-Reese, V. 3
Sanders, E. P. 44–5, 50–1, 53, 55, 66, 75–7, 79–80, 82, 107, 117, 119–20, 122
Sarason, R. S. 84, 85
Schiffman, L. 38, 90
Schmidt, F. 19, 39, 44, 90
Schmithals, W. 117
Schottroff, L. 102
Schwartz, D. 40–1
Scott, J. M. 10, 13
Sellers, O. R. 36
Sheldrake, P. 17
Shields, R. 16

Smith, J. Z. 4, 22, 38, 106, 113, 140
Soja, E. 58
Sommer, B. D. 27
Stemberger, G. 33, 34
Stern, M. 32, 34
Sugirtharajah, R. S. (ed.) 147
Swanson, D. D. 38
Swanson, T. 147

Tan, K. H. 50
Taylor, J. 93–4, 96, 102
Theissen, G. 57, 93, 136
Theissen, G. and D. Winter 18, 98, 99, 117
Tigchelaar, E. J. C. 10
Tiller, P. 54
Tomson, P. J. 97, 101
Trible, P. 110

Tromp, J. 42
Tsuk, T. 73, 74
Tuan, Y.-F. 17

van Aarde, A. 117, 119
Van Seters, J. 29
Vanderhooft, D. 29
VanderKam, J. 10, 53
Vermes, G. 136
Vielhauer, P. 117

Walker, P. 1–2, 21, 60
Webb, R. L. 93
Wenell, K. 2, 49, 56, 140
Whitelam, K. 147
Wilken, R. L. 1, 2, 8, 38, 64–5, 114
Wright, N. T. 133